Forensic Evaluation of Juveniles

Thomas Grisso

PROFESSIONAL RESOURCE PRESS
Sarasota, Florida

Published by Professional Resource Press
(An imprint of Professional Resource Exchange, Inc.)
Post Office Box 15560
Sarasota, FL 34277-1560

The copy editor for this book was David Anson, the managing editor was Debra Fink, the production coordinator was Laurie Girsch, and the cover and text were designed by Carol Tornatore.

Library of Congress Cataloging-in-Publication Data

Grisso, Thomas.
    Forensic evaluation of juveniles / Thomas Grisso.
        p.   cm.
    Includes bibliographical references and index.
    ISBN 1-56887-037-X
    1. Psychology, Forensic--United States--Handbooks, manuals, etc.
2. Forensic psychiatry--United States--Handbooks, manuals, etc.
3. Juvenile delinquents--Mental health services--United States-
-Handbooks, manuals, etc. 4. Juvenile justice, Administration of-
-United States--Handbooks, manuals, etc. 5. Juvenile delinquents-
-Psychological testing. 6. Criminal psychology.   I. Title.
RA1148.G75   1998
614'.1--dc21   98–14684
                                                      CIP

Preface

*F*ew clinicians begin their careers intending to become experts in performing evaluations in the juvenile justice system. I certainly did not. For me it began a few years after graduate studies were completed while I was teaching full time. A chance set of contacts got me an offer to consult weekly to a treatment-oriented residential facility for delinquent youths, part of the Ohio Youth Commission, helping their staff to develop individualized treatment plans.

Child clinical psychology had been a secondary focus of my graduate training, so I was adequately prepared for what was essentially a clinical role in a juvenile correctional setting. This exposure to delinquent youths then drew me toward evaluations in juvenile court cases and a special interest in juvenile law and its implications for youths. For many years I accepted a broad range of referrals, but eventually I focused primarily on assessments for waiver to criminal court in juvenile murder cases.

Like most academic clinicians whose clinical or forensic cases are only a small part of their professional work, I have never quite developed the fine-tuned clinical skills of my more seasoned colleagues in full-time clinical practice. In exchange, I have had more time to think about what we need in order to improve our evaluations for the courts—ways to conceptualize what we do, research to make our assessment methods more relevant for legal questions, and data that can increase our value to juvenile courts. My research activities have given me the opportunity to become familiar with juvenile courts across the country, and I have been fascinated with their diversity and similarities, as well as the particular demands they make on clinicians.

Out of this experience, I began several years ago to organize and integrate my research and clinical perspectives about forensic evaluations of juveniles so that I could teach them to my students and to clinicians in continuing education workshops. That led to this book. In writing it, I have tried to envision what I would have liked to have had available to me when I began performing evaluations in juvenile courts 25 years ago.

Many people have played important roles in my own development as a student of juvenile law, juvenile forensic evaluations, and juvenile justice systems. This book provides a fitting context in which to thank them because in one way or another it is an integration of what they taught me. I thank

- Jesse Goldner (Saint Louis University Law School) and the crew (in the 1970s) of the National Juvenile Law Center of St. Louis, for guiding my first attempts to learn juvenile law.
- Dick Barnum (Boston), Gene Kissling (St. Louis), and Todd Flynn (Tucson) whose everyday performance as juvenile court clinicians became my definition for thoughtful, professional practice of the highest quality in juvenile courts.
- Jay Blitzman and his colleagues at the Roxbury Youth Advocacy Project, from whom I learned much about the intricacies of the legal defense of juveniles by watching how they made use of my evaluations of their clients.
- Administrators and staff in the Massachusetts Department of Youth Services for their support and encouragement across the years.
- Pam Casey and Alan Tomkins, for helping me study how juvenile court judges think about their decisions in delinquency cases.
- Randy Borum, Kirk Heilbrun, and Lois Oberlander for their very helpful comments on earlier drafts of several of the chapters in this book.
- Members of the newly formed John D. and Catherine T. MacArthur Foundation Research Network on Adolescent Development and Juvenile Justice, with whom I have begun to think through ways in which developmental psychology can influence juvenile court policy and practice.

- The many professionals who have attended my workshops, many of them sponsored by the American Academy of Forensic Psychology, and whose questions and reflections helped me refine my notions about what forensic evaluations of juveniles ought to be like.
- The National Institute of Mental Health and Saleem Shah for supporting and encouraging my research on psychological issues in juvenile justice for several years.

Finally, special thanks to Larry Ritt and the crew at Professional Resource Press for their support and guidance in the production of this book. It is a privilege to be associated with their dedicated efforts to develop high-quality products that will improve clinical practice.

Thomas Grisso
University of Massachusetts Medical Center
Worcester, MA
March, 1998

Table of Contents

Chapter 6 *(Cont'd)*

Introduction

This book is a practical guide that summarizes concepts and methods for performing several types of forensic evaluations in delinquency cases. The aim is to help mental health professionals perform evaluations that will (a) offer information to courts relevant for legal decisions, (b) meet the needs of youths and society, and (c) satisfy legal, ethical, and scientific standards for the mental health professions.

Why Was the Book Needed?

This book is being published at an important juncture in the history of the juvenile justice system in the United States. The juvenile justice system, having begun a year before the twentieth century, now approaches its centennial. Throughout that history, juvenile courts have relied heavily on mental health professionals to guide them in their response to delinquent youths, especially to provide information to assist judicial decisionmaking. Some of those decisions are intended to protect youths' rights in the adjudication process. Other decisions focus on providing services to youths for their rehabilitation, while assuring adequate protection for society.

Despite this long history of forensic mental health evaluations for juvenile courts, there have been few resources to guide clinicians' performance of those evaluations. A number of textbooks have described the work of mental health professionals in juvenile courts, including a series of edited volumes by Schetky and Benedek (1980, 1985, 1992) and by Rosner and Schwartz (1989). Other helpful references include certain chapters in works with broader objectives, such as the recent sourcebook on serious, violent youthful offenders by Howell et al. (1995) and the forensic evaluation handbook by Melton et al. (1997). A recent book on the assessment of youthful offenders by R. Hoge and Andrews (1996) provides an excellent resource for identifying psychological instruments and interview methods relevant for delinquency evaluations.

All of these references are recommended for the forensic clinician's library. None of them, however, offers a systematic, conceptual approach to the various evaluations that are described in this book, moving from the planning stage of the evaluation through data collection to the communication of the evaluation's results.

The need for a book of this type has become more critical in recent years because of the ever-increasing number of clinicians who are evaluating youths for the courts. Beginning in the late 1980s, a substantial increase in violent offenses by youths created a wave of legislative changes that were designed to "get tough" with delinquent youths. Legislators focused on creating stiffer penalties in juvenile courts and increasing the number and types of youths who, despite their age, would be sent to criminal court to be tried and sentenced as though they were adults. An increase in the state's power to punish youths has heightened concerns for youths' rights in the adjudication process. For example, youths' competence to stand trial received little attention until recently, creating unfamiliar demands on juvenile court and criminal court clinicians alike.

Therefore, a combination of increases in juvenile violence and new questions that are being raised about their adjudication is increasing the need for clinicians who are prepared to perform evaluations for use in juvenile courts.

Who May Find the Book Helpful?

The book was developed with many types of users in mind:

- Advanced clinical psychology graduate students, psychiatry residents, and fellows in forensic psychology and psychiatry.
- Clinical psychologists and psychiatrists who are or wish to be engaged in evaluations for juvenile courts, whether in the public sector or in private practice.

- Juvenile justice and mental health administrators, as well as lawyers, who seek a standard with which to evaluate and improve the quality of forensic clinical evaluations in delinquency cases.

The book focuses only on evaluations in delinquency cases. Clinicians interested in other types of juvenile court evaluations (e.g., abuse and neglect of children, child custody, child witness capabilities) need to consult other sources. Although evaluations of delinquent adolescents in juvenile court are the primary focus, clinicians evaluating adolescents who are being tried in criminal court will also find the book helpful, especially the chapters on youths' capacities to waive Miranda rights and for competence to stand trial, and the chapter on evaluating youths' risk of future violence.

In order to put into practice the concepts and methods described here, clinicians must have or acquire sufficient knowledge of child psychology or child psychiatry. The book does not describe basic principles of child and adolescent development or the fundamentals of child psychopathology, which form a foundation for competence to perform any evaluation of youths for juvenile courts.

Legal scholars and behavioral science researchers generally will find this book of only limited use in meeting their needs. Legal citations and references to research are provided only very selectively, having been chosen to alert the practitioner to literature that is basic and essential.

How Is the Book Organized?

Chapter 1 is a general introduction to some fundamentals that provide a background for all delinquency evaluations for juvenile courts: (a) basics of juvenile law, the nature of juvenile courts, and the legal process in delinquency cases; (b) the role of the forensic mental health professional in delinquency cases; and (c) some key concepts in adolescent development, adolescent criminal behavior, adolescent psychopathology, and the assessment of adolescents.

Chapters 2 to *5* then describe four types of evaluations for juvenile courts:

- Capacities of juveniles to waive Miranda rights
- Juveniles' competence to stand trial
- Risk of harm to others
- Assessment of rehabilitation needs

Chapter 6 describes evaluations for hearings on the potential waiver of youths to criminal court for trial and sentencing as adults. The standards for waiver to criminal court typically require an examination of the youth's risk of harm and potential for rehabilitation. Therefore, Chapter 6 expands on the evaluations described in Chapters 4 and 5, describing them in the special context of evaluations for waiver hearings. In *Chapter 7* the book discusses a number of professional and ethical issues that frequently arise in evaluations for juvenile courts.

Major sections of each chapter are numbered consecutively, with subsections designated by one or two decimals for first and second level subheadings. When sections are cited, the first number is the chapter, followed by the section number (e.g., 4-1.3 is Chapter 4, Section 1, Subheading 3).

How Should the Book Be Used?

The book is intended especially for use in training programs (e.g., workshops, seminars, or professional-academic settings) where mental health professionals obtain predoctoral or continuing education for their own performance of forensic evaluations for juvenile courts. When used for this purpose, the information should be supplemented by the following types of information and experience in order to implement the procedures that the book describes.

Modeling and Experiential Training

The process of learning any clinical activity involves three stages: (a) acquiring an understanding of the relevant definitions, concepts, and methods; (b) "cognitive practice" in the use of the concepts and information (e.g., reasoning about hypothetical cases), usually with modeling and guidance from experienced colleagues; and (c) "experiential learning," involving supervised experience in carrying out all steps in at least a few actual assessment cases.

Most of the book is designed to provide only the basic understanding involved in Stage (a) of this process. Some of the material will contribute also to Stage (b) by providing case examples.* For clinicians with little previous experience in delinquency evaluations, Stage (c) will require obtaining consultation or supervision when beginning to implement the book's material in actual forensic assessment cases.

Obtaining Information on Local Rules and Procedures

The information in the book must be supplemented with the applicable legal definitions and procedural requirements in one's own jurisdiction. These requirements differ somewhat from state to state, and the book was not designed to describe the specific requirements of each jurisdiction in the country. The definitions and procedures it uses were selected for their general applicability across the widest range of states and local jurisdictions.

Professional Development and Continuing Education

Mental health professionals are obligated to keep themselves informed of new developments that arise in their field of practice. This obligation is especially important when approaching any type of forensic issue. References cited in this book will provide more detailed discussions of many of the definitions, issues, and methods it discusses.

Taking Responsibility

No book can tell a professional exactly how to perform any clinical task. It can offer definitions, provide guidelines, recommend methods, and suggest strategies. Yet were one to follow the

---

*All names and identifying information have been changed to protect the privacy of the participants.

procedures described here to the letter, this would not ensure quality practice and in certain cases might even jeopardize it. In the end, professionals must make their own individual judgments concerning how and when the book's recommendations are to be applied when faced with the specific demands of their own work settings and the circumstances of individual cases.

The book, therefore, should not be read and used as a cookbook. It is far more important to gain an appreciation of the legal demands, issues, and objectives that the book's approach seeks to satisfy, as well as the options that are available to do it. Given this, professionals will be in an informed position to be responsible for their final judgments about how they will perform forensic evaluations in delinquency cases.

Forensic Evaluation
of Juveniles

Chapter 1

Preparing for Evaluations
in Delinquency Cases

*F*orensic mental health evaluations for delinquency cases require a challenging combination of professional knowledge and skills. Typically, mental health professionals wishing to perform these evaluations are well prepared to meet some of these demands but not all of them.

For example, the well-trained child clinical psychologist is prepared to deal with the diagnostic questions raised in many delinquency cases but may be unfamiliar with the specific legal questions involved or with the juvenile justice system and its resources. The experienced forensic mental health professional may have a better understanding of the law, the legal system, and their implications for the role of the examiner in forensic cases but, having applied these skills primarily to adult criminal cases, may know relatively less about the developmental and clinical characteristics of adolescence. As a consequence, most clinicians who approach the forensic evaluation of delinquent youths for the first time need to prepare themselves by augmenting their knowledge in one or more areas.

The purpose of this chapter is to identify those areas of knowledge that delinquency evaluations require. Like a pocket guide for the traveler to a foreign country, it identifies what one should plan to explore and how to get to various places, but it does not try to describe in detail everything that one will find there. Thus this chapter identifies the areas of content that a clinician should know or plan to learn, sketches the content, and provides sources to which one can go. But it is not a substitute for learning the relevant content from other sources.

The chapter begins with a *brief history of the juvenile justice system* (Section 1.0), including its original philosophy and how that has recently changed. Then it reviews three fundamental areas of knowledge required for competent practice in performing forensic mental health evaluations in delinquency cases: the juvenile justice system's *laws, procedures, and court structure* (2.0); *the role of the forensic mental health professional* in the juvenile justice process (3.0); and the *nature of adolescents* and their clinical and behavioral dysfunctions (4.0).

1.0   A BRIEF HISTORY OF THE
JUVENILE JUSTICE SYSTEM

The first special system of justice for juveniles in the U. S. was established in Cook County (Chicago), Illinois, in 1899. Within 30 years, almost all states had followed Chicago's model by enacting special laws and a system of special rehabilitation services for responding to the needs and misbehaviors of youths who came before the new juvenile courts. Excellent descriptions of the foundation of the juvenile justice system may be found in Cicourel (1968), Platt (1969), and Stapleton and Teitelbaum (1972).

The notion of a juvenile justice system arose in the context of late nineteenth century changes in the way that children were regarded in society. The U.S. was beginning to develop its public educational system, was instituting child labor laws, and had begun a system of child welfare. G. Stanley Hall was promoting the new concept of "adolescence," identifying the teen years as a distinct developmental stage during which children were in transition to adulthood. During this period, youths were seen as still in formation—still malleable—so that their transgressions did not have to be considered a sign of inevitable criminality in adulthood. The purpose of a juvenile system of justice was to meet the needs of children and adolescents in order to redirect their development in positive ways.

Juvenile courts' objectives, therefore, were beneficent, not punitive or retributive. They would operate according to the doctrine of *parens patriae*, or as expressed by one founder of the system, "as a wise, merciful father handles his own child whose errors are not discovered by the authorities" (Mack, 1909). Gaining an understanding of the individual child was important in this response; what the court decided for the child was to be based on what the child needed, not what he or she had done. Thus rehabilitative decisions for an abandoned youth, a truant youth who was disobedient to parents, and an assaultive youth might all be the same if their developmental needs were similar, rather than "sentencing" them differently on the basis of the relative seriousness of their offenses.

Consistent with this philosophy, juvenile courts evolved more or less as social service agencies that had the authority and structure of legal institutions. The broader juvenile justice system of which juvenile courts were a part usually included a state's training schools and reformatories, homes in the community for wayward youths, and a variety of clinical services.

To create a justice system in which a rehabilitative objective was paramount, laws had to exempt juveniles from criminal court adjudication. American law had long followed English Common Law in exempting youths under the age of 7 from criminal prosecution, under the presumption that they had insufficient abilities to form criminal intent. In 1899, the Illinois legislature raised that age, so that inability to form criminal intent was presumed below age 17. This cleared the way for a special system of juvenile justice that did not involve questions of criminal guilt (Bernard, 1992; Breckinridge & Abbott, 1912/1970).

Because youths would not be found guilty of crimes, the juvenile court was allowed to make its decisions about youths without the usual legal constraints associated with the constitutional rights of defendants and procedural due process that applied in criminal court for adults. These requirements of law are necessary when trying criminal defendants because the consequence of conviction is a restriction of individual liberties in the form of incarceration or other punishment. In the jurisprudence of the early juvenile court, these protections were considered unnecessary when the juvenile court's objectives were to meet the child's needs, not to punish or to exact retribution. As a consequence, the early juvenile courts were not required to hear detailed evidence to determine a youth's "guilt" or to assure that youths were represented by attorneys who would argue in their "defense." These protections were considered irrelevant because the youth in juvenile court was convicted of no crime and was assured anonymity that would not establish any public record of offending.

During its nearly 100-year history, the juvenile court has undergone two major reforms that make its current laws and procedures very different from those that prevailed during the first half of the century. One of these reforms was signaled by U.S. Supreme Court decisions of the 1960s. The other was a series of changes in juvenile laws that occurred in all states during the 1990s in response to a wave of violent offenses by youths that began in the previous decade.

The U.S. Supreme Court cases of the 1960s, *Kent v. U.S.* (1966) and *In re Gault* (1967), assured that the juvenile justice system could not continue to function as it had during the first half of the century. *Kent* involved the claim that youths should have many of the same procedural due process rights associated with criminal proceedings when faced with hearings that might lead to their transfer to criminal court for trial. The question in *Gault* was whether youths should have the right to avoid self-incrimination and to consult legal counsel when questioned by police, and to be informed of those rights as the Court had affirmed for adults in *Miranda v. Arizona* (1966) a year earlier.

The consequence of both cases was the legal recognition of constitutional rights for youths in proceedings against them in delinquency cases: for example, the right to legal counsel in their defense, to the privilege against self-incrimination, and to confront and cross-examine opposing witnesses. The state now had to prove its allegations in delinquency cases in order to have the authority to take custody of delinquent youths to provide for their rehabilitation. The Court reached this conclusion by recognizing the claim that (a) constitutional rights were not for adults alone, and (b) the juvenile justice system had failed to deliver on its promise of rehabilitation for delinquent youths. The outcomes of delinquency cases typically resulted in confinement in training schools or reformatories that offered little more than custodial care, which was simply punishment in the absence of any demonstrable rehabilitative efforts. Given that outcome, the juvenile court could not continue to take custody of delinquent youths without providing them the rights that would protect them against unlawful deprivation of freedom by the state.

It is important to realize, however, that the Court did not abandon the original purpose of juvenile courts. It specifically recognized a continuing need for the juvenile court to operate in the rehabilitative interests of the youth. Thus over the next 20 years, juvenile court proceedings took on a bifurcated quality consistent with the Court's decisions. In the first stage of the proceedings from arrest until the finding of delinquency at the adjudication hearing (or trial on guilt), the relation between the court and the youth was much like that of an adult accused of a crime. Jury trials were not required, but most other protective rights, including representation by defense counsel and procedural due process in the adjudication of the offense, made delinquency hearings more like criminal court hearings in form and process. Then, after the youth had been found delinquent, the juvenile court could use its traditional discretion in deciding what rehabilitative disposition would best meet the youth's needs.

The second legal reform came in stages and reached its apex during a dramatic increase in violent juvenile offenses that began in the mid-1980s. This reform has been motivated by a desire to redirect the objectives of the juvenile justice system, asserting a punitive objective as primary in cases involving serious violent offenses by juveniles (see Grisso, 1996, for a more detailed explanation). The reform has resulted in legislative changes in juvenile law in every state during the 1990s. These laws take various forms, including restatements of the purposes of juvenile justice (e.g., acknowledging objectives pertaining to the protection of society and punishment of youths), changes in statutes that make it easier to waive juveniles to criminal court for trial as adults (for a wider range of offenses and for youths of younger ages), and the creation of extended sentences for youths who are tried in juvenile court.

From the perspective of youth advocates, these new laws strengthen even further the claim that youths in delinquency cases must be provided due process and full constitutional rights in juvenile court proceedings. This is because (a) the consequences of the new laws often are as severe as if youths were tried in criminal court, and (b) the promise of rehabilitation that once justified a "softer" form of protection of individual rights has been further eroded.

Even in this latest stage of the juvenile court's history, however, rehabilitation continues to play a considerable role in judicial decisions. For example, a finding that a youth is incapable of being rehabilitated is still required in most states in order for a judge to order waiver to criminal court for trial. And rehabilitation is still the legal standard for judges' decisions about what to do with a youth in the postadjudication (disposition) phase of most delinquency proceedings. On the day that I edited this chapter, I listened to a judge in an urban juvenile court in the Midwest agonizing over the proper placement—a boys' ranch in Colorado, or a more "clinical" setting—for an assaultive and suicidal youth. While legislators have become more punitive in their response to youths, many juvenile court judges still make their decisions based on what they believe may save the youth.

Some observers of the juvenile justice system have called for its abolition and for placing all adolescent defendants in criminal court to be tried as adults (e.g., Feld, 1980, 1988). The argument has been made on advocacy grounds (i.e., their rights will be better protected) as well as for retributive reasons (i.e., youths should have to pay for their crimes like adults). No cataclysmic reform of this type is expected in the near future. But recent laws that transfer youths to criminal court have so substantially blurred the distinctions between juvenile and criminal justice that a continuation of the present trend would drift in that direction. Were the reform to come, it is likely that youths could not merely be processed in criminal court without any changes in criminal law. Despite their offenses, adolescents are adolescents, and it is likely that society would continue to require that the law respond to their transgressions differently than to adults' crimes. Placing all delinquent youths in criminal court, therefore, would in effect require a reform of criminal law itself in order to accommodate the special circumstances of youthful offenders. (See Zimring, 1982, for a defense of reduced penalties for adolescent offenders.)

2.0   THE CONTEXT FOR FORENSIC EVALUATIONS: JUVENILE LAWS, COURTS, AND REHABILITATION PROGRAMS

Every state has a juvenile justice system that includes a variety of social institutions and agencies with interlocking functions that respond to youthful offenders. Clinicians must be familiar with this complex system, to ensure that their evaluations are legally relevant and can be used with maximum effectiveness by various parts of the system.

Because there are variations from state to state, the system can only be described in general terms. The best sources of information on the juvenile justice system in one's own state are other local clinicians or attorneys who have worked in it.

At the most basic level, a state's juvenile justice system includes

- *The laws* that authorize the state's response to youths accused of delinquencies and adjudicated delinquent (2.1)
- A *system of detention* for the temporary custody of youths who have been charged with delinquencies (2.2)
- A *system of courts* that controls the detainment of accused youths, adjudicates delinquency charges, determines the disposition of delinquency cases, and often provides some rehabilitative services (2.3)
- A *system of attorneys* for the prosecution and defense of youths in delinquency cases (2.4)
- A *system of rehabilitative and correctional services* for youths found delinquent (2.5 and 2.6)

2.1 *Delinquency Laws*

Laws that control delinquency cases may be found in statutes, administrative rules (the rules established by a governmental department to regulate its own functions and procedures), and case law (decided on appeal by courts).

Most states' statutes define the *jurisdiction* of juvenile courts. Typically these laws indicate when the juvenile court can or cannot intervene in the lives of youths and their families. For example, juvenile justice jurisdiction is limited to persons below certain ages (typically the 16th, 17th, or 18th birthday) and to youths charged with certain offenses.

Specific jurisdictional ages and offenses vary considerably from state to state, and they differ within a state for different purposes. Thus a state's statutes may define the general jurisdictional age but may have any number of other age limits for various specific purposes, such as the minimum age at which a youth may be waived to criminal court. Other exceptions sometimes allow juvenile court intervention above the general age of minority. For example, youths who are 18—above a state's juvenile jurisdictional age—may fall under juvenile court jurisdiction if they are arrested for an offense committed when they were younger. Laws in some states also allow extension of jurisdiction beyond the general age limit in certain circumstances that will be discussed later in the book. Moreover, the age limit may be different for parts of the system that adjudicate delinquency (the courts) and those agencies that are responsible for the rehabilitation of youths in custody.

Other laws control the *legal procedures* that courts must follow in adjudicating a youth's charges (e.g., procedural requirements that ensure protection of the youth's rights as a defendant), as well as the legal standards that must be met for various judicial decisions (e.g., that the court may not waive a youth to criminal court unless it is shown that the youth is "not amenable to rehabilitation"). Specifically what these standards mean, and what factors will be applied in deciding whether they have been met, are often part of a body of law built on the decisions of the state's appellate courts.

States' statutes and administrative laws also define the *conditions of custody* when youths are adjudicated and remanded by the juvenile court to the custody of the state's "youth authority," the agency that is responsible for the youth's rehabilitation. In some states, judges merely determine that a youth will be remanded to the youth authority's custody, while the youth authority is responsible for deciding on the specific services and placements for a given youth. In other states, judges are given discretion to specify the rehabilitation services a youth will receive, or are required to determine the length of time that a youth must serve while being rehabilitated (typically for adjudication of more serious offenses).

State laws sometimes specify the necessary *qualifications of mental health examiners* who perform evaluations for juvenile courts, the procedures that must be followed to ensure that the youth's rights are protected in the evaluation process, the time that is allowed for the evaluation, the types of information that are desired, and the nature of the report that must be submitted. Typically these statutory requirements (except for those pertaining to defendants' rights) are neither very specific nor restrictive. One must usually seek guidance from juvenile court personnel or attorneys to learn about the evaluation standards that have been established in one's local juvenile court (i.e., by specific juvenile court judges).

2.2 *Detention*

All states have secure detention centers where youths may be held temporarily prior to their adjudication. Typically a state's laws provide for very short-term emergency detention (e.g., 48 hours). Any further detainment must be authorized by the court after hearing evidence on the need for detention. Legal standards typically require that the youth may be detained if he or she is likely to flee prior to adjudication, may be of serious danger to self or others, or may be placed in danger if not detained.

Detention centers typically are regulated and/or operated by juvenile courts themselves or by the state's youth authority. They may be located within or adjacent to juvenile court buildings, or they may be at a distance from the communities that they serve. Laws typically require that juveniles and adult offenders cannot be held together; however, this still happens in many places. Similarly, some states have separate detention facilities for pretrial and adjudicated youths, but often they are held in the same detention facilities. Detention centers typically are staffed by social workers and line staff with college degrees. They are required to provide educational programs for youths who may be in residence longer than a week or two.

Length of stay in detention centers often shows a tri-modal pattern. Many youths are in detention only a few days, another group is detained between 2 and 4 weeks, and another smaller group of youths facing serious offenses and lengthy legal proceedings remains for 6 to 12 months or longer.

Often detention centers have arrangements with a mental health professional who can provide emergency mental health services related to youths' mental conditions, such as responding to suicidal ideation or to the need for transfer to an acute mental health service for adolescents (typically operated by the state's department of mental health). Sometimes these professionals also are responsible for performing evaluations related to legal questions about a youth's need for detention. Mental health professionals and other detention staff, however, usually are limited by law or administrative rules in the degree to which they can provide "counseling" services while a youth awaits trial. As agents of the state, their interactions with youths do not provide confidentiality; therefore, information they obtain from the youth might compromise the youth's defense if they were called to testify.

2.3 *Juvenile Courts*

Each state has an administrative agency to operate and control its courts, often with a separate division for the administration of juvenile courts. Juvenile court structures and functions vary from state to state and may even vary considerably within a state (e.g., in urban and rural areas of a state, where the demand for delinquency adjudications often is quite different).

Many urban areas have "juvenile and family courts" that have jurisdiction over a wide range of legal cases involving the welfare of children and adolescents. These courts may hear not only delinquency cases but also allegations of abuse and neglect of children, the need for foster placements, divorce custody issues, and adoptions. Juvenile and family courts typically have complex administrative structures, with staff that includes professionals who are specialized in social services related to the needs of families and children. These professionals are "officers of the court," and they often are formally identified as probation officers when they handle delinquency cases.

In contrast to a single court system for all juvenile matters, some states have separate court systems for "domestic" and "delinquency" cases (as a colleague of mine has put it, "kids who are done unto" and "kids who do unto others"). Delinquency matters in those states may be handled by juvenile courts that hear only delinquency cases or by criminal court judges who periodically "sit in juvenile session," applying juvenile laws but in the same courtrooms that are used for criminal cases. The latter arrangement is more often found in jurisdictions with moderate or small populations.

Juvenile courts typically have jurisdiction over their detention centers and probation services, the latter provided by probation officers—often specialized social workers—who process all referrals to the court by police and parents. Probation officers' case loads typically include not only youths charged with delinquencies but also "status offenders. " These are youths who are referred for misbehaviors that are not official delinquencies because they would not be crimes if committed by adults—for example, truancy, running away from home, or "incorrigible" behavior in school or at home.

As will be discussed in more detail later, juvenile courts in urban areas often have juvenile court clinics, including one or more mental health professionals who meet the evaluation needs of the court. These court clinicians may be employees of the court, or they may be private providers who have obtained a contract from the court to provide evaluation services and sometimes detention and treatment services as well. An alternative mechanism, often employed in smaller jurisdictions but sometimes in larger ones as well, is to obtain mental health evaluations from private practitioners who are on an authorized list of professionals registered with the court.

2.4 *Prosecution and Defense Attorneys*

Juvenile courts are required to ensure that youths facing delinquency charges are appointed legal counsel for their defense. Typically states have a public defense fund that compensates attorneys for their representation of juveniles. Some attorneys specialize in providing these services, while many attorneys take juvenile cases as a small part of their private practice. Urban areas sometimes have a special office of attorneys who defend juveniles on a full-time basis. The office of the district attorney in larger jurisdictions also is likely to have a separate department for the prosecution of delinquency cases.

2.5 *Juvenile Rehabilitation and Correctional Systems*

States typically have a government agency that is responsible for the welfare, rehabilitation, and correction of juveniles who are committed to their custody by the juvenile courts after they are adjudicated delinquent. It is the counterpart of the criminal justice system's department of corrections, prisons, and parole for adult offenders. Often called the state's "youth authority" or "youth commission," this department typically manages one or more secure facilities for incarceration and rehabilitation of juveniles, in many states known as "training schools." Youth authorities may also operate a network of community programs such as open group residential facilities, half-way houses, and probation services for youths who do not require secure placement.

The youth authority is required to meet the basic physical, educational, and medical needs of youths in its custody. Typically it is also required to document by periodic review the rehabilitation progress of youths, the need for continued custody, and changes in the youth's status that might allow services to be provided in the least restrictive environment consistent with the youth's rehabilitation and public safety. Youth authorities often operate a state's pretrial detention facilities as well. They may also operate special screening or assessment centers through which youths pass soon after their assignment to the youth authority in order to determine the proper placement for each youth among the youth authority's available options.

2.6 *Mental Health Services*

States vary considerably in the degree to which their juvenile court and youth authority services are able to provide for the needs of youths with serious mental disorders, although most are quite limited in their ability to do so. The juvenile justice system often interfaces with the state's department of mental health in such cases, transferring to its adolescent inpatient facilities youths whose mental illnesses are too serious for juvenile justice facilities to manage and treat. It is important for clinicians to know the adolescent mental health inpatient options in their state in order to provide the referral linkage between the juvenile justice and mental health systems. This complicated issue will be discussed later.

2.7 *The Process of Delinquency Cases*

Most cases in which youths are referred to the court are never tried, because intake probation officers and courts have at their disposal a variety of ways to divert youths from official adjudication. Thus only a minority of youths pass through all of the stages leading to a full adjudication and commitment to the youth authority. The process is best considered by describing options in each of the following stages: (a) arrest, referral, and detention; (b) intake and diversion; (c) petitions for waiver or adjudication; (d) adjudication hearings; (e) disposition hearings; (f) custody during rehabilitation; and (g) special circumstances involving referral for mental health services.

2.71   Arrest, Referral, and Detention

Upon a youth's apprehension by police officers, the officers may wish to question the youth about the youth's involvement in or knowledge of the offense being investigated. In some states, police questioning will first require bringing the youth to an officer of the juvenile court (often the staff of the court's detention center) although many states do not require this and allow questioning to occur at a police station or at a youth's home. Most states require that the officers must notify parents and provide them an opportunity to speak with their child before presenting the Miranda warnings and obtaining the youth's waiver of Miranda rights (as discussed further in Chapter 2).

When youths are taken into custody, police officers may return them to their homes or request their admission to the court's juvenile detention center. In either case, officers may also refer the youth to the juvenile court. A "referral" notifies the juvenile court of the allegations and sets in motion the court's intake process. As noted earlier, a youth may be held in secure detention on an emergency basis for only a few days unless the court finds sufficient evidence to meet certain criteria justifying continued detention.

2.72 Intake and Diversion

The intake process is conducted by the court's intake probation staff, who begin a process of contacts and interviews with the youth and the youth's parents. Unless prosecutors have made a decision to file charges against the youth in juvenile court, intake probation officers typically have considerable discretion concerning how to handle referrals. Based on the information that they collect (past records, interviews with the youth and parents), they may believe that an "informal adjustment" is preferable to petitioning the court for an adjudication. An informal adjustment is often possible when the parents and youth are willing to seek proper services on their own while maintaining continued contact with the intake probation officer. This procedure is often used for youths who are referred to the court for the first time, especially when the alleged offense is of low to moderate seriousness. Many cases never proceed further if the probation officer believes that the youth is unlikely to engage in further illegal behavior or is satisfied that the youth and parents have complied with their agreement with the probation officer.

There are three other ways that youths may be diverted from further processing by the juvenile court: by *dismissal* of the charges, *civil commitment to psychiatric care*, and *automatic referral to criminal court*.

Prosecutors might decide to *dismiss the charges* because there is insufficient evidence regarding the allegations, witnesses have refused to testify, or victims have refused to press charges. Sometimes prosecutors agree not to press for adjudication because they are satisfied that the intake probation officer has found a satisfactory alternative in the form of an informal adjustment.

Concerning *civil commitment*, it may become apparent to intake probation officers (e.g., through observations by detention staff) that a youth is in need of psychiatric attention. (See 1-2.77.) In such cases, youths may be temporarily transferred to a department of mental health acute inpatient psychiatric service. If their condition is serious enough to require longer-term psychiatric care, courts may civilly commit them and their cases are likely to proceed no further in the juvenile court's adjudication process.

Concerning *automatic referral to criminal court*, about three-quarters of the states automatically exclude certain serious offenses from adjudication in juvenile court when charged to juveniles who are above a certain age (often 14 or older). Those cases are filed in criminal court. Other states allow prosecutors to decide whether to file charges against youths in juvenile or in criminal court for certain offenses. Youths whose cases are filed in criminal court often remain in juvenile detention while awaiting criminal court trial. Sometimes a youth whose case was automatically filed in criminal court will be transferred back to juvenile court for trial rather than proceeding in criminal court (see Chapter 6).

2.73 Petitions for Waiver or Adjudication

For juveniles whose cases are not informally adjusted, dismissed, or referred in the ways described previously, prosecutors and/or intake probation officers may decide to *file a petition* for the case to proceed to a judicial hearing. They may request two broad types of hearings. The most typical request is for an *adjudication hearing* to find the youth delinquent on the alleged charges. In certain cases, however, the petition may request the *juvenile court's waiver of jurisdiction*. This is a form of referral to criminal court that is available in almost all states. Its consequences are the same as automatic referral to criminal court noted earlier, but it requires a juvenile court hearing at which evidence presented by the prosecutor must convince the judge that certain criteria have been met. Typically these criteria include a showing that the youth is a danger to others and is not amenable to rehabilitation in the juvenile justice system. The juvenile court holds a *waiver hearing* on the evidence, and the youth is represented by legal counsel to defend against the assertions by the prosecution (as described in Chapter 6).

Some states recognize a youth's right to be *competent to stand trial*, requiring that the youth be able to understand the nature of the proceedings and to assist legal counsel in preparing a defense (as discussed in Chapter 3). If this question is raised, it is decided by the juvenile court judge at a competence hearing prior to the waiver or adjudication hearing (or sometimes as part of the waiver hearing).

2.74 Adjudication and Disposition Hearings

The adjudication hearing provides the opportunity for presentation of evidence by prosecution and defense, including cross-examination of all witnesses, on which the judge bases a decision that the youth is or is not delinquent on the alleged charges. Rules of evidence and procedure are similar to those in criminal court in most states although the formality with which the proceedings are conducted will vary across jurisdictions. Judges in juvenile courts typically must make written findings, describing the evidence relevant for their decisions.

Juries are not available in juvenile court (although there are exceptions, as in Massachusetts), and typically the press and public are excluded from juvenile court hearings. In recent years, however, a number of states have opened juvenile waiver and/or adjudication hearings to the public, often restricting this to cases involving the most serious alleged offenses.

When juveniles are adjudicated delinquent, most states require that the juvenile court then hold a separate disposition hearing to hear evidence regarding the proper legal response to the youth's delinquency. Evidence is heard from both sides, often including the testimony of probation officers and mental health professionals (as discussed in Chapter 5) regarding the disposition that meets the needs of the youth and adequately protects the safety of the public.

2.75 Disposition Alternatives

Juvenile court judges have several dispositional options. One is for "continuance" of the disposition hearing. This involves judicial notice that the disposition decision will be delayed for several months and informing youths that if they are arrested before that time they will immediately be committed to the state's youth authority on the offense for which they have already been found delinquent. This is thought to provide strong motivation for avoiding further delinquency, while offering the court the ability to respond swiftly—without the need for pretrial and adjudication proceedings—if the youth is arrested again.

If the disposition decision is not "continued," one option is to place the youth on *court probation*, assigning the youth to the case load of the court's probation staff. The probation officer develops a rehabilitation plan with the youth and family, involving whatever educational, recreational, vocational, counseling (e.g., substance abuse programs), or mental health services are considered important. Many courts also have the option to require restitution as part of the probation plan. Court probation generally will include periodic monitoring by the probation officer (the frequency of monitoring varying with the nature of the case), and some jurisdictions have intensive monitoring programs involving special case workers' daily contact with youths in the community. Failures to carry through with the plan for use of the preceding resources, or re-arrest for new offenses, are considered violations of probation, to which the court may respond with a more restrictive disposition.

The other primary option available to the juvenile court is to relinquish the court's custody of the youth by *commitment to the state's youth authority*. In recent years, some states have amended their statutes to require that juvenile court judges "sentence" youths to mandatory periods of time in secure juvenile facilities for certain serious offenses. Commitment to the state's youth authority, therefore, is required in such instances. In the remainder of cases it is a discretionary option for the court.

2.76 Commitment to Youth Authority

Upon taking custody, the youth authority often will engage in a screening or evaluation process to determine the appropriate rehabilitative program for the youth. Unless the state's laws require secure incarceration, a state's youth authority may choose to return youths to their homes and provide services much like those already described for court probation. Alternatively, the youth authority may place youths in one of a variety of residential settings. In many states, these include open but "staff-secure" (structured) group homes in the community, residential facilities that are outside the community but have minimal security (e.g., forestry camps), and secure residential facilities. Secure facilities across the country range from relatively small programs, sometimes with more intensive counseling and clinical emphases, to very large training schools or reformatories. All secure facilities must offer education, medical services, and recreational activities, and they may include various group or individual counseling services.

Youths remain in the youth authority's custody for varying periods of time. In many states there are no limits to the time that a youth may be in custody other than the statutory maximum age of jurisdiction for the system although secure custody may require periodic review of the continued need for the youth's confinement due to danger to self or others. Youths in secure custody often will "transition" through a series of gradually less restrictive rehabilitation plans that aim for eventual re-entry into the community.

Youths in the custody of the youth authority must be discharged at a maximum jurisdictional age defined by law (often the 17th or 18th birthday). Various states, however, have three types of exceptions to this discharge rule.

First, in some cases youths may *request continuation of their custody* for a limited time beyond the maximum jurisdictional age in order to continue to obtain services that they need (e.g., in order to finish their education or vocational training or to receive disability-related services that would otherwise not be available). Second, some states provide for *special sentences* that extend well beyond the usual maximum age of jurisdiction. For example, a few states provide for special "youthful offender" sentences (for youths found delinquent of very serious charges) that may continue their custody well into their twenties. Third, many states allow the youth authority to petition the juvenile court for an *extension of jurisdiction* under certain circumstances. For example, some states allow extensions of custody (ranging from 1 to 3 years beyond the maximum jurisdictional age) when it can be shown that discharge would present a serious danger to society and when the youth is making rehabilitative progress.

This sketch describes only the most general features of the manner in which delinquency cases are processed so that the description can offer guidance across the greatest number of jurisdictions. Most states will have exceptions and additions to this description, and it is very important that clinicians discover the specific rules and procedures that apply to their own local juvenile courts.

2.77 Referral to Mental Health Services

Throughout the process of delinquency cases, some youths are transferred to adolescent inpatient psychiatric services, often in the department of mental health, when they are in need of psychiatric care that cannot be provided by juvenile justice facilities or programs. When youths in detention need emergency psychiatric services, often they will be transferred to department of mental health facilities and then, when they have stabilized, returned to detention for a resumption of the adjudication process. But if they need continuing intensive psychiatric care, it is not uncommon for charges to be dismissed in favor of a long-range plan of psychiatric care in the mental health system.

Clinicians must be aware of the tension that often exists between a community's juvenile justice system and mental health system regarding the diagnosis and care of youths who are delinquent and who show signs of mental disorder. Often juvenile justice personnel will consider these youths too disordered to care for and manage properly in the nonclinical context of most detention or juvenile justice rehabilitation programs, especially when these youths manifest signs of bizarre thinking or suicidal ideas and behaviors. Yet when a youth is referred to an inpatient psychiatric facility, often the youth is seen by mental health staff as "inappropriate" for psychiatric inpatient services. In contrast to many other youths in psychiatric facilities, the delinquent youth may appear to mental health staff as more antisocial than mentally ill, and the youth's aggressive or disruptive behavior may present difficult management issues.

For some youths, this develops into a series of referrals, shuttling the youth back and forth between the juvenile justice and mental health systems, both of which see the youth as more appropriately belonging in the other system's care. The subset of delinquent youths who are caught in this systemic conflict often are both mentally ill and conduct disordered, a group for which many states do not have programs that effectively serve the interface between juvenile justice and mental health systems.

3.0 THE ROLE OF FORENSIC MENTAL HEALTH EXAMINERS IN DELINQUENCY CASES

The previous discussion said little about the role of forensic mental health professionals and the place of their evaluations in the processing of delinquency cases through the juvenile court. This will be addressed now, beginning with a brief history of psychology's and psychiatry's interactions with juvenile courts, then turning to a consideration of the ways in which clinicians provide their evaluation services and the types of evaluations they perform.

3.1 *Historical Perspective*

Psychologists and psychiatrists played an important role in juvenile courts from the time that such courts began early in the twentieth century. The early model for clinical evaluation services to juvenile courts was an institute developed in 1909 by Healy, a neurologist, and Fernald, a psychologist, to serve the Cook County (Chicago) juvenile court (Schetky & Benedek, 1992). Their evaluations are said to have been comprehensive, multidisciplinary studies of youths' complete life situations, not the narrower assessments of mental disorder or cognitive functioning that would have been typical of their professions in other clinical settings.

Together with social workers, psychologists and psychiatrists readily found a place in the juvenile justice system because their abilities were so closely related to the new juvenile court's philosophy. As noted earlier, the juvenile court's mission was to determine what was needed in each individual case to further a youth's rehabilitation. This required understanding of the youth's background, personality, strengths, and deficits. Typically, the new juvenile courts embraced the expertise of professionals whose stock in trade were theories and assessments that could contribute to that understanding.

The role of mental health professionals in juvenile courts continued relatively unquestioned until the 1960s and 1970s. This was an era when juvenile courts themselves were being transformed by the new recognition of youths' rights (in the wake of *Kent* and *Gault*). Courts were under attack for having failed to live up to their promise of individualized rehabilitation, having made decisions about youths that deprived them of freedom without attending to the individualized needs of youths to form the logic of their disposition decisions. Similarly, the services of mental health professionals to juvenile courts came under scrutiny, questioning the validity of their predictions about youths' dangerousness and their potential for rehabilitation. These were the very issues upon which a youth's potential deprivation of freedom was based, and judges often used clinicians' recommendations as the guide for their disposition decisions. Disenchantment with clinicians' abilities to provide valid guidance in these matters was fueled by research reports of the 1970s concerning serious limits in clinicians' predictions of violent behavior (e.g., Ennis & Litwack, 1974). Others argued that clinical predictions about rehabilitation were questionable, because research reviews of that time (e.g., Martinson, 1974) were reporting that there was no evidence supporting the effectiveness of any rehabilitation efforts with delinquent youths.

Despite these concerns, clinicians are just as evident in juvenile courts today as they were in past decades. The types of evaluations that they perform, however, appear to be changing as a function of recent changes in juvenile law, as discussed in 1-1.0. For example, legislation that has created ways to transfer youths to criminal court "automatically" (i.e., on the basis of their offense and age alone) has decreased the volume of cases involving judicial waiver to criminal court, thereby decreasing the need for waiver evaluations that assist the court in such cases. On the other hand, new laws have substantially increased the potential penalties for youthful offenders, which has raised the need for evaluations related to the protection of their rights as defendants—for example, their capacities to waive Miranda rights (Chapter 2) and their competence to stand trial (Chapter 3).

Juvenile justice policies have been cyclical for over one hundred years, moving from periods in which individualized rehabilitation was emphasized to periods that focused on punishment based on the nature of the offense, and back again (Bernard, 1992). Clinical evaluations for the courts tend to be more important during the rehabilitation cycles that focus on the individual needs of the youth, and less relevant when policy favors punishment and nondiscretionary legal responses to youthful offenders. Currently we are in a punitive phase of the cycle, and it is very likely to give way to a rehabilitative phase within the next 10 to 15 years.

3.2 *Types of Evaluations*

Juvenile courts and juvenile defense attorneys may request clinical evaluations at a number of points in the processing of delinquency cases. They will be considered briefly here, and they will be discussed in more detail in other chapters devoted to each type of evaluation.

At the point of *secure pretrial detention*, staff may request clinical evaluations for two purposes. One is to deal with the potential needs of youths on an emergency basis: for example, concerns about the imminent risk of a suicide attempt, psychotic-like behavior that may require immediate hospitalization, or current intoxication or withdrawal. More focused forensic evaluations may be requested for hearings at which the court will determine the need for continuing detention. Evaluations for these purposes usually are brief and focus on short-range predictions. Typically they are based on a review of detention staff observations, records that are immediately available, and clinical interviews.

During *intake procedures by probation officers*, a consultation or evaluation by clinicians will occasionally be requested to help the probation officer assess the likelihood that an informal adjustment of the case will be an appropriate response. This type of evaluation usually arises only when the juvenile court has its own clinicians who routinely work with the probation staff (see 1-3.4).

Evaluations are often requested by the court, prosecutor, or defense attorney in preparation for hearings on *waiver to criminal court*. As described in Chapter 6, these evaluations can be quite comprehensive, focusing on issues of short-range and long-range risk of harm to others, as well as the youth's amenability to rehabilitation in the juvenile justice system.

In cases proceeding to juvenile court adjudication, defense attorneys who wish to question the admissibility of evidence that the youth provided to police at the time of arrest may request an evaluation of the youth's ability to have understood and made decisions about the Miranda warnings, and therefore the youth's *capacity to have waived Miranda rights* "knowingly, intelligently, and voluntarily." If the defense attorney decides to raise the issue, the prosecutor sometimes will request a similar evaluation by another clinician. The youth's *competence to stand trial* is another pretrial question for which an evaluation may be requested by the court (i.e., for use by the judge), the prosecutor, or the defense attorney. These two evaluations are discussed in Chapters 2 and 3.

There is virtually no role for the clinician in the majority of adjudication hearings in juvenile court. The legal question is whether the youth committed the offense as charged, and this rarely raises issues for which psychological or psychiatric evidence is relevant. Although the potential for an insanity defense in delinquency proceedings has been discussed (e.g., Drukteinis, 1986; Harrington & Keary, 1980), it has rarely had a place in juvenile court determinations, and most clinicians in juvenile forensic work have never been asked to perform an insanity evaluation for juvenile court. This is partly because the very existence of a special system of law for juveniles recognizes that juveniles—because of their youthful status and apart from any mental disorder—are not held responsible for their offenses in the same manner as are adults.

Evaluations to assist courts in *disposition decisions* are probably the most common evaluation in delinquency cases. They focus on the needs of the youth and provide the court a recommendation regarding a rehabilitation plan. Often these rehabilitation evaluations (discussed in Chapter 5) are performed prior to the youth's adjudication hearing so that the results will be ready for the disposition hearing without the need for a delay between hearings. Laws usually provide, however, that the results cannot be used at the adjudication hearing itself.

When courts place youths in the custody of the state's youth authority, the first step in the youth authority's program often involves *a rehabilitation evaluation to determine proper placement*, especially if there has been no disposition evaluation in the case. Clinicians who work in the state's youth authority often perform these evaluations. After a youth has been in a program of rehabilitation, clinicians may be asked to evaluate the youth's *rehabilitation progress*. The referral may seek recommendations regarding changes in the youth's program (e.g., transitioning from a secure facility to programs in the community) or opinions as to whether the youth meets legal criteria for *extension* of the youth authority's custody beyond the maximum jurisdictional age.

3.3 The "Forensic" Quality of Evaluations for Delinquency Cases

Evaluations like those described earlier typically are called "forensic" (or "forensic mental health") assessments. What makes them forensic, and how are they different from "clinical" evaluations?

The term "forensic" can refer to *any evaluation that is performed specifically for use in a legal forum or agency to assist decisionmaking about a case*. In some cases—for example, rehabilitation evaluations for use in delinquency disposition hearings—the evaluation will be similar in many ways to evaluations performed in many other clinical contexts. The main difference is the need to take into consideration the treatment resources of the juvenile justice system.

Some forensic assessments, however, require a very different way of thinking about the evaluation than would be applied in purely clinical contexts. This is true when the evaluation must be designed to help the court address a specific legal standard. For example, to determine a defendant's competence to stand trial, a court must decide whether the defendant "has sufficient present ability to consult with his attorney with a reasonable degree of rational understanding and a rational as well as factual understanding of the proceedings against him" (*Dusky v. U.S.*, 1960). A clinician who performs an evaluation to assist a court in addressing this legal standard must

- translate the legal standard into constructs that have relevance for both law and psychology/psychiatry;
- evaluate the defendant with regard to those constructs; and
- interpret and communicate the results in a way that will ensure that they can be applied by the court in addressing the legal standard.

There are other ways in which all forensic evaluations for juvenile courts are somewhat different from evaluations in clinical contexts. They must always be interpreted and communicated in a way that will be useful for decisionmaking by people who are not clinicians (e.g., judges and attorneys). In addition, the evaluation's use in a legal context often means that the evaluation report must provide more documentation, and a more detailed description of one's logic, than would be necessary for most clinical settings. And often the information will not be protected by rules of confidentiality that apply to most clinical relationships.

Clinicians can never merely transport their clinical skills to the juvenile court and carry out their evaluations as though they were in a clinical setting. Every evaluation for juvenile court is transformed by the legal context in which it is being performed and used.

3.4 *Contractual Arrangements for Evaluations*

Clinicians perform evaluations in delinquency cases in the context of either of two broad contractual relationships: as a professional in a *court clinic service* or on a *case-by-case contractual basis*. These two arrangements are important to understand because they constitute an essential background for examining the practical and ethical issues that arise in providing evaluations in delinquency cases (which will be discussed in Chapter 7).

A *court clinic service* is any individual or group of practitioners responsible for meeting the daily evaluation needs of a juvenile court. Some court clinics are within the organizational structure of the juvenile court so that the clinicians are employees of the court. In other cases, the court clinic is a private practice group (or "vendor") with a contract to meet whatever evaluation needs arise for the juvenile court on a continuing day-to-day basis. In either case, the court clinic's offices may be in the same facility as the juvenile court or may be located in office space outside yet near the juvenile court. The functions and obligations of professionals in these two arrangements are often exactly the same, and in both types of arrangements the professionals must follow the same rules of the court. The differences are primarily administrative and financial.

Professionals providing *case-by-case contractual services* are private practitioners who accept referrals for evaluations in delinquency cases as they arise. They have no continuing contractual obligation to provide evaluations for any party. Their referrals may come from defense attorneys, prosecutors, or the juvenile court. In some communities, all of the delinquency evaluations that are requested by the court are performed by private practitioners, sometimes chosen on a case-by-case basis from a court list of professionals in the community. (In addition, some court clinics use a mixed model in which they perform some evaluations themselves and contract with private practitioners for some evaluations on a case-by-case basis.) These professionals may be on the court's list by prior agreement with the court, and perhaps they have had to meet certain qualifications to be included on the list.

When defense attorneys or prosecutors seek independent evaluations in delinquency cases, typically they will contact clinicians with whom they have worked in the past or who are recommended by their colleagues. Financial compensation for the clinician's services to prosecutors typically are paid by the prosecutor's office. Youths' families typically cannot afford to pay for clinical services provided to their defense attorney. Therefore, clinicians performing independent evaluations (e.g., not court-ordered) for defense attorneys usually are paid out of special state or court funds that are earmarked for defense services for indigent defendants.

3.5 *Professionals Who Perform the Evaluations*

Remarkably little is known with any certainty about psychologists and psychiatrists who perform evaluations in delinquency cases. Few clinicians perform delinquency evaluations as their sole practice; even full-time juvenile court clinicians typically perform a substantial number of evaluations in other areas of juvenile law, such as evaluations for child abuse and neglect, child custody, and child witness issues. In addition to juvenile court clinicians, many clinical psychologists and psychiatrists perform such evaluations as some part of their practice or occasionally find themselves testifying in delinquency cases.

The number of juvenile court clinics in the U.S. is not known, and I know of no published surveys of juvenile court clinics. I am aware of no national "networks" that would offer clinicians in these settings a sense of shared professional identity beyond their associations with local colleagues. Over the years, however, the American Psychiatric Association has sponsored working groups on issues in child psychiatry and the juvenile court which have provided a sense of recognition for this subfield of psychiatry that is not found in clinical psychology. Organizational interests in the practice of child psychology and the law tend more often to have focused on evaluations for questions of child custody and other legal issues related to child welfare.

It is unlikely that most psychologists or psychiatrists who perform evaluations in delinquency cases were formally trained for this specialty. Many were trained in child psychiatry and child clinical psychology, but few psychiatry residency or graduate psychology programs are available for specialized training in evaluations of children in legal contexts. A small number of child forensic psychiatrists obtain training in psychiatry and law fellow programs. But until recently there have been only a handful of forensic psychology postdoctoral training programs, and they usually provide experience in juvenile court evaluations only as a rotation, not as a specialty.

We know almost nothing, therefore, about the body of clinicians who have gravitated toward juvenile court evaluations: how many there are, their typical career tracks, their satisfaction with their roles, or how they have organized their services to meet the needs of juvenile courts and juvenile defense attorneys. This ignorance stands in stark contrast to society's growing alarm at the increase in violent offending among youths, the undoubtedly large number of forensic evaluations that are being performed daily in the processing of delinquency cases, and the importance of these evaluations in light of the juvenile court's traditional reliance upon them to make far-reaching decisions about the rehabilitation and confinement of youths.

4.0 FUNDAMENTAL KNOWLEDGE ABOUT YOUTHS

Clinicians who perform evaluations in delinquency cases must have specialized knowledge and experience regarding children and adolescents. Fundamental aspects of this knowledge include (a) theories and empirical information about *adolescent development*; (b) theories and understanding of aggression, delinquency, and *adolescent offenders*; (c) the nature and diagnosis of *adolescent psychopathology*; and (d) the *assessment of adolescents*.

The literature in each of these areas is vast, including decades of theoretical and empirical contributions within developmental, clinical, educational, and social psychology, as well as psychiatry, criminology, and sociology. This section will not review or cite this literature even in a general sense. It simply highlights some of the ways in which information in these four areas is relevant for evaluations in delinquency cases. These comments for the most part are previews of issues discussed in greater detail in subsequent chapters in the context of their relevance for specific types of forensic evaluations of juveniles.

4.1 *Adolescent Development*

Nothing about the behavior of adolescents can be understood without considering it in the context of youths' continued biological, psychological, and social development. Youths are continually in transition to adulthood in all of these areas, a fact that has a number of general implications for understanding their behavior at a given time and judging what it will be in the future.

Some aspects of development, especially cognitive abilities and psychosocial characteristics, are age related. The average 12-year-old is not like the average 15-year-old, who in turn is not like the average 20-year-old. Yet there is much variability at any given age in youths' abilities, perspectives, and social capacities, too great to be able to say much that is really important about them individually on the basis of their age alone. This intra-age variability is due to many things:

- Youths' tendencies to develop at different rates in general, and to develop in spurts, delays, or temporary regressions
- Their development of new abilities in a specific social context, with a delay in their application of that ability to other social contexts
- Youths' tendencies to "enact" a persona to "try it out," only to discard it after a few weeks, perhaps retaining some fragment of it as part of a developing self that will not crystallize until much later
- The likelihood that stress and emotion interfere with their capacities to use abilities that they have recently acquired, more so than for adults who have had greater experience in exercising those capacities across a variety of circumstances

All of these phenomena together make the usual course of development anything but linear and smoothly progressive, and this has important implications for the assessment of youths. Compared to the assessment of adults, the erratic quality of youths' development increases the likelihood of error when generalizing from the youth's behavior today—at the time of the assessment—to future points in time. This is not to say that adolescents do not have enduring individual characteristics. But those characteristics often are not yet shaped to their final form and tend to be comingled at any given time with some behaviors, attitudes, and perceptions that will not be enduring in the long run. This, in fact, is precisely what has maintained the traditional perception of adolescents as malleable and potentially responsive to intervention that can positively direct their development.

Some clinicians who choose to embark upon forensic evaluations of juveniles may have been away from the field of developmental psychology since their graduate school or residency days. If so, they should be warned that the developmental contributions of Piaget and Erikson that may have formed the basis for their early education in this area are no longer the dominant theoretical perspectives for adolescent development. Clinicians who need to explore newer developmental theories are advised to obtain and read a very current advanced textbook on developmental psychology, perhaps the one that is used in the psychology graduate school at their local university.

4.2 *Adolescent Offenders*

Clinicians will find that their abilities to perform assessments in delinquency cases will be improved if they have basic information on

- Theories of delinquency
- Statistics on the prevalence of delinquency and serious violent offenses among youths
- Empirical information about the relation of delinquency to demographic and historical factors in youths' lives
- Data that help to conceptualize developmental "pathways" to delinquency

The literature contributing to our knowledge in these areas has grown tremendously in the past two decades. For clinicians to obtain a basic foundation for performing delinquency evaluations, I would recommend starting with a review of two references: a recent textbook (perhaps the one used in one's local university courses on delinquency) on sociological and psychological theories of delinquency, and a book by Howell et al. (1995) entitled *A Sourcebook: Serious, Violent, and Chronic Juvenile Offenders*. The latter is a very effective compilation of crime statistics and social science research on factors and developmental pathways related to delinquent behavior. It will also guide the clinician to references on specific topics that the clinician may want to examine in more detail.

Empirical information on the causes and development of delinquency is continuously being refined, and information such as prevalence for various types of offenses naturally changes across time. One way to keep abreast of such changes is to request to be on the mailing list of the Office of Juvenile Justice and Delinquency Prevention (Department of Justice, Washington DC 20531), which frequently publishes monographs that summarize juvenile justice statistics.

Although new information continues to refine our knowledge of patterns and causes of delinquency, certain general observations that have stood the test of time form a foundation and context for delinquency evaluations. Many of these are reviewed in the other chapters in this book. Examples include the following:

- By self-report, the majority of adolescent males engage in behaviors which, if they were arrested, would be charged as misdemeanors or felonies (e.g., see Elliott et al., 1983). Those whom we call "delinquents," therefore, are not necessarily a psychological or social subset of adolescents; they are adolescents whose delinquent acts have been detected and who have been arrested and "found" delinquent.
- Arrests per 1,000 youths at a given age begin to increase at about age 12 and decline rapidly after age 18 (Howell et al., 1985; Moffitt, 1993). *Most youths who are arrested in adolescence do not continue offending past the adolescent years.* This "desistance phenomenon" apparently is due to the effects of maturation and a transition to adult psychological and social status (see 4–1.5).
- Arrests per 1,000 youths at a given age for violent offenses follow the same pattern as above and are higher for ages 15 to 20 than for the rest of adulthood. The pattern is the same for white and minority youths, except that the actual prevalence per 1,000 is about 50% higher for African-American males than for White males in the peak years (16 to 19) (Howell et al., 1995).
- Most youths who are arrested for violent offenses do not engage in further violence. Those who do engage in a second or third violent offense tend to be at high risk of many future violent acts and arrests. Based on self-reported offending, *chronic* violent offenders account for only about

15% of all youthful violent offenders but are responsible for about 50% to 70% of all violent offenses by youths (Howell et al., 1995).

- Chronic youthful violent offenders (in contrast to youths with violent offense arrests who do not engage in further violence) tend more often to have early childhood disruptive and aggressive behavior problems and to engage in their first official delinquent acts prior to age 12 (Moffitt, 1993).
- Key background risk factors during childhood for serious and chronic delinquent youths are family conflict, economic deprivation, and related community disorganization. Key risk factors related to the immediate context for delinquency include the availability of guns and drugs, community/family attitudes that favor (or do not effectively discourage) crime and substance use, and the influence of peer groups (see Chapter 4).

4.3 *Adolescent Psychopathology*

Clinicians who perform delinquency evaluations must be familiar with the criteria for childhood mental disorders that are most prevalent in delinquent populations. These include Conduct Disorder, Attention-Deficit/Hyperactivity Disorder, Substance Abuse and Dependence, affective disorders, personality disorders, and Posttraumatic Stress Disorder. Psychotic disorders are not frequent, but their prevalence is slightly greater than in the general population of adolescents. Clinicians must also be able to identify youths who might meet criteria for Mental Retardation or might need to be examined for specific learning disabilities.

The prevalence of these disorders among delinquent youths is not easy to discern. There has been only a small number of epidemiological studies of mental disorder among delinquent samples, and they have produced widely discrepant results. Currently the best review of this research is by Otto et al. (1992). This is a chapter in a monograph edited by Cocozza (1992), which, unfortunately, may be hard for clinicians to find because it was not published by a publishing company. (Inquiries may be made by contacting Dr. Otto at the Florida Mental Health Institute at University of South Florida in Tampa, FL or Dr. Cocozza at Policy Research Associates in Delmar, NY.)

31

The following observations about the prevalence of mental disorder among youths in the juvenile justice system are drawn from Otto's review:

- The prevalence rate of psychiatric disturbances for *adolescents in general* is probably between 14% and 22%.
- Among delinquent youths, studies find that Conduct Disorder is the most prevalent diagnosis (probably about 50% to 60%), followed by Substance Abuse/Dependence (probably 25% to 50%).
- Many delinquent youths manifest Attention-Deficit/Hyperactivity Disorder (prevalence rate uncertain, but probably more than 20%).
- The prevalence rates for affective disorders among delinquent youths have ranged from 30% to 75% in various studies.
- The prevalence of Posttraumatic Stress Disorder among delinquent youths has been reported as ranging from just under 10% to 40% in various studies.
- Psychotic disorders among delinquent youths have been reported at prevalence rates of 1% to 6%.
- Comorbidity among delinquent youths is very common, especially Conduct Disorder together with one or more other psychiatric disorders.

Child mental health specialists have long recognized that it is often much more difficult to diagnose adolescents' mental disorders than those of adult psychiatric populations. The stability of personality disorder diagnoses in adolescents has been shown to be especially poor (Hertzig, 1992; Mattanah et al., 1995). Often this has been blamed on our diagnostic classification systems for children's and adolescents' disorders. Yet the difficulty is also related to the nature of adolescents' disorders themselves. Adolescents' developmental status causes their disorders to be manifested in ways that make differential diagnosis quite difficult. For example, while anger and aggression are typical of youths with Conduct Disorder or developing personality disorders, they are also one of the most common presentations of youths who have serious affective disorders.

Moreover, many adolescents manifest affective and cognitive states that are like the symptoms of formal disorders, but which in time prove to be temporary manifestations related to developmental processes. For example, instability in mood and affect is typical of many adolescents at various stages in their development, whereas it would have a more pathological significance in adults. These developmental phenomena complicate the diagnostic process and produce a higher risk of false positives when assessing adolescents compared to adults.

The high prevalence of Conduct Disorder as a diagnosis in delinquency cases warrants mention of three pitfalls that clinicians should avoid when applying *DSM-IV* criteria in the diagnostic process.

First, some clinicians have a tendency to stop the diagnostic process when they find that the youth meets the formal criteria for Conduct Disorder (which consist primarily of the presence of a variety of delinquent behaviors in the youth's past history). This ignores the fact that Conduct Disorder is often comorbid with one or more other psychiatric disorders. The job is not to find "a diagnosis" but to discover and describe the youth's psychological condition. Rarely is this job completed by establishing a diagnosis of Conduct Disorder.

Second, clinicians should recognize that not all youths who meet the formal criteria for Conduct Disorder—even perfectly— should be given a diagnosis of Conduct Disorder. Most of the criteria for Conduct Disorder are specific aggressive, destructive, deceitful, or oppositional behaviors. *DSM-IV* commentary points out, however, that "the Conduct Disorder diagnosis should be applied only when the behavior in question is symptomatic of an underlying dysfunction within the individual and not simply a reaction to the immediate social context" (American Psychiatric Association, 1994, p. 88). This requires that the clinician explore the causal relationships between the criterion behaviors and (a) the youth's personality as well as (b) the social and cultural conditions in which the youth's past criterion behaviors occurred. In at least some instances, youths who meet all of the formal criteria for Conduct Disorder should not be given the diagnosis.

Third, clinicians who are unaccustomed to diagnostic work with adolescents should very carefully identify the relation of

Conduct Disorder to Antisocial Personality Disorder. I have had the painful experience of hearing psychologists and psychiatrists testify to a misinterpretation of that relationship in the following ways:

- "Kids with Conduct Disorder (CD) become adults with Antisocial Personality Disorder (APD)."
- "Conduct Disorder is the adolescent version of Antisocial Personality Disorder."
- "Antisocial Personality Disorder is what youths with Conduct Disorder become—after all, according to *DSM-IV* criteria, an adult can be APD only if he was CD in adolescence."

This misassociation was so strong for one clinician that he testified that a 15-year-old boy should be diagnosed Antisocial Personality Disorder, even though criterion "B" for APD requires that the individual must be at least 18 years of age. The clinician claimed that this could be overlooked when, as in this case, the youth met all criteria for Conduct Disorder as well as all 7—not just the required 3-out-of-7—specific indicators in criterion "A" for Antisocial Personality Disorder.

The simple key to avoiding this misinterpretation is on page 89 of the *DSM-IV*. The majority of youths who can be diagnosed Conduct Disorder "remit by adulthood." *DSM-III-R* estimated that this was true for about two-thirds of them (American Psychiatric Association, 1987). Conduct Disorder is a necessary precondition for APD, but it does not predict APD.

4.4 *Adolescent Assessment*

One of the adjustments for clinicians whose experience has focused mostly on the assessment of adults is the need to learn and use a different set of psychological tests developed specifically for adolescents and offering adolescent norms. A recent book by Hoge and Andrews (1996), *Assessing the Youthful Offender*, provides a good "menu" of tests for assessing adolescents' aptitudes and achievement, personality traits, psychiatric disorders, and risk of future delinquency. Tests related to specific types of evaluations are recommended in each of the following chapters in this book and discussed in terms of their role in the context of the evaluation process. Although the tests are not reviewed in detail, sources are provided where clinicians can obtain information about their application with adolescents. Heilbrun (1992) has outlined several criteria that can guide the clinician in selecting test instruments for use in forensic settings.

Interviewing delinquent youths presents certain challenges less often encountered with adults. The sullen, oppositional attitude of many youths makes the going difficult at times, requiring adjustments in style that probably differ considerably from one clinician to the next. On the other hand, more commonly than one might expect, youths charged with serious offenses are often forthcoming regarding various aspects of their life, even showing signs of developing a relationship with the examiner if the evaluation requires several sessions.

Finally, forensic examiners who are accustomed to assessing adult defendants will find that their evaluations of youthful offenders must have a broader focus that includes the assessment of families. This is a natural consequence of youths' social and emotional dependence on their parents, for which reason youths' behaviors rarely can be understood adequately without having a picture of their parents. Parents also are a primary source of information about the youth's past development and present behaviors, and they often articulate issues in family dynamics that youths either cannot or do not want to discuss.

In conclusion, clinicians who wish to perform evaluations in delinquency cases must become familiar with the *legal context* for their work, their *professional role* in that legal context, and specialized information about *adolescents*, especially their development, delinquency, psychopathology, and assessment. This is a challenging but feasible task for most well-trained clinicians if it is done as a continuing process rather than a crash course.

Beyond this background for doing evaluations in delinquency cases, one must be able to conceptualize clinical evaluations for the various specific legal questions that are raised in juvenile courts. This is the objective of Chapters 2 through 6.

Chapter 2

Juveniles' Waiver of Miranda Rights

*W*hen juveniles are arrested on suspicion of committing serious offenses, they are often questioned by police who seek a statement—usually a confession—concerning the alleged offense. Defense attorneys sometimes challenge the validity of these confessions, seeking to exclude them as evidence in delinquency proceedings. The challenge often is based in part on a claim that the juvenile was not capable of waiving rights to silence and counsel "voluntarily, knowingly, and intelligently" when the "Miranda warnings" were presented to the youth.

In this context, mental health professionals may be asked to evaluate the youth to assist the court in a decision about the youth's capacities to waive Miranda rights. This chapter provides guidance for those evaluations. Section 1.0 describes the legal, theoretical, and contextual background for such evaluations. Section 2.0 conceptualizes the purpose of the evaluation, and 3.0 describes the evaluation process. Section 4.0 discusses the use of standardized assessment methods in these evaluations, especially forensic assessment instruments that have been developed specifically for Miranda waiver evaluations. Interpretive issues are discussed in Section 5.0, and reports and testimony in 6.0.

1.0 THE LEGAL AND SOCIAL CONTEXT FOR MIRANDA WAIVER EVALUATIONS

1.1 *Validity of Juveniles' Confessions*

In *Miranda v. Arizona* (1966), the U.S. Supreme Court affirmed and defined an important right of criminal suspects. If their confessions are to be used as evidence at trials, the confessions must be made with suspects' knowledge that they have certain rights while in custody. These include the right to avoid self-incrimination (Fifth Amendment) and the right to advice of counsel (Fourteenth Amendment) prior to or during in-custody legal proceedings such as police questioning. Defendants' confessions cannot be used against them in criminal proceedings if it is found that they could not have waived these rights "voluntarily, knowingly, and intelligently."

In *Miranda*, the Court established a procedural requirement that was intended to augment this protection of fundamental rights. Confessions would be considered invalid as evidence if police failed to provide certain information to suspects prior to their confession during police questioning. The information included notification of the right to silence, the potential for use of their statements in later court proceedings, the right to legal counsel prior to and during interrogation, and the availability of free legal counsel. Soon after the Court's decision, police departments across the nation constructed and put into effect what came to be called the "Miranda warnings," most of them patterned after the Court's wording of suggested warnings in an appendix to the *Miranda* decision.

Miranda was an adult case. Its protections were soon extended to youths by state courts' interpretations of the U.S. Supreme Court's decisions in *Kent v. U.S.* (1966) and *In re Gault* (1967). These cases affirmed that the relevant constitutional rights applied to juveniles at all stages of delinquency proceedings.

This almost immediately raised another issue in the courts: Even if juveniles were provided Miranda warnings, were they capable of waiving rights voluntarily, knowingly, and intelligently? Were they "competent" to waive Miranda rights? The prevailing legal approach to this question was first outlined in *People v. Lara* (1967), elaborated in *West v. U.S.* (1968), and affirmed by the U.S. Supreme Court in *Fare v. Michael C.* (1979).

These cases acknowledged that the mere fact of being a juvenile did not invalidate a waiver of rights. They also recognized, however, that juveniles as a class were at greater risk than adults of having deficiencies in the intellectual or emotional characteristics required to satisfy the standard for valid waiver. Juveniles' waiver

of rights would thus require greater scrutiny and special considerations not usually raised in adult cases. The validity of a juvenile's
waiver was not based on any single factor alone—for example, age,
intelligence, or developmental status. Instead, each case was to be
decided in light of the "totality of circumstances." As will be
discussed later, legal descriptions of the *totality of circumstances*
have focused on two broad types of case factors: (a) *features of the
situation* in which the youth made the confession, and (b) *characteristics of the youth* that might diminish (or augment) abilities to
understand and apply the Miranda warnings.

During the 1970s and 1980s, many states' legislatures or courts
added a procedural requirement for juvenile interrogations that is
not available to adult defendants. They required that police officers must arrange for the youth's contact with a parent, guardian,
or other "interested adult" prior to waiver of Miranda rights in
order to provide the opportunity for the youth to be advised
regarding the waiver of rights during police questioning. This
added protection was intended to reduce the risk of invalid confessions due to juveniles' questionable capacities to understand the
warnings and weigh their significance.

1.2 *The Process of Police Questioning and Miranda Warnings*

Police officers question juveniles about their activities in various circumstances. These range from almost casual street-corner
discussions to formal, videotaped statements at police headquar-
ters. Between these two extremes are semi-formal investigative
activities, such as a visit to the youth's home to gather information
related to an offense about which police believe the youth might
have information.

Any of these encounters may lead to a youth's confession, but
not all of them require Miranda warnings. The warnings must be
given when the questioning occurs while the youth is in police
custody. What constitutes "custody" is a legal question that
continues to be refined, but generally it is that point when the
suspect has been "apprehended"—is not free to walk away from
the encounter. When street-corner confessions occur during
noncustodial encounters (and without Miranda warnings), they
may be valid if they were truly spontaneous. If they were derived

from noncustodial questions by police, however, their validity more often depends on whether the police officers' questions were directed toward obtaining a confession and whether they subsequently took the youth into custody, endeavored to meet all procedural requirements (e.g., provided the Miranda warnings about rights), and the youth then waived the rights and repeated the confession.

A study in one jurisdiction (St. Louis) found that police officers formally questioned youths in about two-thirds of all felony arrests (Grisso, 1981). Attorneys were almost never present. As noted earlier, many states require that a parent, guardian, or interested adult must be present during the questioning process, or at least that the opportunity for consultation between youth and adult was offered. In addition, some states require that the questioning must occur in a setting such as a station house or a facility controlled by juvenile court regulations (e.g., a juvenile detention center). In these settings, typically one or two officers provide the Miranda warnings and offer the parent and youth the opportunity to talk them over. It is best for them to be allowed to do this in private, but sometimes police officers remain in attendance. Having obtained the waiver, police officers proceed to question the youth with or without the parent present.

Even when these general procedures are followed, the conditions under which arrests and questioning occur may vary considerably across police departments and from case to case. These conditions deserve comment because, as described later, they may play a significant role in the examiner's efforts to interpret a youth's capacities to have made a competent waiver of Miranda rights and a valid confession.

1.21 Prequestioning Conditions

Police officers arrest and question youths at any time of day or night. I have evaluated cases in which youths and parents were roused from their beds at midnight, with questioning of the youth at the station house occurring at 3:00 a.m. or 4:00 a.m.

Youths sometimes will not be questioned immediately upon arrest and transportation to the station house. Parents may not be available immediately, or police officers may wish to obtain relevant information from other youths who have been arrested simultaneously because of suspected involvement in the offense. Therefore, the youth may be placed for some time in a holding cell or special unit of a detention facility prior to questioning.

In some cases, courts have been interested in the nature of this prequestioning confinement as it might be related to the emotional condition of the youth when questioning was finally initiated. Facts that courts have considered in this regard include

- the length of time the youth was held "incommunicado" (without opportunity to communicate with others or obtain social support)
- the physical conditions of the holding cell
- the degree of contact with other incarcerated persons (especially the adults)
- whether the youth was provided food and other necessities
- whether anything was done by officers that might be seen as an attempt to instill fear

A review of courts' decisions does not make clear specifically how each of these conditions was weighed and under what specific circumstances they made a difference in judicial decisions about the validity of youths' waivers. Moreover, there is no research on their actual effects on youths' capacities at the time of police interrogation.

1.22 Social Structure of the Questioning

Station-house questioning usually occurs in an interview room designated for that purpose, but the physical and social arrangements of questioning will vary. Typically the room holds a desk or conference table and several chairs. Present are the youth and one or two officers although cases have been recorded in which a large number of uniformed and armed officers have been present, increasing the intimidating effect of the encounter.

The "interested adult" may or may not be present during police questioning and during reading of the Miranda rights to the youth. When the parent is there, often the parent and youth are placed across the table from an officer. But I have observed cases in which the parent was given a chair that was behind the officer or away from the line of conversation, which has the subtle effect of placing the parent in the role of observer rather than participant-advisor. The absence of windows, dim or harsh lighting, hard benches, and other architectural factors may have significance depending on the length and intensity of the questioning.

1.23 How the Warnings Are Given

The general content of the warnings is similar across police jurisdictions, but they may be worded in somewhat different ways. The following is a typical example:

1. You do not have to make a statement and have the right to remain silent.
2. Anything you say can and will be used against you in court.
3. You have the right to consult an attorney prior to any interrogation (sometimes "questioning") and to have an attorney present at the time of interrogation.
4. If you cannot afford an attorney, one may be appointed to you free of charge.

A fifth statement not specifically recommended by the *Miranda* court is often included:

5. If you decide to answer questions, you may stop at any time during the questioning.

These warnings typically are on a printed form. Suspects might be asked to initial each warning, and there is a space to sign their name at the bottom of the page. A colleague has informed me of a procedure she encountered in which the youth is asked to sign the Miranda form and the telephone card (explaining the right to make a telephone call) at the same time. In her evaluations, some youths have seemed confused about which form was the Miranda form, and their simultaneous presentation could make the Miranda form seem less significant when presented together with another form that merely discloses that one is entitled to a telephone call.

When giving Miranda warnings, police officers typically place the page in front of the youth and parent, an officer reads the warnings aloud, then requests the youth's signature at the end after giving the youth and parent time to confer.

I have encountered many variations, however. Officers may recite the warnings carefully and slowly, or they may present them in a rapid and rote fashion. Police officers sometimes recite all the warnings *before* the page is placed in front of the youth. Sometimes they do not recite the warnings, but place the page in front of youths and ask them to read it, sometimes to themselves and sometimes aloud. Although it may not be typical, some officers go beyond reciting the warnings to provide the youth explanations or interpretations of them. Less frequently, they may ask youths to "tell me what it means" in order to evaluate their understanding of the warnings.

When and how the warnings are given in relation to questioning about the offense will vary. Often a recitation of the warnings precedes any questioning. But sometimes considerable questioning occurs before the Miranda warnings are offered. In those situations, enough information is obtained to recognize that a confession will be forthcoming ("Okay, okay. I guess I'll tell you what really happened"), at which time the warnings are given and the waiver is documented. If an initial recitation was given, the formal reading and signing of the form may occur after the confession, with a repetition of the confession statement after the formal waiver. Indeed, it is not uncommon to find that the Miranda warnings have been given two or more times, in various ways, during a single questioning session.

Most Miranda forms end with a sentence stating that "I have read my rights, I understand them, and I wish to waive these rights and make a statement." This is followed by a place for the youth's and parent's signature. Sometimes police officers' instructions to the youth are "Read everything, initial each of these statements, and sign at the bottom." Such instructions do not clearly indicate that the youth has a choice *not* to waive the rights. This may increase the likelihood of signing without comprehension of its significance. Some forms more clearly indicate that youths have a choice. For example, some police departments use forms that include "do" and "do not" boxes, so that youths are asked to check whether they do or don't wish to waive their rights.

1.24 Parents' Involvement

Although most states require that parents (or guardians or another "interested adult") be present, this is not meant to allow the parent to decide for the youth. Neither parents nor attorneys may waive the constitutional rights of youths in delinquency cases. The youth must make the decision.

States have required that parents be involved in the waiver in order to offer assistance to youths in understanding and deciding about waiver of their rights and to mitigate the potentially intimidating effects if they were to face police officers without adult support. Although the absence of any involvement by an interested adult invalidates youths' waivers and confessions in those states, their presence does not necessarily guarantee that the waiver is valid. At the time of their children's arrests, many parents themselves are anxious, fearful, or confused during the police encounter. Others are angry at the youth and contribute to the coercive pressure of the interrogation.

There is empirical evidence questioning the presumption that parents provide youths assistance in understanding the Miranda warnings and protection from coercive intimidation during police interrogations (Grisso, 1981; Grisso & Ring, 1979). In a survey study, many parents expressed the belief that they should put pressure on their arrested children to cooperate with police officers. Their reasoning focused on childrearing principles that teach respect for authority and acceptance of responsibility for wrongdoing. However, a study by Grisso (1981) of parents' actual communications with their children during interrogation found that 70% to 80% of parents offered *no* advice. In fact, no words at all were exchanged between parent and child in 66% of 390 juvenile interrogations. (Advice was given in about 20% of the cases, and it favored waiving vs. asserting the right to silence by a ratio of about 3:1.)

1.25   Style of Questioning

How police officers present their questions to the youth is relevant for the validity of waiver of rights. As noted previously, significant interchanges between police officers and the youth often occur prior to the waiver of rights. The nature of those discussions, as influenced by the officers' investigative strategy, might influence the voluntariness of the youth's waiver.

Reportedly, police officers rarely question juvenile suspects with abusive "rubber hose and bright light" tactics that once were said to characterize police interrogations. Modern training for police investigation (Inbau, Reid, & Buckley, 1986) stresses the value of a firm but "considerate" approach. For example, the officer can impress the youth with how bad the situation looks, express the opinion that the youth does not seem like a "bad kid," and then offer a way that the youth can provide a confession that allows the youth to foster that impression:

> "Look, I don't think you killed him in cold blood. You just don't seem like that kind of kid. Sometimes these things just happen without anyone wanting them to. I have a feeling that your shooting him was like that— just something that happened, not something you wanted. Is that the way it was?"

Strategies like this can foster a suspect's perceptions of the officer as a potential source of assistance—someone with whom to cooperate—in the face of the extreme jeopardy of the suspect's legal situation. The investigator is abiding by all legal requirements, while still having a reasonable chance of fulfilling the necessary objective to obtain a statement.

Occasionally one hears of cases in which this tactic takes extreme forms that result in false confessions by youths. In *A Death in Canaan*, the true story of a small-town Connecticut youth's interrogation and trial, Barthel (1977) described in detail a youth's questioning by local detectives concerning the murder of his mother. The boy discovered her mutilated body upon returning home one night, and in later years (after his conviction) it was determined that he could not have committed the offense. But over a period of several days following the murder, during which the boy at first denied any involvement, detectives endeavored to help him recover his "repressed memory" of killing his mother. Expressing extreme concern for his welfare, they urged him to "remember" the event lest its repression cause him to "go insane." They falsely reported to him that he had failed a lie detector test, and during questioning they provided details of the crime scene to help him reconstruct the event that never occurred. After a few days, he believed that he had killed his mother. He expressed relief and thanked the detectives for their help.

Other matters of procedure that are sometimes relevant are the length of interrogation sessions, the number of sessions, and the number of days during which sessions are held. If the youth's friends are being interviewed regarding the same offense, information from those interviews is sometimes used to heighten the sense of jeopardy and of risk in failing to cooperate while one's friends might have done so.

There have been no recent studies describing the frequency with which youths waive their rights during police questioning. In one study (Grisso & Pomicter, 1977), about 90% of youths who were asked to make statements about suspected felonies had waived their rights to silence and counsel. By comparison, other studies of adult suspects (e.g., Seeburger & Wettick, 1967) have reported waiver rates of about 60%.

1.26 Documentation of Rights Waiver

Police officers typically are careful to record that the suspect was given the Miranda warnings and to include the suspect's signed waiver as documentation. Yet rarely will police records describe the specific context of the rights waiver and the manner in which the Miranda warnings were given (see 2-1.22 and 2-1.23).

Most police departments are equipped to audiotape or video-tape sessions with suspects although mechanical recording tends to be used primarily in cases involving more serious allegations. Sometimes the whole questioning process will be audiotaped, and occasionally it will have been transcribed. When videotaping is used, it tends to be done after the questioning has achieved a statement by the youth. Videotape equipment is then set up, usually with a clock visible in the background, and a formal question-and-answer process recapitulates the prior statement.

Many police records will contain written versions of the youth's statement. Sometimes the youth is asked to write it. More often, police officers write their own account based on the youth's statement during questioning. Then the youth is asked to read it (or officers read it aloud), with instructions to the youth to correct anything that is in error or that the youth does not wish to say. Because these statements are not the youth's own words, the degree to which they reflect the youth's own thoughts and ways of describing the event is often questionable.

1.3 *Referral for Evaluation*

On rare occasions a clinician in a juvenile court clinic might be asked to "screen" a youth for the capacity to provide a meaningful waiver of Miranda rights at the time that police officers intend to pursue questioning. Typically, however, the legal question and the referral for evaluation arise after questioning and waiver have occurred but before the adjudication hearing on the charges. The clinical questions to be addressed, therefore, are usually retrospective; they refer to the youth's capacities in the past, at the time of the interrogation and the circumstances that surrounded it.

The question is usually raised by the defense attorney as a pretrial motion to exclude the confession, seeking a court ruling that it is inadmissible as evidence against the youth. The mental health examiner may receive the evaluation request from the defense attorney as a privileged consultation, but sometimes it may come from the court itself or from the prosecutor in anticipation of a defense expert's testimony.

Unfortunately, requests for evaluations related to youths' capacities to waive Miranda rights often arise months after the time of the youth's waiver and confession. Often it takes some time before attorneys learn about the nature of other evidence available to the prosecution. Whether the confession will be of ultimate significance depends in part on the strength or weakness of direct evidence that accumulates as the case proceeds. If direct evidence is strong, it may be in some youths' best interest to acknowledge rather than challenge the confession. Strategic issues of this type often mean that a decision about challenging the confession is delayed until a full picture of the evidence is developed or other challenges have been exhausted.

The delayed nature of the request has consequences for the examiner's task. The longer the time between the confession and the evaluation, the greater is the possibility that youths' performance at the time of the evaluation might not reflect their knowledge or emotional state at the time of the questioning when they were arrested.

1.4 *Presumptions about Validity of Juveniles' Waiver of Rights*

The U.S. Supreme Court last summarized in *Fare v. Michael C.* (1979) the legal precedent that guides judges in weighing the validity of juveniles' waiver of Miranda rights. The applicable laws of most states conform to this summary.

The question of a juvenile's capacities to waive Miranda rights begins with a rebuttable presumption of competence. The mere fact of being a juvenile does not invalidate a waiver of Miranda rights. As noted earlier, whether the confession may be used as evidence will depend on a judicial consideration of the "totality of the circumstances" in the instant case.

The totality of circumstances typically includes two broad classes of variables: (a) circumstances of the interrogation and (b) characteristics of the youth. These constitute the two general types of data with which the examiner will be concerned during an evaluation to assist the court in its determination about the validity of the waiver of rights. By implication, the eventual product also requires inferences about the interactions of these two types of variables: for example, the effect that the circumstances of the interrogation may have had on the performance of a youth who has certain characteristics identified by the examiner.

The Court in *Fare v. Michael C.* (1979) listed a number of factors for judges to consider within both of these categories. Although courts have been told to weigh these factors, the law has always resisted the development of formulas based on these variables. For example, no particular variable is considered more important than any others, and courts have generally refused to support any particular level of any variable (e.g., a particular age) as determinative of the legal question. Moreover, most courts consider lists of "factors to consider" as nonexclusive; judges are instructed to consider them, but they may consider other variables as well if they believe there is logical reason to do so.

1.41 Circumstances of the Interrogation

Various courts, including the Court in *Fare v. Michael C.*, have commented on the circumstances of police questioning that may be relevant to the inquiry. A composite of these circumstances has already been described in 2-1.2, where we have examined the ways in which these circumstances may vary from case to case, and they are outlined later in 2-3.3.

1.42 Characteristics of the Juvenile

Age is the most frequently cited juvenile characteristic. Appellate cases involving youths 12 years of age or younger have usually—but not always—resulted in opinions that they lacked requisite understanding of the Miranda rights. In contrast, appellate cases involving juveniles 16 to 18 years of age have most often resulted in opinions that the youths could understand the warnings. Cases of youths 13, 14, and 15 years of age have been associated with more variable outcomes.

Intelligence of the youth is frequently cited. Yet no particular level of intelligence—even mental retardation—has been seen by itself as indicative of incapacity to waive Miranda rights voluntarily, knowingly, and intelligently. While many youths with very low IQ scores (e.g., below 75) have been considered to have the requisite capacities, the majority of appellate cases in which juveniles' capacities were considered deficient have been youths with low IQ scores.

Judges have often considered *prior experience* with police officers and courts when weighing juveniles' capacities to waive Miranda rights. Less experience has been said to suggest possible naïveté, while more experience has led to presumptions of more sophisticated knowledge of rights and their significance in legal proceedings.

Extent of *education* has sometimes been considered, especially when youths have been in classrooms for students with developmental cognitive deficits. Achievement test scores affirming a youth's lack of academic ability sometimes are considered relevant.

Keep in mind that these are factors that judges have *presumed* are related to capacities relevant for comprehension and waiver of rights. As we will see later, the *empirical* relations between these factors and measures of youths' actual comprehension of Miranda rights do not always support judicial presumptions.

2.0 CONCEPTUALIZING THE EVALUATION

Planning the evaluation requires taking stock of one's objectives, as well as one's theoretical and empirical perspective on youths' characteristics that may be relevant for the Miranda waiver issue.

2.1 *Objectives of the Evaluation*

In an earlier work (Grisso, 1986), I described a scheme for analyzing the essential features of all legal competencies. Every type of legal competency can be seen as having four components, which I call (a) Functional (referring to functional abilities), (b) Causal, (c) Interactive, and (d) Judgmental. These concepts can be used to formulate the objectives of an evaluation for juveniles' capacities to waive Miranda rights.

2.11 Describing Functional Abilities

Evaluations should describe to the court the status of the youth's abilities that are relevant for the legal question. On what types of abilities should the evaluation focus? An examination of courts' concerns about juveniles' abilities in the context of waiver of Miranda rights suggests the following:

- the ability to *comprehend* the Miranda warnings
- the ability to *grasp the significance* of rights in the context of the legal process
- the ability to *process information* in arriving at a decision about waiver

The ability to *comprehend the Miranda warnings* refers simply to juveniles' capacities to understand what they are being told when the warnings are given to them. When the youth is told that "You do not have to make a statement and have the right to remain silent," does the youth understand that this conveys the message that he or she is not required to answer police officers' questions?

The ability to grasp the *significance of the Miranda warnings* goes beyond understanding of the warnings themselves to address the youth's relevant beliefs and perceptions. For example, some youths may understand that they have the right to have an attorney present. Yet this does not necessarily indicate that they understand or believe the function of defense counsel as an advocate. Without that foundational perception, understanding of one's right to have legal counsel may have little functional significance or relevance for the youth's decision about waiver of the right to counsel. The assessment, therefore, must include some indication of the youth's grasp of the function and significance of the Miranda rights during the legal process, not just an understanding that the rights exist.

Comprehension of the Miranda warnings, and a grasp of their significance, is related in theory to cognitive development and experience. Some words and phrases may simply not be understandable to some youths due to their immaturity or intellectual deficits. Moreover, as will be shown later, the concept of a legal right may be understood differently by youths at various stages of cognitive or moral development.

The ability to *process information,* or problem-solving capacity, refers to the youth's ability to use knowledge of the rights in a decisionmaking process aimed at making a choice about waiver of the rights. Here we are concerned with the youth's ability to engage in a process that involves comparisons of the consequences of optional choices that are available during the police investigation. This requires some degree of intellectual capacity. It also requires the ability to think in the abstract about hypothetical outcomes and to employ a sense of time perspective that considers both short-range and long-range consequences. These capacities are associated with the process of maturation and may be impaired by cognitive developmental disabilities.

An evaluation related to the question of rights waiver, therefore, aims to provide a description of the youth's status regarding these abilities. As we proceed, we must also remember that it is not just the youth's abilities at the time of the evaluation that are in question but also the youth's functional capacities at the time the rights were waived during police investigation.

2.12 Causal Explanations for Deficits in Abilities

If youths show deficits in the abilities noted previously, an additional objective of the evaluation is to explain the probable reasons for those deficits. Perhaps the most common reasons are cognitive and developmental: for example, developmental immaturity, intellectual deficits (e.g., mental retardation), and specific learning disabilities.

Other reasons, however, should be considered. For example, mental disorders, various types of emotional disturbance, and anomalies in psychosocial development may interfere with deployment of cognitive functions. Such conditions may be responsible for delusions, anxiety, anger at authority, depression, or attentional difficulties that will distort or inhibit the manifestation of a youth's cognitive capacity.

Malingering must also be considered as a "cause" of observed deficits in youths' cognitive performance. Like adults, youths are often capable of trying to appear to have deficits in order to achieve an advantage (e.g., suppression of the confession). The importance of assessing the potential for dissimulation in evaluations for capacities to waive Miranda rights cannot be overstated. Even when there are fairly convincing explanations for deficits based on intellectual or mental disabilities, it is still necessary in every evaluation of this type to address the possibility of dissimulation and to explain why it is or is not a reasonable explanation for the youth's poor performance during the evaluation, especially regarding understanding of the Miranda warnings. Suggestions for assessing dissimulation in Miranda waiver evaluations are offered in 2-5.2.

The "causal" objective, therefore, will require more than an evaluation of the youth's functional abilities that are related to competence to waive rights. One must also assess general intellectual, developmental, and emotional characteristics of the youth, as well as the possibility of dissimulation, as potential explanations for deficits in understanding of and reasoning about Miranda warnings.

2.13 Interaction of Abilities and Situational Demands

As noted earlier, the question before the court is retrospective: Was the youth competent to waive Miranda rights at the time of the police investigation? This question refers to a person-environment interaction. It requires a consideration of the abilities of the youth in the context of the specific demands of the interrogation situation that he or she faced.

This component is related to a basic maxim of all legal competencies. Whether a person is considered legally competent is not decided on the basis of the person's level of ability alone. It depends on *the degree of match or mismatch between the person's abilities and the demands of the situation.* One person may be found incompetent to make a particular decision even if the person is more capable than a second person who is found competent, given that the first person is facing more demanding circumstances (e.g., a more complex decision). Similarly, a relatively immature youth with limited abilities may be found competent when an older and more capable youth would not, if their specific interrogation situations presented very different demands.

This means that the evaluation must include an investigation of the specific circumstances of the events surrounding the police questioning and waiver of rights. It is especially important to realize that one of those circumstances is the role that the parent or guardian may have had in the process of making the decision about waiver of Miranda rights. In summary, part of the work of the examiner will involve an interpretation of the youth's capacities in light of the demands of the specific circumstances of the youth's questioning and Miranda decisionmaking process. This process will be discussed later in the chapter.

2.14 The Judgment about Competence to Waive Rights

Ultimately it must be decided whether the youth's abilities were *sufficient* to make a "voluntary, knowing, and intelligent" waiver, given the circumstances of the interrogation. Were the youth's abilities *enough* to meet the demands of the situation? In my opinion, this component of the process for arriving at competence decisions is not the clinician's responsibility.

The clinician's objective is to provide the court whatever clinical and psychological information is available to assist the court in making that judgment. This includes the information related to the Functional, Causal, and Interactive components described previously. This does not mean, however, that the examiner is responsible for answering the ultimate question: that is, whether the juvenile "is (or was) competent," or whether the waiver "was or was not valid." These are not clinical questions and are not

properly a matter for expert opinion by a mental health professional. They cannot be decided on the basis of psychological or
psychiatric expertise. Once all the facts are known and interpreted, whether the youth's capacities were *sufficient* to meet the
demands requires the application of moral values, the concerns of
society for the apprehension of offenders, and a sense of what is
just or unjust. Judges, not clinicians, are authorized by society to
apply those values to decisions about legal competence. (See
Grisso, 1986, pp. 26-29 for a full explanation of this position.)

Having said this, I must note that not all (perhaps not most)
forensic mental health professionals agree with this view. Many
of them believe that it is important for the court to hear the
clinician's opinion concerning the application of clinical data
to the final legal question. Thus my opinion is not supported by
a consensus of the profession and does not represent the field's
view of standard or adequate practice. This issue is discussed
further in Chapter 7.

2.2 *Theoretical Guidance for the Evaluation*

Developmental theory and past research on youths' capacities
can provide guidance for the examiner in preparing for the evaluation. They suggest hypotheses that need to be tested during the
evaluation, as well as the types of data that would address them.
These will be discussed at greater length in the section on
Interpretation (2-4.0), but some general points can be offered here.

Grisso (1981) has provided empirical data about understanding
of the Miranda warnings by adolescents in custody in juvenile
detention facilities. These results suggest that they have greater
difficulty than criminal adults (matched for IQ) in comprehending
the warnings and grasping their significance. Especially at risk
are younger adolescents and those with general intellectual or
cognitive developmental deficits.

Some younger adolescents may still be in the process of acquiring capacities that allow them, while making decisions, to think in
terms of hypothetical future situations and abstractions, which are
capacities associated with Piaget's (1972) "formal operations" stage
of cognitive development. Similarly, some adolescents may not
yet have acquired the capacity to think of a "right" in the abstract,
as something that is guaranteed by law and society rather than

controlled by persons in authority (Kohlberg, 1976; Melton, 1980).

Decisionmaking about rights requires not only cognitive capacity, but also judgment concerning the weights to be placed on the consequences of one's possible choices. Judgment may be influenced by factors that are related to psychosocial development: for example, time perspective that allows one to consider the longer-range future, and attitudes toward risk taking and personal vulnerability. To the extent that these psychological characteristics are still developing in adolescence (see Cauffman, 1996; Furby & Beyth-Marom, 1992; Scott, Reppucci, & Woolard, 1995; and Steinberg & Cauffman, 1996, for reviews of theory and empirical evidence), youths are at greater risk than adults of making decisions based on incomplete development in their perspective on the consequences of their Miranda waiver decisions.

How well youths are able to deploy their abilities after they are acquired may be dependent at any given time on their emotional states, such as moodiness, the influences of mental disorder, or stress associated with conditions under which the Miranda waiver decision is being made. Janis (1982) has described the effects of stress on decisionmaking, and there is considerable evidence that adolescents on average may have greater fluctuations in mood and emotion than adults and are therefore at greater risk of difficulties in understanding or decisionmaking as a result of current emotional states (Steinberg & Cauffman, 1996).

In summary, theory and research indicate that the examiner should be concerned with much more than merely the adolescent's capacities for understanding the Miranda warnings. The evaluation will also need to attend to questions of psychosocial maturity, mental disorder, and emotional disturbance.

3.0   THE EVALUATION PROCESS

Given these objectives, let us examine the process of data collection for an evaluation of a youth's abilities related to the waiver of Miranda rights during police questioning. This begins with the referral question, and continues with the review of records, interviews with the youth and parents, and psychological testing of the youth.

3.1 _Taking the Referral_

As noted earlier, typically the request for the evaluation will come from the youth's defense attorney or from the court. If the court is requesting the evaluation, it is usually because the defense has filed a motion to present evidence challenging the validity of the Miranda waiver, possibly including another examiner's evaluation of the youth. If the request comes from defense counsel, the evaluation will be conducted under the auspices of client privilege; one's report should be available to the court only with the eventual decision of the youth on advice of counsel. Most experienced forensic examiners, however, can describe instances in which a juvenile court judge has allowed a defense report to be admitted into evidence against defense counsel's objections and contrary to law (i.e., due to judicial error). Therefore, defense counsel's desire for a written report, especially if the results do not support the arguments of defense, should be discussed with the attorney if the referral is accepted.

When defense counsel first requests the evaluation, the examiner should carefully explore the attorney's specific questions and objectives. Typically this process begins with a brief description by the attorney concerning the police questioning process, as well as a description of the attorney's perceptions of relevant characteristics of the youth. This leads to a statement of the attorney's specific concerns.

In my experience, attorneys tend to frame their concerns in ways that imply one or more of three distinct questions:

- Did the youth _understand and appreciate_ the significance of the Miranda warnings? Was the waiver invalid because of a lack of understanding of the rights, appreciation of their significance, or ability to make judgments about their consequences?
- Was the youth capable of _exercising autonomous choice_ about waiver of the Miranda rights? Given the characteristics of the youth and the nature of the situation, was the waiver invalid because of undue intimidation or pressure?
- Was the youth's confession _reliable_? Given the characteristics of the youth and the nature of the situation, was the youth's confession false or distorted—for example, due to fear or confusion?

It is important to realize that these questions are conceptually distinct, not repetitious. Hypothetically, any one of them can be answered "yes" while answering the others "no."

The attorney may be interested in only one or two of these questions, but sometimes all three questions are implied in the request. The examiner should endeavor to determine which of these questions is (or are) the focus of the referral. Even if the attorney wants all of them explored, the discussion should seek to differentiate them in order to frame the request clearly.

If the examiner does not feel comfortable accepting any of these questions as an objective for the evaluation, that should be communicated to the attorney at this point. For example, when I receive the third question—the reliability of the youth's confession—I almost always warn the attorney that I am not likely to be able to address it. If nonpsychological facts will answer the question (e.g., if there is empirical evidence that the youth was not at the scene of the offense to which he or she is confessing), there is no reason to ask for a clinical opinion about it. If nonpsychological evidence is not available, I rarely find that psychological evidence and circumstances of the interrogation alone allow me to form a confident opinion concerning the proposition that a youth offered a distorted or fabricated confession. I prefer to warn the attorney that the likelihood that I will be able to form a confident opinion on this question is remote.

3.2 *Obtaining Records*

The examiner should arrange for the attorney to obtain and provide to the examiner any past records that might be of help in meeting the objectives of the evaluation. The following types of records often are relevant:

- *School Performance*: Recent school marks are very important. Records for the entire school history may be less relevant, but elementary school marks with which to compare current (e.g., middle school) marks sometimes reveal consistency or inconsistency of a youth's present cognitive difficulties.
- *Academic Evaluations*: Any special academic testing (e.g., intelligence and achievement tests, special education evalu-

ations) for the entire academic career of the youth should be obtained.

- *Mental Health Evaluations*: The attorney should be asked to obtain all psychological evaluations (and reports of mental health treatment) that have occurred at any time in the past.
- *Delinquency Records*: A complete list of arrests and adjudications should be obtained, bearing on the youth's prior involvement with police and legal procedures.
- *Police Investigative Report*: The attorney should obtain a copy of all reports in police files documenting the current arrest, questioning, and investigation of the case. This would include copies of any audiotapes and videotapes that were made of the youth's questioning and confession.

Some examiners prefer to engage in their first interview with the youth before reviewing documents, in order to form a first impression without potential bias. I prefer to review documents before proceeding with interviewing and testing of the youth and third parties. Their contents may significantly influence the nature of the questions that I want to pose in interviews, and they allow me to form hypotheses to be tested during the evaluation. I also feel at a distinct disadvantage to explore questions of dissimulation and falsification if I embark on interviews without this background information.

3.3 *Interviewing Parents*

The examiner should interview as many people as possible who were involved in the arrest and interrogation events. Typically this will include the youth's parents (or guardian). Parents should be interviewed even if they were not involved in the events at the police station, because they can often provide background information about the youth, as well as information about the youth's life circumstances and mental status during the days prior to the arrest.

Interviews with parents should be conducted without the youth's presence, in order to provide independent reports of the relevant events. There are three broad types of information that the examiner seeks to obtain in the parent interview: (a) life-course developmental information, (b) observations about the arrest and questioning, and (c) the parent as a resource for the youth during the arrest and questioning process.

The *life-course developmental information* that the parent may provide is similar to that which would be gained in many other clinical situations, but should focus on areas that are most likely to be relevant for the cognitive and psychosocial questions raised by the Miranda waiver evaluation. This might include, for example, birth/medical/injury history, social developmental milestones, educational history, and a history of emotional disturbances and mental health concerns, especially those resulting in contacts with mental health agencies.

The examiner should engage the parent in a detailed chronological report of *events surrounding the arrest and questioning*, as the parent observed them. This should begin at some point a few days prior to the arrest, then carry on through the arrest itself, events at the police station (or wherever questioning and Miranda waiver occurred), and the day or two following those events.

I find a two-stage process helpful in doing this. The first stage allows the parent to provide a general account that is structured by the examiner only in terms of periods of time (e.g., "Tell me what you observed about Joe during that day, before the arrest that occurred that night"). The second stage involves an inquiry that uses the first report as an outline but includes much more probing, going into the events in greater detail.

For example, in one case, the mother's initial report of prearrest events went something like this:

> "The officer came to the house in the afternoon and said he wanted to question Joe. When I told him Joe wasn't there, he said he wanted to wait there until Joe came home. So he did, and when Joe came in, he took him to the station."

In the second stage, when she was guided by detailed questioning about specifics, she offered the following concerning one part of this event:

> "It was about 4:00 in the afternoon. I invited the officer into the kitchen to wait. He sat at the kitchen table. I offered him coffee and we talked about kids. He told me

> about his kids, and we got to talking about how everyone's kids get into trouble. He told me how he sees his job not just as arresting and punishing kids, but also trying to help them. He seemed like a nice guy."

This more detailed description provided a significant context for the mother's response to later events during the Miranda waiver, because this police officer eventually was the one who was involved in the youth's questioning at the police station.

The examiner also will be seeking information to gauge the *parent as a resource for the youth* during the Miranda waiver and arrest events. This would include the parent's own intellectual capacities, familiarity or naïveté regarding police arrests and legal issues, and emotional or motivational characteristics that would increase or decrease the parent's abilities to assist the youth in the Miranda waiver decision. For example:

> "I was pretty scared when they took us in there (the room used for questioning in the police station). But the officer seemed to really care about kids—I just told Joey to tell them what they wanted to know and it would work out for the best."

Much of what needs to be learned about the parent as a resource can be obtained by proper questioning while the detailed chronology of the events is being reviewed (e.g., "And how were you feeling [what were you thinking] when that was happening?").

The examiner should ask parents about the specifics of their involvement in all stages of the arrest and questioning. Sometimes parents are present for some parts of the process but not others. For example, they may or may not have been present when the Miranda warnings were presented to the youth, and they may have been present for all, certain parts, or none of the questioning itself. If questioning is lengthy, parents often step outside for a cigarette or coffee and thereby are not available to provide the youth assistance in the questioning process.

The following is a suggested list of points to be covered during the chronological review although it is not exhaustive and will need to be supplemented or altered depending on the nature of the specific case.

- *Circumstances in Days Prior to Arrest*
  Significant stressors in youth's and family's life
  Mental status of youth

- *Circumstances at Time of Arrest*
  Time of day
  Where and how arrest occurred
  Officers involved, what was said
  Mental/Emotional state of youth (including alcohol/drugs)
  Parents' involvement and actions

- *Transportation to Police Station*
  Mode of transportation
  Who went
  When they arrived

- *At Station Prior to Questioning*
  Time of arrival and time of questioning
  Physical conditions during waiting period

- *Questioning*
  Physical properties of room
  Who was present
  Physical arrangement of seating (who was where)
  What was said in preparation for questioning
  How Miranda warnings were given

- *Parent and Youth Communications Prior to Waiver*
  Whether youth asked parent any questions
  What parent advised, and why

- *Sequence and Description of Questioning Process*
  Observations of behavior and emotion of youth
  Observations of behavior and emotion of officers
  Parents' reflections on their own behavior, thoughts, emotions, and expectations

Occasionally the examiner may want to use standardized methods to assess parents' intellectual abilities or psychological status. Generally this should be reserved for cases in which the examiner already believes that the parent may have serious deficits that could have impaired the parents' ability to assist the youth in the Miranda waiver decision.

3.4 *Other Third-Party Interviews*

Police officers' official written descriptions of the arrest, Miranda waiver, and confession often are too general to provide the detailed picture that the examiner hopes to obtain. Therefore, if the defense attorney approves, an effort should be made (e.g., by telephone) to obtain a more detailed description from the police officers who were involved. The examiner can use the preceding outline as a guide for probing the details of the event with the police officer.

Attorneys should also be interviewed about the arrest and Miranda waiver events if they were present. Typically they were not present. In most cases in which waiver is questioned, the waiver and interrogation events proceeded without assistance of counsel after the youth waived his or her right to have counsel present.

3.5 *Interviewing the Youth*

3.51 Preparing the Youth for the Evaluation

Prior to interviewing the youth, some thought should be given to how the attorney will prepare the youth for the interview. The youth is entitled to know the purpose, nature, and potential implications of the evaluation. From a clinical perspective, this creates concerns about how the youth will use the information—for example, whether the youth will attempt to feign relevant incapacities or fabricate reports of the relevant events in order to obtain support for suppression of the confession.

Examiners cannot control how attorneys discuss the pending evaluation with their clients. They can, however, inform attorneys that when discussing the evaluation with the youth, it is best to advise the youth simply to answer all questions truthfully and to do his or her best on testing. Clinicians can tell the attorney that they are very attentive to any evidence of dissimulation in this type of evaluation. They can warn attorneys that if evidence of dissimulation arises, this will weaken the likelihood that the examiner can form any opinion about the youth's capacities relevant to the referral questions.

When first meeting with youths, examiners should ask them to describe what they understand about the purpose of the evaluation, based on discussions with their attorney. This report then can be used as a context for verifying or clarifying the purpose of the evaluation. The evaluation can be described simply as an effort to learn about the circumstances surrounding the arrest, the police investigation, and the youth's own ability to make decisions about what to say or not to say to the police. The limits and extent of confidentiality and privilege should be discussed (see Chapter 7). The examiner might also wish to inform the youth that the best approach is simply to be truthful and try one's best.

After this preparation, I have found the following sequence most useful for this type of evaluation:

- General life background information and rapport
- Psychological testing and instruments assessing abilities specific to Miranda waiver
- Review of past legal and juvenile justice experience
- Two-stage discussion of the chronology of events in the present arrest and police investigation, and challenges (if any) to the youth's report

3.52   Background Information

The first part of the process often is much like other clinical interviews, observing the youth's behavioral presentation and focusing on the youth's responses to questions about social, family, and educational history. In this context, the examiner is also taking note of any information related to mental status, both historically and at present. Many examiners may wish to include a formal "mental status exam" focusing on current mental and emotional state. I generally postpone discussion of past or current delinquency and involvement with law enforcement or courts until after testing.

3.53   Psychological Testing

Next, I typically administer psychological tests and specialized forensic assessment instruments, which are described later in 2-4.0. A colleague of mine suggests that sometime during this process, it is helpful to have the youth read aloud the Miranda warning form and the printed statement that the police officers recorded, to time the youth, and to record the youth's errors ("typing madly on my word processor," she says). Then she compares these errors to what she knows about the manifestation of developmental reading disorders.

3.54 Legal Experience

After testing, the interview can be resumed with a more or less chronological discussion of the youth's past encounters with police, arrests, and experiences with attorneys and courts. Often this discussion allows the examiner to begin to gauge the degree of sophistication or naïveté of the youth regarding such matters, outside the context of the current offense and arrest. Detailed exploration of one such encounter in the past sometimes helps to obtain this information.

3.55 Report of Current Legal Incident, and Challenging the Report

The youth's report of the present arrest and police questioning can be obtained in the same two-stage manner that was described earlier for interviews with parents, using roughly the same outline (see 2-3.3). If police reports and parents' accounts have already been obtained, the clinician will be watching for consistencies and differences between the youth's report and third-party descriptions.

Differences can be expected because of attentional, perceptual, and memory differences between multiple observers of a common event. In addition, each party has something different to gain or lose from the examiner's and the court's interpretation of the arrest, waiver, and interrogation events. Therefore, when youths provide descriptions that vary from those heard previously, the examiner will want to question their reports on implausible or discrepant points.

Youths' reports may be different from those of others for many reasons. Youths may be trying to manipulate the clinician's impression of the situation for personal gain. But differences in reports can also occur because the youth is confused about the specifics of the event or has a distorted memory of it for reasons that are not manipulative.

Discussion of questionable parts of the youth's account need not occur in a negatively confrontive way. If it is, this may establish a combative and oppositional reaction that signifi-cantly decreases the clinician's ability to obtain further data. "Challenging" certain aspects of the youth's report can be done firmly and matter-of-factly without being accusatory. "Wait a minute—help me get this straight . . ." is generally preferable to "We both know you're lying." "But your mother said . . ." should not be the first line of questioning; first determine whether the discrepancy can be explained without challenging the youth with others' contradictory reports.

4.0 <u>STANDARDIZED ASSESSMENT METHODS</u>

Three types of standardized measures may be helpful in evaluating youths' capacities to waive Miranda rights: instruments that assess understanding and appreciation of the Miranda warnings (4.1); standardized tests of cognitive abilities (4.2); and personality measures (4.3).

4.1 *Measuring Functional Abilities to Waive Miranda Rights*

When there are questions about a person's legal competence to perform specific tasks, a clinician's assessment ought to include direct observations of the person's ability to perform the tasks in question. Standardized tools to fulfill that objective for assessments related to capacities to waive Miranda rights were developed in a research project I directed some years ago (Grisso, 1980, 1981). Professional Resource Press has published these instruments under the title *Instruments for Assessing Understanding and Appreciation of Miranda Rights.* This publication provides all the necessary stimulus materials, instructions for administration and scoring, and norms based on the original research with over 400 youths in juvenile detention centers. The following subsections briefly describe the instruments themselves, the research project within which they were developed, and comments on administration of the instruments in the evaluation of juveniles.

4.11 The Miranda Measures

With resources from the National Institute of Mental Health, the study developed ways to measure individuals' understanding of the Miranda warnings, as well as their appreciation of the warnings in the context of legal proceedings against them. Four measures were developed.

The primary measure of understanding, *Comprehension of Miranda Rights (CMR),* requires that the examiner present each of the four main Miranda warning statements to the youth. The examiner reads the first warning to the youth while the youth is shown the warning in printed form. The youth is then asked to tell the examiner what it says, but "in your own words." The process continues for each of the Miranda warning statements. The youth's responses are scored "adequate," "questionable," or "inadequate" according to detailed scoring criteria provided for each warning, and a total CMR score is calculated (range 0-8).

A second understanding measure, *Comprehension of Miranda Rights–Recognition (CMR-R),* is intended as an adjunct procedure that does not require youths to paraphrase the warnings as does the CMR. Some youths may understand the warnings but may not have the verbal ability to express what they know. The CMR-R deals with this by requiring no verbal paraphrase. For each warning statement the youth is told that the examiner will offer other statements that mean either the same thing or something different from the warning that the youth is shown. The youth need only answer "same" or "different." The examiner presents three of these statements for each Miranda warning (a total of 12 statements), half of which are the same and half different from the Miranda warnings to which they are being compared. The number of correct responses constitutes the total CMR-R score (range 0-12).

The third understanding measure, *Comprehension of Miranda Vocabulary (CMV),* is a vocabulary test that uses six words taken from the original Miranda warnings. Objective scoring criteria are used to score the youth's definitions and produce total CMV scores (range 0-12). This method was intended to provide additional information with which to interpret the source of youths' poor understanding when manifested in the CMR and CMR-R.

A final instrument, *Function of Rights in Interrogation (FRI),* was developed to assess youths' appreciation of the relevance of the Miranda warnings in the context of the legal process. For example, a youth may clearly understand that the third Miranda warning means, "I can have a lawyer to talk to before and during the time that police ask me questions." Yet this does not tell us whether the youth appreciates the function of a defense attorney—for example, that the attorney is intended to be an advocate. Without this background knowledge (which is not offered by the Miranda warnings themselves), the understanding that one can "have an attorney" has little meaning.

To assess this background appreciation, the FRI uses four situations that are described by brief vignettes and accompanied by drawings, as well as a series of questions about each situation. The situations are (a) a youth about to be questioned by police officers after arrest, (b) a youth consulting with defense counsel, (c) a youth being pressured by police officers to make a statement, and (d) a youth in a hearing before a juvenile court judge. Questions for each of these situations, respectively, focus on the youth's appreciation of (a) the adversarial nature of the encounter with the police officers (that the youth is in jeopardy), (b) the advocacy nature of the attorney-client relationship, (c) the protective nature of the "right to silence" despite the authority of the police officers, and (d) the role of an earlier confession or assertion of the right to silence at a later court hearing. The youth's responses to these questions also are scored according to objective criteria.

The research demonstrated very high inter-scorer reliability among pairs of raters for all of these instruments (CMR: .92-.96; CMV: .97-.98; FRI: .94-.96; the CMR-R has perfect inter-scorer reliability since it is completely objective, relying only on "yes" and "no" answers).

4.12 The Miranda Comprehension Study

In the study for which these instruments were developed, they were administered to (a) 431 male youths in juvenile detention centers (within 2 to 4 days after their arrest) and delinquency treatment programs, and (b) 203 male adults who were in halfway houses while re-entering the community after serving prison terms. The two samples did not differ in race or socioeconomic status, and comparisons between juveniles and adults were controlled for IQ (measured with a short form of the WISC or WAIS).

The manual for the Miranda measures provides a number of tables that present the data from this study, especially the percent of inadequate responses on various items for juveniles and adults. Results are also shown for age-by-IQ groups, across each juvenile age (12 through 16) and for various age groups of adults. The clinician will be interested in these results primarily because they provide a point of comparison for the scores obtained in individual clinical cases.

While providing clinically useful data, the research study also was intended to test hypotheses concerning the capacities of juveniles as a group compared to adults, as these might address law and policy. In general, youths 14 and younger in this study performed significantly more poorly than did older adolescents or young adults. Youths who were 15 to 16 did not perform more poorly than adults as a group. However, youths at that age with lower IQ scores (below 80) performed more poorly than adults with similarly lower IQ scores and showed no better understanding of the Miranda warnings than did youths who were 14 years old or younger.

Details concerning these results can be found in Chapters 4 to 6 of *Juveniles' Waiver of Rights: Legal and Psychological Competence* (Grisso, 1981), and in a journal article in the *California Law Review* (Grisso, 1980).

4.13 Administering the Miranda Instruments

There is no specific sequence of administration for the Miranda instruments. I usually administer the CMR first, then the CMV and CMR-R, followed by the FRI. This is the sequence used in the manual for the Miranda measures.

Sometimes the clinician knows the mode of presentation of the Miranda warnings that was used by police officers with the youth in question. In such instances, the clinician might wish to set aside standardization to present the CMR in a manner similar to the presentation by police officers in the instant case. For example, if officers merely handed the youth the card and asked him to read it to himself, the clinician might wish to do the same, then use the standard inquiry ("In your own words, what does that first statement mean?") without first reading the warning to youth as the standardized CMR instructions suggest. If this is done, the clinician will want to administer the CMR in the standardized way after the nonstandardized presentation has been completed.

Some police departments use versions of the Miranda warnings that employ different words than those in the CMR version. For example, the CMR statement uses the term "interrogation," while many police department forms use the words "questioning" or "interview." In these cases, clinicians have two options. One is to give the CMR as it is worded, which allows the clinician to compare the youth to the research norms, but with diminished relevance for the wording used by the police officers. The other option is to substitute the terms used locally, in which case there are two additional options. The first is to forego comparison to the norms (which were based on a different wording) and merely to evaluate the adequacy of the youth's response on a common sense basis. The second option is to apply the CMR scoring criteria for the warning statement in question despite change in wording of the statement. Some youths may understand the term "questioning" better than the word "interrogation," in which case they will simply score higher than similar youths in the Miranda waiver research study (as they should, if the simpler wording has made the warning more comprehensible).

The examiner should observe the youth's demeanor carefully during the administration of the Miranda instruments. Youths' behaviors on these instruments may be the beginning of a number of potential hypotheses (e.g., that the youth was not really trying, or that the youth was dissimulating poor understanding). A youth I once examined looked at each CMR statement as I read it, but invariably shrugged his shoulders and said nothing whenever I asked for a paraphrase of it. As it turned out, he could not read but was too embarrassed to tell me. Moreover, he had significant hearing loss, which I began to suspect when he failed even to shrug after I asked questions with my head down.

4.2 *Measures of Cognitive Ability*

Standardized measures of intellectual ability and reading or comprehension achievement tests are logical adjuncts in these evaluations, in light of the relevance of cognitive capacities when attempting to explain poor comprehension of Miranda waiver information. As will be noted later, such tests also may be useful in addressing suspicions of dissimulation.

In addition to the better known measures of intelligence for adolescents (e.g., the *Wechsler Intelligence Scale for Children-III*,

Wechsler, 1991), portions of various achievement tests also may be appropriate depending on hypotheses raised in individual cases: for example, the *Wide Range Achievement Test-Revised* (S. Jastak, Wilkinson, & J. Jastak, 1984), the *Kaufman Test of Educational Achievement* (A. Kaufman & N. Kaufman, 1985), and the *Peabody Individual Achievement Test-Revised* (Markwardt, 1989). For example, a measure of auditory comprehension might be especially helpful when the youth was given the Miranda warnings aloud by police officers but did not have the capacity to read the warnings simultaneously or was never given a printed version to read.

The need for additional cognitive testing is reduced when a youth performs very well on the Miranda measures. Such testing becomes more important when the youth has manifested significant deficits on the Miranda measures, raising the need for additional data with which to form opinions concerning the cause of the youth's difficulties in comprehending the Miranda warnings. Even more specialized testing may be necessary in a small minority of cases: for example, when one suspects that a specific learning disability may be interfering with the youth's comprehension.

4.3 *Objective Personality Measures*

When the major referral question is the youth's cognitive capacities to understand the Miranda warnings, personality measures typically are of limited value in addressing the question. They may be of assistance, however, in cases raising questions that go beyond cognitive and intellectual abilities.

For example, despite the youth's adequate comprehension during the evaluation, an attorney (supported by observations by the youth's parents) might suggest this particular youth has always had abnormally strong fear reactions to persons in authority, such as teachers and doctors. Might an exceptional degree of fear of police officers have interfered with the youth's comprehension at the time of the Miranda waiver and confession? In other cases, the referral question might focus not so much on youths' understanding of the warnings when they were given but on the claim that they were impaired in their ability to assert the rights because of extreme acquiescence related to dependency and immature conformity to authority.

In such cases, personality testing may be helpful in providing an independent, standardized measure of personality traits associated with these hypotheses. Potentially relevant personality dimensions can be found in many instruments designed for use with adolescents: for example, the *Millon Adolescent Personality Inventory* (Millon, Green, & Meagher, 1982), the *Millon Adolescent Clinical Inventory* (Millon, 1993), the *Personality Inventory for Children* (Lachar & Kline, 1994), and the content or supplemental scales of the *Minnesota Multiphasic Personality Inventory-Adolescent* (Butcher et al., 1992).

For cases in which acquiescence and potential suggestibility of youths' are the primary questions, examiners might also wish to look into the *Gudjonsson Suggestibility Scale* (Gudjonsson, 1984, 1992). This procedure involves reading a standardized one-paragraph story to the youth and first asking the youth to recall as much as possible. After about 30 minutes (during which other testing can be done), the youth is asked 20 questions about the story, some of which are worded to provide the opportunity to acquiesce to inaccurate information. This provides a "Yield" score (yielding to suggestion). The youth is then told that he or she made a number of errors (regardless of whether or not this is true), that it is necessary to go through all of the questions again, and that the youth must try to do better. Changes in the youth's answers compared to the original questioning produces a "Shift" score, suggesting degree of acquiescence to the situational demand produced by the authority figure (the examiner).

Instructions for administration, scoring, stimuli, and normative data are provided in Gudjonsson's book, *The Psychology of Interrogations, Confessions and Testimony* (1992). Unfortunately, adolescent norms for the method are a good deal less complete than those for adults.

5.0   INTERPRETATION

Earlier in this chapter, four characteristics of all legal competencies were offered to identify objectives of the Miranda waiver evaluation. Let us return to these objectives to structure our discussion of the interpretation of results of the evaluation.

5.1 *The Functional Component: Describing Performance on the Miranda Instruments*

The most basic step in the interpretive process involves the comparison of a youth's summary scores on the Miranda measures to the normative data provided in the Miranda study (or in future studies that provide other statistical norms). The presence or absence of deficits in a youth's performance is determined by comparing the youth's scores to those of adults and of other youths of similar age in the normative samples.

From the perspective of many judges, however, just as important is a description of the specific warnings that the youth did not seem to comprehend, as well as the specific type of errors that the youth made. Hearing this, judges may form their own opinion concerning the degree to which the youth's errors should raise concerns.

5.2 *The Causal Component: Explanations for Deficits in Miranda Performance (Including Dissimulation)*

If a youth manifests errors on the Miranda instruments, the clinician must then offer reasonable explanations for them. Poor performance may be due to poor cognitive abilities in general, specific disabilities, psychological deficits, or simply immaturity. But in some cases, poor performance may be due to factors that do not suggest an inability to understand and waive Miranda rights: for example, poor test-taking motivation, feigning a lack of understanding, or malingering cognitive deficits.

5.21 Relating Miranda Scores to Cognitive Deficits

The logical process of relating poor performance on the Miranda instruments to cognitive deficits or immaturity involves the same type of interpretations with which clinicians are accustomed in their general diagnostic practice with children and adolescents. The clinician takes notice of the youth's cognitive deficits and clinical condition and by logical inference forms hypotheses about how these might account for the youth's deficits on the Miranda measures.

For example, in one case involving a 15-year-old boy, his performance on the Miranda measures was markedly poorer than the average for youths of his age and level of general intelligence (according to the Miranda research norms). His strong subtests on the WISC-III included the Performance subtests generally. He had relatively lower performance on tasks requiring reception and processing of verbal information, unless the information included content that was familiar and likely to have been learned by rote repetition (e.g., Information subtest). Teachers had observed that the youth had particular difficulties processing novel information, and past testing in the school noted such problems especially in stressful situations (e.g., timed tasks).

The youth's deficits on the Miranda instruments, therefore, were interpreted not as a function of intellectual deficits or immaturity but were hypothesized to be a consequence of a learning disability involving processing of novel verbal information, manifested especially under stress. The youth had never been arrested before, was only vaguely familiar with the Miranda warnings, and was cooperative but highly anxious during the evaluation.

5.22 Feigning Poor Understanding

When youths show poor understanding or appreciation on the Miranda instruments, it is important to rule out the possibility that the youth is feigning a lack of understanding. Youths potentially have something to gain by appearing to have poor comprehension on the Miranda instruments. There are a few strategies that one can use to identify potential feigning of deficits in Miranda comprehension.

First, one can examine *consistencies and inconsistencies* in the types of errors that the youth has made. When a youth makes similar errors across the various Miranda instruments, performance on each instrument might "validate" performance on the other. For example, in the CMR, a youth interpreted the first warning ("You do not have to make a statement and have the right to remain silent") to mean that you must not talk until you are told to do so. On the CMV, he interpreted the word "right" as meaning "the right thing to do." On the FRI, he answered "yes" when asked whether a person had to tell a judge what he'd done if the judge told him to do so in court. Therefore, the youth apparently thought that a right was an obligation one had to fulfill and that authorities controlled the nature of that obligation. The consistency of this erroneous interpretation across tests that tap understanding of a concept in different ways suggested that the youth's misinterpretations probably were not feigned. In contrast, suspicions of feigning are raised when there is less consistency in errors across the Miranda measures.

Second, the clinician can *compare the youth's performance on the Miranda instruments to other indices of cognitive ability*. In general clinical work, examiners typically test their hypotheses about potential feigning by looking for inconsistencies between the patient's performance in various contexts. For example, occasionally I have examined youths who seemed not to be able to comprehend simple words in the Miranda warnings, yet defined more complex words in general vocabulary tests. Examining a youth's performance on other measures of cognitive ability, one might sometimes find that the youth has made far more errors on the Miranda measures than is typical for other youths of similar age and intelligence.

Some youths perform very poorly on the Miranda measures, yet in separate interview sessions they manifest considerable knowledge of how "the police violated my rights." When their descriptions of police officers' obligations are detailed and accurate when describing their own circumstances, their poor performance on the Miranda instruments is suspect.

It is important, however, not to infer automatically that a youth is "sophisticated" about legal terms and procedures simply because the youth has an extensive delinquency record. Data from the Miranda study (Grisso, 1981) suggested that there is not a simple relationship between Miranda instrument performance and amount of prior experience with courts and police. Some youths apparently learn a great deal from their past experiences and some do not. Thus when a very experienced youth performs poorly on the Miranda instruments, there is no more reason to presume dissimulation than to presume that the youth is naïve despite his or her frequent involvement with police.

Finally, the clinician's *observations of the youth's behavior during testing* sometimes provides clues. Youths who are feigning poor understanding often give themselves away by the same behaviors that have long been identified with adult malingerers (Resnick,

1984; Rogers & Resnick, 1988). For example, they may attempt to draw attention to their difficulties in understanding the Miranda warnings. They may also "over-act," producing exaggerated errors or errors more numerous than are found even among youths who are very young or very deficient in general intelligence.

The CMR-R may sometimes be helpful in detecting a youth's attempts to feign poor understanding. Of the 12 CMR-R items, 6 are true and 6 are false. Even random responding should produce scores of 5 or 6. Scores below that should alert the examiner to the possibility that the youth knows the right answers and is trying to give the wrong ones, resulting in even poorer performance than most youths who truly do not understand.

5.23 Malingering Cognitive or Neuropsychological Deficits

Dissimulation is also possible in the form of malingered deficits on measures of general intelligence and neuropsychological functions. Rogers, Harrell, and Liff (1993) and McCann (1998) offer several strategies for identifying potential malingering in neuropsychological evaluations. For example, on tasks that are arranged from very easy to increasingly more difficult, the test taker who deviates markedly from the usual pattern of errors (i.e., performing well until a certain point in the series, then tailing off until a series of items is missed) may be suspected of malingering. This is known as the "performance curve" strategy. Another strategy, the "floor effect," raises suspicions of malingering when the individual misses items that would be performed adequately even by most severely impaired individuals.

5.3 *The Interactive Component: Making Inferences about Comprehension at the Time of Police Questioning*

Once a youth's current level of comprehension of the Miranda warnings and their significance has been determined and explained, the clinician must entertain the retrospective question: What can be said about the youth's probable understanding at the time of the encounter with the police officers? Level of comprehension during the evaluation, of course, may not be the same as comprehension in the past, at the time of interrogation.

5.31 Considering Situational Demands

One key to entering this interpretive territory is to take stock of the demands of the relevant situations: specifically, the context in which the youth was informed of the Miranda warnings by police and the context of the evaluation itself. These two contexts usually vary in important ways.

In 2-1.41 and 2-3.3 we reviewed a number of variables for which the clinician will have obtained information concerning the police encounter. These included details about such matters as the time of day of the encounter, the youth's condition, steps in the process, the involvement of other parties in the event, and a host of other variables. This becomes the information with which the clinician now must build a picture of the demands of the situation, as a context within which the youth was required to comprehend the Miranda warnings and their significance.

Special attention should be paid to variables that are known to interfere with attention and comprehension. This might include the specific manner in which the Miranda warnings were given, any stressful and fearful external conditions, as well as conditions of the youth (e.g., intoxication or lack of sleep). It should also include any conditions that may have augmented the youth's capacities to understand: for example, the assistance of caring and helpful parents.

Similarly, the clinician should build a picture of the context in which the clinician examined the youth's present capacities. Often the testing conditions themselves were far more favorable toward understanding the Miranda warnings than was the police encounter, in terms of relatively fewer distractions, clearer presentation of information to the youth, and the less threatening quality of the examiner. Nevertheless, testing is never stress free, and the clinician should carefully assess the testing conditions, not merely presume that they were optimal for obtaining the youth's best performance.

5.32 Making Inferences about
Capacity in the Two Contexts

Given the relative demands of these two contexts, there are several possibilities for making inferences about the meaning of youths' present performance for their capacities to understand Miranda warnings in the earlier police encounter. (In the following, we presume that dissimulation of poor comprehension has been ruled out as a cause for deficits in performance during the evaluation process.)

If a youth has *shown significant difficulties in understanding* the Miranda warnings in the evaluation, it is often reasonable to assume that the youth would have comprehended no better under the (usually) less favorable conditions of the police encounter. Exceptions can be imagined: for example, when concerned and knowledgeable parents were there to explain, and when it is possible that the youth has not retained those explanations in the time between the encounter and the evaluation. Ordinarily, however, this inference can stand up to scrutiny.

If a youth has *shown minimal deficits in understanding* during the evaluation, however, it is not as safe to infer that the youth would have had similar understanding at the time of the police encounter. That likelihood needs to be weighed in light of the specific demands of the police interrogation, many of which may have been far less conducive to comprehension than in the evaluation session. Moreover, it is possible that the youth's encounters between the time of the interrogation and the examination (e.g., discussions with peers or conversations with the attorney) may have increased his or her understanding of the Miranda warnings.

Finally, this weighing of contexts often may support the inference that youths' adequate comprehension at the time of the evaluation is a good estimate of their comprehension at the time of the police encounter. Indeed, probably the majority of older adolescents that I have evaluated for these purposes not only have manifested adequate understanding, but they themselves claim that they did understand the warnings at the time that they waived them. In contrast, they identify other problems: for example, that they "didn't really have a choice," or that they were "just not thinking at all." Clinical inferences about such claims of reduced autonomy require further discussion.

5.4 *Inferences about Voluntariness and Choice*

In *In re Gault* (1967), the U.S. Supreme Court warned that special care was required in examining police procedures for taking confessions in juvenile cases, in order to ensure that juveniles did not waive Miranda rights due to "adolescent fantasy, fright, or despair." Adults, too, may sometimes waive rights to silence and counsel due to fear and confusion. The Court recognized, however, that adolescents may be at greater risk because of immaturity and the status difference between youths and adults in authority.

Adolescents will vary (both within an age group and across ages) in characteristics that may reduce or increase their fearfulness in such circumstances. Among these variables, for example, are self-esteem, assertiveness, dependency, and tendencies toward conformity to adult requests. When particular youths are significantly different from their peers on such personality dimensions, those differences may be relevant for making inferences about their increased risk of acquiescence to police pressures.

The clinician may want to attend to a variety of personality dimensions for making these judgments. It is strongly recommended, however, that clinicians base their opinions on solid empirical evidence of the personality characteristics in question. This usually will mean evidence from several reliable personality measures, with further support by clinical observation and social history data.

Youths with mental retardation may be especially vulnerable to the pressures of police interrogations. Persons with mental retardation often have learned to adapt to complex and frightening social demands by being cooperative and acquiescent. This tendency may be even greater for youths with mental retardation than for mentally retarded adults.

Special attention to potential differences between adolescents and adults in their modes of decisionmaking is also required. As noted earlier in this chapter, both theory and research suggest that younger adolescents—and a substantial proportion of middle adolescents as well—are less likely than adults to consider longer-term consequences when making important choices. Despite their adequate reasoning capacities, they may also tend not to employ them—or to employ them less well—in stressful situations.

Clinicians should exercise great caution when attempting to form opinions about the degree of autonomy that youths may have been able to maintain in past police encounters. We know very little empirically about the relation of personality character-istics to past functioning in such circumstances and about the effects of social pressures on youths' ability to deploy whatever decisionmaking abilities they have.

6.0 REPORTS AND TESTIMONY

6.1 *Contents of the Report*

There is no single outline for reports of evaluations related to questions of Miranda waiver. Many clinicians will employ sections to describe social history, current mental status, and descriptions of cognitive and personality characteristics of the youth. The special forensic nature of these evaluations, however, will require additional sections for the following basic discussions:

1. First, a section must be included that describes the youth's current ability to comprehend the Miranda warnings and their significance (the Functional question). This will report results of the Miranda instruments and compare those findings to normative data. It should also include similar data derived from any other sources.

2. Second, a section should interpret the reasons for any deficits that were discovered in the youth's capacities to comprehend and appreciate the Miranda warnings (the Causal question). This will include opinions about rela-tionships between deficits on the Miranda measures and psychological conditions—for example, what intellectual or clinical variables can best account for the deficits. This should include a discussion of dissimulation as well. If the clinician believes that the youth was not dissimulating, the reasons for this belief should be clearly described.

3. Third, a section should describe all that the clinician has been able to learn about the conditions and circumstances surrounding the police encounter, disclosure of the Miranda rights, and the youth's response. This is in preparation for dealing with the Interactive question, which should describe the relevance of the Miranda

comprehension deficits that were observed, in light of the demands of the situation (i.e., the nature of the police encounter). Are the deficits more or less important in light of the specific conditions surrounding the youth's interrogation?

6.2 *Challenges to the Miranda Instruments*

Occasionally attorneys on cross-examination may challenge the admissibility of evidence based on the Miranda instruments because they are not "traditional" psychological measures such as the MMPI-A or WISC-III. Sometimes attorneys will cite federal cases (e.g., *Frye v. U.S*, 1923; *Daubert v. Merrell Dow Pharmaceuticals, Inc.*, 1993), or similar case law within one's state, that refer to criteria for admissibility of evidence based on scientific methods. Usually the inquiry focuses on some combination of several factors: for example, (a) whether the instruments have demonstrated reliability and validity; (b) whether they have been peer reviewed; (c) whether they are relied upon by other experts in the field; and (d) whether other courts have recognized the utility and relevance of the instruments in similar cases.

The following information may prepare the clinician to deal with these questions. The Miranda studies (Grisso, 1980, 1981) were the product of a research grant from the National Institute of Mental Health (NIMH). NIMH grant proposals undergo highly stringent scientific peer review by NIMH review panels, and only those with very sound scientific designs are awarded research grants. The Miranda studies underwent such a review and were conducted precisely as they were proposed and approved by NIMH.

Moreover, the work has been widely cited and positively reviewed in major publications by scientific peers during the past 15 years (e.g., see Melton et al., 1997). Further recognition of the research that produced these instruments is suggested by awards the author has received from national organizations based partly on this work (e.g., from the American Academy of Forensic Psychology, and the American Psychological Association). Finally, the Miranda studies and instruments have been cited as scientific authority by a number of state appellate courts throughout the country, and defense counsel who is calling the examiner to testify may want to locate some of those cases using a legal research computer database (e.g., Lexus).

6.3 *Stating Expert Opinions about the Validity of Juveniles' Waiver of Miranda Rights*

Either early or late in direct examination, the attorney offering the clinician's testimony must establish that the clinician has an opinion relevant to the legal question. "Doctor, do you have an opinion on . . ." may be followed by a variety of phrases: for example,

- "the youth's ability to have understood the Miranda warnings"
- "the youth's ability to have made a voluntary, knowing, and intelligent waiver of rights"
- "whether the youth's confession was valid"

These questions are not synonymous. With adequate data, one can often form a clinical opinion about what a youth probably could and could not understand (the first question). It is quite another matter to have an expert opinion on "whether the confession was valid." How much do defendants need to understand, and how well do they need to understand it, in order for their waiver and confession to be "valid"? Is it necessary to understand each of the four Miranda warnings perfectly? Or is it satisfactory if only one is misunderstood? What if two of them are only partially understood? Are some "partial understandings" more important than others? What if they are all understood, but the youth has difficulty using them in a logical process of reasoning about waiver?

The reason that these are such difficult questions to answer is not that they are unanswerable but that clinical theory or logic offers no guidance for answering them. They constitute the fourth component of all legal competencies: the Judgmental component. After learning all the clinical and circumstantial facts of the case, courts must address the matter of validity of the waiver by posing a final question: "Were the youth's deficits, together with the demands of this particular Miranda situation, of an extent and type that it would be *unfair* to accept the youth's waiver and introduce the confession as trial evidence?" What is fair or unfair, of course, is a *legal* (some say moral) question, not a matter of *clinical* opinion.

For this reason, no matter how I am asked the "opinion" question, I always answer in a way that foreshadows the limits of my expert opinion. For example, if asked, "Doctor, do you have an opinion about the validity of this youth's waiver," I would reply: "I have an opinion, to a reasonable degree of clinical certainty, about the youth's *capacities* that are *relevant* for deciding the validity of his waiver of rights."

Clinicians are free to answer otherwise, of course, and sometimes judges will insist that they do. But I know of no way—within the boundaries of scientific theory and method—to assist the clinician in deciding that a youth's waiver of rights is valid or invalid.

In conclusion, the legal purposes and standards for determining whether a juvenile's waiver of Miranda rights was made voluntarily, knowingly, and intelligently have been reviewed. Addressing the clinical questions related to these standards requires a consideration of the youth's characteristics and condition, as well as the social context of the police questioning, at the time the rights were waived. Assessment methods were reviewed, including special instruments that evaluate functional abilities directly related to comprehension of Miranda rights. Interpretation of results must pay particularly close attention to the possibility of dissimulation of deficits.

Clinicians who perform evaluations in delinquency cases can expect an increase in requests for evaluations to address questions of waiver of Miranda rights. The recent trend toward more punitive sanctions for juvenile offenders is causing defense attorneys and courts to look more closely at questions of due process and the protection of youths' rights as defendants. Clinicians' "Miranda evaluations" have a significant role to play in assisting courts by providing reliable information that is directly relevant to the "voluntary, knowing, and intelligent" standard for waiver of Miranda rights.

Chapter 3

Juveniles' Competence to Stand Trial

The law requires that criminal defendants must be able to understand the nature of the proceedings against them and be able to assist their attorney in their defense as their trials proceed. Mental health professionals often are asked to perform evaluations of defendants' relevant capacities in order to assist the court in determining whether the defendant is competent to proceed to trial and to make important decisions during that process.

Adolescents may be evaluated for their competence to stand trial in two different legal contexts. First, all states try some juveniles in *criminal court* if they are charged with certain serious offenses. Once they are arraigned in criminal court, the question of their competence to participate in their defense is sometimes raised. Second, many states provide that juveniles whose delinquency cases are heard in *juvenile court* must be competent to participate in delinquency proceedings. As we will see, most of the same basic concepts and procedures for competence to stand trial evaluations will apply in both of these circumstances. The present chapter, therefore, is concerned with evaluations of trial competence of adolescents, whether they are being tried in criminal or juvenile court.

This chapter describes the relevant legal, theoretical, and contextual background for competence to stand trial evaluations (1.0), conceptualizes the purpose of the evaluation (2.0), describes the evaluation process and standardized methods (3.0 and 4.0), then discusses interpretive issues (5.0) and special issues of report writing and testimony (6.0).

The approach to competence to stand trial evaluations outlined here is described in greater detail in an earlier manual, *Competency to Stand Trial Evaluations: A Manual for Practice* (Grisso,

1988), published by Professional Resource Press. That reference, however, did not address special issues in trial competence evaluations of juveniles.

1.0 THE LEGAL AND SOCIAL CONTEXT OF COMPETENCE TO STAND TRIAL EVALUATIONS

1.1 *The Law of Competence in Criminal Court*

The American system of criminal law adopted the doctrine of competence to stand trial from English common law. When defendants' mental incapacities seriously reduced their ability to defend themselves, it was considered unfair to require them to stand trial. When a defendant is found incompetent to stand trial, the trial is delayed in order to provide treatment that will restore the defendant to competence and allow the trial to resume.

Every state's laws require that defendants must be competent to stand trial in criminal court, including adolescents when they have been transferred to criminal court for trial. Every state employs a legal definition of competence patterned after the one stated by the U.S. Supreme Court in *Dusky v. U.S.* (1960):

> "whether he [the defendant] has sufficient present ability to consult with his attorney with a reasonable degree of rational understanding and a rational as well as factual understanding of the proceedings against him." (p. 402)

Many states' statutes add that deficits in these abilities, if they are to be considered reasons for incompetence to stand trial, must be due to mental illness or mental retardation. In fact, most adult defendants who are found incompetent to stand trial have serious (usually psychotic) mental disorders or mental retardation (Nicholson & Kugler, 1991). It is very important to realize, however, that incompetence is not synonymous with mental disorder; a defendant may be seriously mentally ill yet be competent to stand trial. The issue is whether, and how, the mental disorder actually affects the defendant's abilities to perform those functions that are required for the defendant's trial participation. Not all defendants with mental disorders, even those that involve psychotic delusions, necessarily experience symptoms that interfere with their trial participation.

As the *Dusky* standard indicates, competence requires a degree of understanding of the trial process, as well as the capacity to consult with and assist counsel. When working with counsel, defendants may have to make decisions related to defense strategy, pleading (guilty, not guilty, not guilty by reason of insanity), responding to plea bargains, and waiving the right to be represented by counsel.

Intuitively, understanding the trial and making decisions related to it may seem like separate psychological functions requiring different types of abilities. Bonnie (1992), for example, has suggested that some defendants who have a basic understanding of the trial process could be considered competent to proceed to trial with the assistance of counsel, but possibly incompetent to make certain decisions (e.g., a psychotic defendant's refusal of an insanity plea due to the defendant's denial that he or she is mentally ill). Some federal and state courts have accepted this view in the past. Nevertheless, the U.S. Supreme Court in *Godinez v. Moran* (1993) decided that there is only one competence for purposes of trial participation. Therefore, when states apply the *Dusky* standard for trial competence, they do not violate constitutional requirements if they use this standard to cover all of the psychological functions that might have to be addressed in deciding whether the defendant has sufficient capacity to be fairly tried.

1.2 *Competence in Juvenile Court*

In contrast to the long history of competence to stand trial in criminal court, the concept received little attention in juvenile courts during the first 60 years of the juvenile justice system's history. This is because it was considered unnecessary. In philosophy and intent, our separate system of juvenile justice presumed that delinquent youths were to be rehabilitated, not punished, and that the court's purpose was to meet the needs of wayward youths. The proceedings were not construed as adversarial, youths did not have to be represented by legal counsel, and there was no need for a defense against the state's beneficent interventions. Youths' competence to participate in a defense, therefore, was irrelevant.

Then in the 1960s, the U.S. Supreme Court's decisions in *Kent v. U.S.* (1966) and *In re Gault* (1967) required that juvenile courts begin providing many of the same due process rights in delinquency proceedings as in adult criminal proceedings, including the rights to counsel, to avoid self-incrimination, and to challenge evidence presented in court. These cases were silent on the right of juveniles to be competent to stand trial in the new adversarial proceedings in juvenile court. But within 20 years, about one-third of the states had recognized, by statute or case law, the legal concept of competence to stand trial in juvenile court (Grisso, Miller, & Sales, 1987). This has now increased to about one-half of the states, and others undoubtedly will produce a majority over the next few years.

Few appellate cases have interpreted the standard or concept of competence to stand trial in juvenile court. Most states appear to have employed the same *Dusky* standard for competence in juvenile court as is applied in criminal court. Later we will discuss ways in which the standard may be interpreted somewhat differently in juvenile court. For example, a few appellate courts (e.g., *In re Causey,* 1978) have ruled that immaturity—not just mental disorder—may be the basis for a finding of incompetence in juvenile court.

The recent increase in rates of violent offenses among juveniles has produced many changes in states' laws that place juveniles in jeopardy of highly punitive sentences in juvenile court, including a greater likelihood of waiver to criminal court for trial as an adult. As a consequence, the issue of juveniles' competence to stand trial began to be raised more frequently in the mid-1990s. This produced new, more definitive appellate decisions in a few states affirming juveniles' right to be competent to stand trial in juvenile court.

For example, a recent Georgia case (*In the Interest of S.H.,* 1996) involved a 12-year-old with an IQ of 40 who was accused of sexually molesting younger mentally retarded youths. Although the juvenile court was of the opinion that the youth was incompetent to stand trial, it denied a motion for incompetence because Georgia law appeared not to provide a statutory framework for finding juveniles incompetent to participate in juvenile court proceedings. The Georgia Court of Appeals reversed this decision. To try juveniles in juvenile court when they are incompetent, the court said, would deny them a fair trial in that they would not be able to exercise other rights that Georgia already recognized as important in delinquency proceedings (e.g., the right to confront opposing witnesses, the right to avoid self-incrimination). In the present case, the youth's incapacities prevented his attorney from mounting any meaningful defense because the youth was unable to communicate to his attorney his own perceptions of the events surrounding the alleged offense.

Not all courts will analyze the issues in the same way, however. In an Oklahoma appellate case, the court decided that juveniles do not have a right to be competent to stand trial in juvenile court because the proceedings are rehabilitative and not criminal (*G.J.I. v. State*, 1989).

In the few instances in which the question has been raised, courts have indicated that the competence of a youth to stand trial in juvenile or criminal court is not determined by any particular age or mental disorder. The matter is weighed according to the totality of circumstances, including any characteristics of the youth that might be relevant for the question.

1.3 *The Legal Process for Determining Competence to Stand Trial*

1.31 Raising the Question

Adult and juvenile defendants are presumed competent to stand trial unless the question is raised by defense, prosecution, or the court. Whether this will happen is a matter of discretion. (A current exception is in Virginia, where juveniles' competence to stand trial in criminal court must be evaluated in all juvenile court hearings on the issue of a juveniles' waiver to be tried in criminal court.) When the question is raised, courts in most states are required to order a competence evaluation by a mental health professional.

Little is known about the circumstances in which the question of competence is raised in juvenile court, except that until recently it has been rare. The question usually is raised because the court or the defendant's attorney has observed some behavior of the defendant that suggests the presence of mental disorder, disability, or other deficiency that seems to be interfering with the defendant's abilities to grasp the nature of the trial process or to communicate relevant information to the attorney (e.g., to provide a coherent account of events related to the charges). Courts in some jurisdictions may misuse competence evaluations, calling for them without any particular interest in the defendant's competence, but merely to obtain a psychiatric or psychological perspective on the defendant for other purposes. This happens less often in courts that have adequate resources and legal procedures for obtaining clinical evaluations without having to "disguise" the referral as a forensic question of competence.

Based on available information about children's and adolescents' abilities as described in developmental and clinical literature, Grisso et al. (1987) recommended that the question of juveniles' trial competence should be asked in cases involving any one of the following conditions:

- Age 12 years or younger
- Prior diagnosis/treatment for a mental illness or mental retardation
- "Borderline" level of intellectual functioning, or record of "learning disability"
- Observations of others at pretrial events suggest deficits in memory, attention, or interpretation of reality

The presence of any of these conditions does not necessarily mean that a competence evaluation should be ordered or performed. They should simply alert the attorney or the court to the potential need to raise the question of trial competence.

1.32 Legal Requirements for the Evaluation Process

The actual process of the evaluation rarely is specified by statute other than to indicate what types of professionals are qualified to perform the evaluation, their time limit for completing it, and where it is to be done. Very few states' statutes currently spell out different procedures for juveniles than for adults.

Most states authorize psychiatrists and clinical psychologists to perform trial competence evaluations, and a few states allow social workers to perform them. Some states also have regulations that require specialized forensic mental health credentials for examiners performing court-ordered evaluations. Although specialized clinical experience in the evaluation of children and adolescents would seem to be important when evaluating juveniles' competence to stand trial, few states have such provisions.

The time limit for completing competence evaluations varies considerably across states, from as few as 10 days to as high as 60 or 90 days. Some states require that the evaluation be performed at an inpatient mental health setting. When the defendant is an adolescent, presumably the inpatient facility would be an adolescent psychiatric unit rather than a forensic psychiatric facility for adults. The majority of states, however, now recognize that trial competence evaluations can be done with most defendants while they are being held in jail and detention facilities or on bail rather than requiring more costly transfers to inpatient facilities (Grisso et al., 1994).

Some states describe broadly the types of information or opinions that the examiner is expected to provide in a report on the trial competence evaluation. While such instructions vary across states, almost all statutes require that the examiner describe the likelihood of restoration of competence if the defendant appears incompetent. The reasons for this are explained in the following discussion.

1.33   Disposition in Incompetence Cases

If the court finds the defendant competent to stand trial, the trial process proceeds. If the defendant is found incompetent, the court must decide whether the defendant can be restored to competence within a specified time (in many states, 1 year). If the court finds that the condition responsible for the defendant's incompetence is not likely to be changed within that period of time (e.g., a deficit due to an unalterable chronic organic brain condition), charges must be dismissed. (See *Jackson v. Indiana*, 1972; defendants who meet criteria for civil commitment can then be committed if they are in need of psychiatric care.) If there is a reasonable prospect of the condition responding to treatment, then the court can authorize the defendant's treatment to restore competence, usually in an inpatient facility.

The trial process is then suspended while the defendant is provided treatment to regain competence. Professionals who are responsible for the defendant's treatment must re-evaluate the defendant's competence status periodically, and they must notify the court at any time that they believe the defendant is competent to stand trial. This will result in a court hearing on the defendant's restoration to competence. If the defendant is found competent, the trial process will resume. If the defendant has not been restored to competence by the end of the period of time defined by statute, most states require that the charges must be dismissed and a hearing held concerning possible civil commitment.

These rules for dealing with incompetent defendants have been developed in the context of adult defendants' incompetence due to mental illness or mental retardation. They have not taken into account the fact that some adolescents may be incompetent not for reasons of mental disorder but simply due to immaturity. To my knowledge, at the time this chapter was written, no state statutes and no criminal or juvenile appellate cases had yet provided specific instructions for the disposition of cases in which adolescents are incompetent to stand trial as a result of developmental immaturity. Potential remedies for law and policy on this question have been described elsewhere (Grisso, 1996), but at this time there is no clear legal guidance for courts' responses to such cases.

2.0   CONCEPTUALIZING THE EVALUATION

A theoretical and empirical perspective for trial competence evaluations of juveniles can be constructed on the basis of past literature on competence to stand trial evaluations with adults, combined with developmental literature on children's and adolescents' cognitive and psychosocial capacities. Clinicians who want a review of research on evaluations for competence to stand trial may consult Grisso (1986) for research through 1985, and two 5-year updates for 1986 to 1990 (Grisso, 1992) and 1991 to 1995 (Cooper & Grisso, 1997). (See also Melton et al., 1997.)

2.1   *Objectives of the Evaluation*

The objectives of a competence to stand trial evaluation can be outlined using the same four components employed in Chapter 2: (a) *Functional* (referring to functional abilities), (b) *Causal*, (c) *Interactive*, and (d) *Judgmental*. To these we will add one more related to the question of restoration of competence: (e) the *Prescriptive* component.

2.11 Describing Functional Abilities

The most fundamental objective of a competence to stand trial evaluation is to describe to the court the status of the youth's abilities that are relevant for the legal question. At the broadest level, these abilities are identified in the *Dusky* standard for trial competence: understanding and appreciating the nature of the proceedings, and being able to assist counsel in developing a defense. Forensic mental health examiners have found it helpful to use a more specific set of abilities to which these two broad domains seem to refer, focusing on matters that appellate courts have suggested defendants ought to know or be able to manage as competent trial defendants. One of the more frequently used sets of abilities was developed by McGarry (1973). They are listed here in four categories that offer additional structure:

- *Understanding of Charges and Potential Consequence*
    1. Ability to understand and appreciate the charges and their seriousness
    2. Ability to understand possible dispositional consequences of guilty, not guilty, and not guilty by reason of insanity
    3. Ability to realistically appraise the likely outcomes

- *Understanding of the Trial Process*
    4. Ability to understand, without significant distortion, the roles of participants in the trial process (e.g., judge, defense attorney, prosecutor, witnesses, jury)
    5. Ability to understand the process and potential consequences of pleading and plea bargaining
    6. Ability to grasp the general sequence of pretrial/trial events

- *Capacity to Participate with Attorney in a Defense*
    7. Ability to adequately trust or work collaboratively with attorney
    8. Ability to disclose to attorney reasonably coherent description of facts pertaining to the charges, as perceived by the defendant
    9. Ability to reason about available options by weighing their consequences, without significant distortion

> 10. Ability to realistically challenge prosecution witnesses and monitor trial events

- **Potential for Courtroom Participation**
  > 11. Ability to testify coherently, if testimony is needed
  > 12. Ability to control own behavior during trial proceedings
  > 13. Ability to manage the stress of trial

There are a few things here that youths need not understand when facing juvenile hearings; for example, most states have no jury trials in juvenile court. Overall, however, the abilities in McGarry's list are as relevant for juvenile as for criminal court.

A somewhat different way to conceptualize functional abilities relevant for trial competence has been offered by Bonnie (1992) and his colleagues (S. Hoge et al., 1997; Poythress et al., 1997). They focus on the same content areas as the McGarry structure, but they group the abilities in a different way.

First, defendants must be able to *understand* a number of things about their legal situation, the possible penalties, the nature of the trial process and its participants, and information that is acquired as the trial proceeds (e.g., what their attorney tells them about the process and what they are observing as events unfold). Second, defendants must have a proper *appreciation* of the significance of what they understand as it applies to their own situation. For example, a defendant might "understand" that defense counsel is intended to be an advocate, yet the defendant may fail to "appreciate" (or believe) that the attorney is on his or her side due to the defendant's paranoid delusional state. Third, defendants must have the *reasoning* ability to make important trial-related decisions using the information that they understand and appreciate. For example, cognitive deficits might interfere with their ability to imagine the consequences of various options that are available (e.g., through plea bargaining), or to handle the complex task of considering several consequences related to several available options.

This brief review indicates that there are several ways to conceptualize the functional abilities that are relevant for competent trial participation by adolescent defendants. A primary purpose of the evaluation is to provide a description of the youth's status regarding these specific functional abilities. The focus is on the youth's abilities now and in the future as the trial process continues.

2.12 Causal Explanations for Deficits in Abilities

If youths show deficits in the abilities noted previously, the clinician must explain the probable reasons for those deficits. As will be discussed in more detail later, the more common sources of deficits in such abilities include mental disorders, mental retardation, specific learning disabilities, and developmental immaturity. Following up on hypotheses about these clinical and cognitive conditions is thus an integral part of the competence evaluation. The clinician's eventual opinions should include a description of the connection between deficits in competence abilities and the youth's clinical and developmental status. This is especially important because of the later question of remediation: that is, if the youth is incompetent, whether the conditions underlying the youth's functional deficits can be modified, and thus whether and how competence can be developed or restored.

2.13   Interaction of Abilities
and Situational Demands

The mere fact that youths manifest deficits in one or more of the functional abilities noted earlier, for whatever clinical or developmental reasons, does not answer the question of their competence to stand trial. These deficits must be considered in light of the specific demands of the criminal or juvenile court proceeding that the juvenile faces. As noted in Chapter 2, competence depends on the degree of match or mismatch between the person's abilities and the actual demands of the situation.

This means the evaluation will be of more value if the examiner has some notion of the specific circumstances of the youth's legal situation and the trial circumstances that the youth might face. For example, greater demand for various abilities might be required when:

- the trial is in criminal court rather than juvenile court
- the juvenile court hearing is for the purpose of deciding whether the youth should be transferred for trial in criminal court

- plea bargaining is likely to be involved
- the evidence against the youth is uncertain so that the youth's own ability to provide a coherent, personal account of the events is especially relevant
- the trial process is likely to involve many witnesses
- the trial is likely to require a more complex legal defense
- the defendant is likely to have to testify
- the trial is likely to be lengthy
- the defendant has fewer sources of social support

An example will illustrate the interactive concept. Imagine two 14-year-old youths with equally marginal intellectual capacities for weighing several options and their consequences during problem-solving. Both youths are charged with first degree murder and both face hearings on whether they should be transferred to criminal court for trial.

One youth acted alone, was seen by several witnesses, and told several of his friends that he was going to do the shooting earlier in the day. He must decide whether to plead guilty or not guilty. The other youth was one of five youths involved in the murder, he has no prior delinquent or aggressive history, and there is contradictory evidence concerning the degree of his involvement. He is offered a plea bargain by the prosecutor: testify against the others and the prosecution will reduce the charges to juvenile (rather than criminal) manslaughter. The youth must now weigh the options of various alternatives. Among them are the potential consequences of a criminal court trial, a juvenile court trial, potential danger in either case if other youths seek revenge when he testifies against his peers, and the possibility that he will have to leave his family to live elsewhere to avoid such danger.

The circumstances of the second youth are much more complex than those of the first youth. It is possible that the second youth might be found incompetent to decide and the first youth competent, despite the fact that their degree of capacity is identical. The evaluation will be of additional help to the court if the examiner can describe the demands of the situation, then comment on ways in which the youth's specific functional capacities are likely to fall short of (or be adequate for) meeting those demands.

2.14 The Judgment about Competence to Stand Trial

After describing relevant deficits in functional abilities, their clinical or developmental causes, and ways in which they might impair the youth's participation in light of the youth's trial circumstances, a conclusion must then be reached: Are the youth's abilities sufficient or insufficient to satisfy the standard for competence to stand trial? The law provides no brightline rule for this judgment. Ultimately the judge must return to the purpose of the legal concept: Weighing all of the evidence, *would it be fair* to try this defendant?

Some examiners believe that reaching a conclusion about what is fair or just is not a function for mental health professionals because it involves a legal or moral judgment that is not essentially clinical in nature. Nevertheless, some judges (and indeed, some states' statutes) expect examiners to express a conclusory judgment concerning whether the defendant is competent or incompetent to stand trial. The implications of this will be discussed later.

2.15 Prescribing Remediation of Competence Deficits

When a defendant is found incompetent, the court must determine whether the conditions responsible for the defendant's incompetence can be changed. Thus it will be important for the examiner to provide information relevant for this question. Specifically, the examiner must form an opinion concerning

- whether *an intervention exists* that could increase the defendant's relevant abilities;
- if there is, the *likelihood of change* if that intervention were employed; and
- the *time that is likely to be required* to bring about the necessary change.

The purpose of this "treatment recommendation" is somewhat different from one that is made in ordinary clinical situations. Here the clinician is not prescribing what would be needed for complete remission of the underlying condition but simply what needs to be done in order to prepare the defendant to participate in the trial process. In some cases, the latter objective is not as ambitious as the former. For example, treatment might reduce the intrusion of delusional ideas that were interfering with the defendant's perceptions of the trial process, while not necessarily having dealt with a wider range of changes that would be necessary to return the person to community life.

The proper remedial prescription for youths who are incompetent due to developmental immaturity rather than mental disorder is an unanswered question. At this writing, no appellate cases have addressed this issue. When incapacities are due to immaturity and the need for further development, the concept of "restoration" of competence is a misnomer. In criminal court, a finding of incompetence due to immaturity could be seen by some judges as a reason to waive the youth to juvenile court (presuming that the standard for trial competence—the amount of ability that is necessary—is perceived as lower in juvenile court than in criminal court). If a youth were considered incompetent to stand trial in juvenile court, this might be a basis for dismissal of the charges, or some judges might simply "continue" the case (postpone the trial) until the juvenile has achieved greater maturity. All of these possible outcomes, however, currently are merely speculations. Examiners will have to seek advice from legal counsel or the court concerning how to address the prescriptive question in cases of incompetence due to developmental immaturity.

2.2 *Theoretical Guidance for the Evaluation*

In a recent article (Grisso, 1997), I reviewed what is known from applied developmental research concerning children's and adolescents' decisionmaking abilities that are important for participating in their trials. The following is a summary of the conclusions from that article, which should be consulted by the clinician in order to understand the basis for the conclusions.

Competence to stand trial inquiries focus on *cognitive* abilities (a) to *understand* information that is provided to defendants regarding the trial process and (b) to *reason* with the information that they acquire or bring to the situation. Developmental theory and relevant research tell us these capacities are still developing in most youths prior to age 14. In general, however, "average" adolescents at around age 14 and above are no less capable than "average" adults in their ability to understand matters pertaining to trials or to perform the mental processes that are required when one engages in decisionmaking about trial-related options. These results, however, are true only for "average" adolescents. Current research suggests that the risk of difficulties in abilities related to trial competence is a good deal greater for youths 14 and above who have mental and emotional disorders or cognitive disabilities that produce delays in their development of capacities for comprehension and reasoning.

In addition to cognitive functions, *psychosocial* factors related to development raise important hypotheses about youths' abilities in the trial process. Very young adolescents, or middle adolescents with developmental delays or mental disorders, will vary in the degree to which they have worked through relatively normal developmental issues concerning self-concept and self-control, relationships with adults in authority, and a capacity for an extended time perspective when making decisions (Cauffman, 1996; Scott, 1992; Scott et al., 1995; Steinberg & Cauffman, 1996). Such factors may influence their judgment about the meaning and relevance of the trial process so that their decisions as juvenile defendants might not be the decisions they would make if they had attained their eventual level of maturity. (As this chapter was being written, studies were in progress to examine relationships between specific cognitive or psychosocial factors and juveniles' capacities to participate in their trials. Results of those studies, however, were not yet available.)

One study has examined the relation between juveniles' trial competence and various demographic, psychiatric, and background variables. Cowden and McKee (1995) examined the records of 136 juveniles, ages 9 to 16, who were referred by juvenile courts to a South Carolina forensic evaluation center. Examiners reached conclusions of incompetence in about four-fifths of cases involving youths who were 9 to 12 years of age and in almost half of those who were 13 to 14. The proportion found incompetent in the 15 to 17 year range (about one-quarter) was no different than the proportion reported in studies of adult defendants (e.g., Nicholson & Kugler, 1991; Roesch & Golding, 1980). In addition, incompetence opinions were significantly more likely to be found for youths with serious psychiatric diagnoses and those with remedial educational histories. No relation was found between competence/incompetence status and gender, race, seriousness and number of charges, mental health history, and the youth's degree of prior experience with the juvenile court.

Studies of this type may be influenced by local patterns of referral for competence evaluations as well as the practices of the examiners in a particular evaluation center. Therefore, the study does not necessarily tell us what proportions of youths are (or ought to be) found incompetent in other jurisdictions. Moreover, the study did not identify the specific functional deficits (whether cognitive or psychosocial) that were typical of youths found incompetent to stand trial. The study's results do suggest, however, that at least three causal factors seemed to be related to clinicians' conclusions about incompetence: severe mental disorder, cognitive and intellectual disabilities, and age-related characteristics.

Among adult defendants, mental disorders most often found in cases adjudicated incompetent to stand trial include psychotic conditions and mental retardation. For adolescents, however, a greater range of disorders should be considered when explaining deficits in youths' functional abilities to participate in a trial. Examples include

- A youth with prepsychotic paranoid ideation that seriously distorts his or her perceptions of the value of legal counsel
- A youth with Attention-Deficit/Hyperactivity Disorder who has significant problems monitoring and making sense of the trial process
- A very depressed youth who lacks motivation to participate in his or her defense and will not discuss matters with his or her attorney

In summary, when a youth manifests deficits in important functional abilities related to competence to stand trial, the examiner's attempts to explain those deficits may require a careful examination of underlying psychopathology, cognitive disabilities, and characteristics related to the youth's psychosocial development.

3.0   THE EVALUATION PROCESS

The process of a juvenile's competence to stand trial evaluation begins with an understanding of the referral question and continues with a review of records, interviews with the youth, interview with parents, and psychological testing.

3.1   *Taking the Referral*

Typically the order for a competence to stand trial evaluation will come from the criminal or juvenile court, the question having been raised by the court or the defense attorney.   Requests for these evaluations may also come directly from the defense attorney.   In criminal court the referral might call not only for a competence assessment but also for a criminal responsibility evaluation ("insanity" or "mental state at the time of the offense").   If so, the examiner should plan to obtain data for both purposes simultaneously.   Sometimes the wording of the order makes it unclear what is wanted (e.g., "to evaluate the juvenile's competence to know right from wrong"), in which case the examiner should contact the court for clarification of the question.

The examiner should request the name of the youth's attorney if the court has not automatically provided it.   It is good practice to notify the youth's defense attorney when a court order for a competence evaluation has been received.   This serves two purposes.   It gives the attorney the opportunity to meet with the youth prior to the evaluation if he or she wishes.   In addition, clinicians can use this telephone contact to obtain important information from the attorney as background for the evaluation.

3.2   *Obtaining and Reviewing Records*

Courts making referrals typically will provide information about the current charges, the type of hearing that the youth faces, and a copy of the youth's offense record.   Any social history data that the court might have should also be obtained.

During the telephone contact with the youth's attorney, the examiner should learn as much as possible about the nature of the juvenile or criminal court process that the youth faces.   The type of information to be sought corresponds to the earlier list of ways in which the demands of trial proceedings may vary (see 3-2.13).

In addition, the attorney may be able to describe the youth's behavior in previous attorney-client contacts or in the courtroom, especially behaviors that raised the question of the youth's competence. Finally, the attorney might assist the examiner to obtain documents and reports regarding the youth's school achievement, past contacts with mental health services, and reports of past psychological or psychiatric evaluations.

Attorneys sometimes ask to be present at the evaluation. Forensic mental health professionals have varying opinions about assenting to these requests. Some argue that attorneys will influence the evaluation process adversely. On the other hand, the attorney's presence sometimes provides a good opportunity for the clinician to watch the attorney and the youth in conversation with each other, thus providing data regarding the youth's capacities to interact with the attorney. Moreover, it seems reasonable to allow the attorney to observe the evaluation so that the attorney can see first-hand what transpires and can protect the defendant's interests (e.g., by being able to raise objections to the examiner's procedures in later court hearings). Some states expressly provide the right for attorneys to be present at their clients' evaluations in juvenile and criminal cases, and the examiner should be aware of this requirement if it exists.

3.3 *Preparing the Youth for the Evaluation*

At the first interview with the youth, the examiner should clearly explain the purpose of the evaluation. For example, the examiner can point out that the court (or the youth's attorney) has asked for the evaluation to be done and that its purpose is to evaluate how well the youth understands and can handle the legal process that he or she is going through. If the evaluation is court ordered, the youth should be told that the examiner will eventually be talking to (writing a report for) the judge, and that the judge's decision will influence how soon the youth has a trial and whether the youth might need treatment before that happens.

It is good practice to ask youths to explain what the clinician has told them in order to check their comprehension. When the evaluation is court ordered, the purpose of this process is not to obtain "informed consent" or a "waiver of confidentiality," neither of which applies in this circumstance. If youths raise the question concerning whether they can refuse, the examiner should indicate that they can although (a) the examiner naturally will have to report this to the court that ordered the evaluation, and (b) the youth should consult his or her attorney about the advisability of refusing.

3.4 *Content of the Interview with the Youth*

Competence to stand trial evaluations may require more than one session to complete although many should not require more than a single session of 45 to 90 minutes.

The following sequence of procedures is used by many examiners:

- Brief inquiry into social history
- Inquiry into past legal and juvenile justice experience
- Youth's report of current legal circumstances
- A "competence interview" focused on relevant functional abilities for trial competence
- Mental status exam and/or psychological testing

3.41 Social History

The social history inquiry can focus primarily on the youth's past and current living arrangements (e.g., family, where youth grew up, present location), past and current academic activities and performance, jobs held, special interests, history of injuries, and history of mental health services. Much of this information can be obtained from other sources. But it opens the interview on something other than legal and offense topics, thus reducing the likelihood of defensiveness on the part of the youth. In addition, youths sometimes will provide social history information that others do not have.

3.42 Past Legal Experience

The examiner should then ask about the youth's past experience with police and courts—for example, whether this is the first time the youth has been arrested, and if not, what the previous experiences were like. This begins to provide some indication of the degree and type of experience the youth has had with legal procedures, attorneys, and courts. If the youth is being held in a detention center or residential mental health facility, the examiner can then inquire about that place and about the events that brought about the youth's admission.

3.43 Current Alleged Offense

This will lead naturally to the youth's description of the circumstances of the arrest, the charges, and the youth's story about the events surrounding the time of the offense. A very detailed description is not necessary. The objective is to test the youth's ability to recount his or her own version of the events in a way that allows someone else to follow the account and grasp the youth's message.

3.44 Competence Abilities Interview

At this point the examiner embarks on a line of questions designed to assess the youth's actual understanding of the nature of the charges and their potential consequences, the nature of the trial process and its participants, and matters pertaining to the youth's capacities to consult with legal counsel on important decisions in the process. The content of this part of the interview should be guided by categories of information like those developed by McGarry (1973) noted earlier in Section 3-2.11. Typically the questions are fairly direct (e.g., "What do you think is likely to happen if you are found guilty of the things they say you did?" "What does a judge do in a trial?" "Tell me about the last time that you talked to your attorney—like what was said, and what you thought about her"). All of the categories of information that were described earlier should be covered. Several methods that can be used to structure this "competence abilities interview" portion of the evaluation will be described later (3-4.0).

If youths seem to do poorly when asked to define certain terms or concepts (e.g., "What is plea bargaining?"), the examiner should not simply presume the youth does not understand and move on to the next question. It is not unusual for youths to have trouble expressing what they know in the abstract, while having less difficulty doing so in the context of actual events or when they are presented with concrete images. For example, some youths who understand the concept of plea bargaining but have difficulty providing a definition may be able to give an acceptable example of it that demonstrates their understanding. Others may be able to tell the examiner how it works after the examiner has set up a concrete example (e.g., "Imagine that the prosecutor comes to your attorney and says, 'Let's make a deal.' What could the prosecutor have in mind?").

Examiners should also remember that mere lack of knowledge about the charges, their consequences, and trial matters is not the critical issue in determining competence to stand trial. If youths do not know something, what really matters is their capacity to learn it if it is explained to them. If they can easily learn such matters with proper instruction, there is no need to conclude that this lack of knowledge will keep them from understanding their legal circumstances or assisting in their own defense, as long as the attorney takes the time to teach the youth.

Therefore, when a youth manifests poor understanding about some matters, the examiner should choose a few concepts with which the youth is not familiar and should explain them (i.e., teach the youth the correct meaning). Questions can then be asked to ascertain whether the youth seems to have grasped the meaning. Finally, at some later time in the interview, the examiner can return to that point and "test" the youth's retention and comprehension of the matter (e.g., "You remember a while ago I was explaining to you what a judge does in the trial? Can you explain that to me now?").

Experienced competence examiners have found that visual stimuli often provide added assistance in discovering what defendants understand and what they can learn. Some examiners use drawings of courtrooms or illustration boards to accompany their discussions of participants and events in trials. One examiner with whom I consulted on a trial competence evaluation of a 12-year-old took the youth on a tour of the juvenile court building, asking the usual "competence ability interview" questions at appropriate times (e.g., discussing the trial process and participants while they sat in an empty courtroom).

Examiners sometimes have a tendency to focus heavily on defendants' understanding of important trial matters but neglect other equally important issues. For example, when discussing things that happen between attorneys and their clients, examiners should explore not only what youths *understand* about these matters, but also how they feel or what they *believe* about them. A youth may comprehend and be able to describe adequately what an attorney is supposed to do yet may believe (e.g., due to delusional, paranoid, or highly oppositional perceptions) that attorneys can never be trusted to do it.

In addition, examiners should assess youths' abilities to *reason and problem solve* about trial-relevant matters. For example, the examiner can present a hypothetical plea bargain offer and ask the youth to think aloud about how one would decide which option to take. Does the youth seem to be considering the various consequences, or merely focusing on one desirable or undesirable consequence? Does the youth seem actually to be comparing the options rather than merely selecting one impulsively and by-passing any real decisional process? Is there any evidence of delusional thinking or other gross distortions of reality woven into the youth's discussion of hypothetical trial events proposed by the examiner?

3.45   Mental Status Exam and/or Psychological Testing

If youths' show deficits in functional abilities related to competence to stand trial, the examiner eventually will need to explain the reasons for those deficits. The reasons might be related to mental disorder, cognitive disabilities, or developmental immaturity. Thus part of the examination must focus on assessing these psychological conditions.

The examiner is likely to obtain a good deal of clinical and developmental information through the review of records and by observing the youth in the preceding parts of the interview. Nevertheless, a formal mental status examination provides a more standardized clinical database and assures that an adequate range of psychological functions has been examined.

Psychological testing often is not performed in routine competence to stand trial cases with adults. It is reserved for cases in which there are diagnostic issues or questions of cognitive disabilities that a review of records, clinical observations, and interview data have not been able to answer. Those cases are likely to be more numerous for adolescents than for adults because of lesser reliability inherent in diagnosis of serious mental disorder in adolescents. In addition, standardized measures are likely to provide a helpful database for examiners' descriptions of some youths' cognitive deficits and developmental immaturity. This point will be revisited in the next section.

4.0   STANDARDIZED ASSESSMENT METHODS

Several structured methods have been developed for obtaining data on defendants' abilities related to the legal standard for competence to stand trial. They are of two types: *semi-structured interview guides* for assessing relevant abilities, and paper-and-pencil *screening instruments* for trial competence abilities. In addition, a variety of *psychological tests* focusing on psychopathology, cognitive deficits, and psychosocial developmental characteristics may be helpful in some cases. This section reviews the use of these three types of structured assessment methods in competence to stand trial evaluations of adolescents.

4.1   *Semi-Structured Interview Guides for Competence to Stand Trial Abilities*

A number of semi-structured interview methods have been developed to assist clinicians in obtaining information on the range of abilities suggested by the *Dusky* standard for competence to stand trial. None of them were developed with the intention that they would be used in evaluating adolescents. Yet most of them can be used with adolescents, in juvenile or criminal court, because they are quite flexible. They only guide the interview rather than require that specific words or items be administered.

The best known is the *Competency Assessment Interview* (CAI) developed by McGarry (1973). The CAI consists of definitions for 13 "functions" relevant for competence to stand trial. These functions make up the list that appeared in 3-2.11, which was adapted from the CAI. The functions as they were originally worded can be reviewed in Melton et al. (1997) or Grisso (1986, 1988). The original manual provides examples of questions that examiners can ask to elicit information from defendants relevant to each function although the procedure does not require any specific, standardized set of questions. It also provides a rating format with which the examiner judges the degree to which the defendant shows deficits on each function. The rating procedure, however, provides no anchors or criteria for examiners to follow in making the ratings. Research with the CAI (reviewed by Grisso, 1986, 1992) suggests that examiners' opinions based on CAI data generally have corresponded to judicial decisions about competence or incompetence, and that a high degree of agreement can be achieved between raters.

The *Fitness Interview Test-Revised* (FIT-R; Roesch, Webster, & Eaves, 1994; Zapf & Roesch, 1997) focuses on questions in three main areas: understanding of the proceedings, understanding of the possible consequences of the proceedings, and the ability to communicate with counsel. It differs from the CAI primarily in providing greater structure for the interview process.

The most recently developed method is the *MacArthur Competence Assessment Tool-Criminal Adjudication* (MacCAT-CA; S. Hoge et al., 1997). Like the FIT-R, it is more highly structured than the CAI, but it uses an objective scoring system. Questions are grouped into four categories, corresponding to four types of abilities: (a) *Understanding* of charges and trials, (b) *Appreciation* of the relevance of information for a defense, (c) *Reasoning* with information during decisionmaking, and (d) *Evidencing a Choice*. For most parts of the MacCAT-CA, hypothetical situations are described and the defendant is questioned about them. For the Understanding items, defendants are "taught" the concepts for which they show deficient understanding and then re-tested. Research (S. Hoge et al., 1997) has shown that the instrument discriminates well between adult defendants whom courts have found incompetent and defendants for whom the competence question was never raised. The instrument could be used with adolescents who are being tried in criminal court, but some of its content would have to be modified for examining competence to stand trial in juvenile court (e.g., its reference to juries, which are rarely involved in juvenile court hearings). Currently there are no MacCAT-CA norms for adolescents.

4.2 *Competence Screening Instruments*

Several highly structured instruments have been developed to assess defendants' understanding of trial-related concepts. Two of the better-known instruments, both paper-and-pencil, are the *Competency Screening Test* (CST; Lipsitt, Lelos, & McGarry, 1971) and the *Georgia Court Competency Test-Mississippi State Hospital* (GCCT-MSH; Nicholson et al., 1988). These methods are brief, and they focus primarily on the defendant's understanding of particular legally relevant information rather than covering the full range of abilities that are involved in judgments about competence to stand trial. Therefore, they are best viewed as screening instruments that may be useful for determining whether the question of competence should be raised and a more complete evaluation performed.

In my opinion, these instruments have limited use when evaluating adolescents' trial competence, especially for trial participation in juvenile court. Their content tends to be oriented to criminal court situations, and they require defendants to respond without the benefit of the flexibility in presentation of questions that is important in the assessment of delinquent youths, many of whom have receptive and expressive language difficulties. Cooper (1997), for example, found that only 1 in 120 youths in a secure detention facility scored above the suggested "cut-off score" (was "competent") on the GCCT-MSH. Moreover, the use of cut-off scores with these instruments is misleading because it suggests incorrectly that the narrow range of abilities that they assess is all that is involved in evaluating a defendant's competence.

If a brief structured instrument is to be used with adolescents, a better choice might be the *Competency Assessment to Stand Trial-Mental Retardation* (CAST-MR; Everington, 1990). Developed especially for use with adult defendants with mental retardation, it attempts to compensate for receptive and expressive language problems, as well as for acquiescent response styles, in assessing what a defendant understands about trial matters.

4.3 *Standardized Psychological Tests*

As noted earlier, psychological testing in trial competence evaluations may be needed more often with adolescents than with adults. It should be considered especially when there are ambiguities regarding youths' mental disorder or cognitive deficits, or for testing the validity of the examiner's clinical judgment about the reasons for functional deficits during the "competence interview." Three general types of measures may be helpful.

Several objective measures of *mental and emotional disorders* are available for adolescents although all of them have limitations with youths encountered in the justice system. The *Minnesota Multiphasic Personality Inventory-Adolescent* (MMPI-A; Butcher et al., 1992) measures a wide range of disorders and personality characteristics, but its length (similar to the MMPI-2) is beyond the attentional and reading capacities of a subset of delinquent youths. (Audiotaped presentation of questions is available; I have found it useful in some cases.) The *Brief Symptom Inventory* (BSI; Derogatis, 1993) is shorter (54 items), provides 9 clinical scales, and (although developed for adults) has been used in research and practice with delinquent adolescents. However, BSI results in research studies with youths have raised questions about whether it can adequately discriminate between clinical and nonclinical samples. Moreover, its way of asking about symptoms ("How much have you been troubled by . . .") may focus more on youths' feelings about their symptoms (i.e., whether they have been "troubled" by them) than on the presence or absence of the symptoms themselves.

The *Millon Adolescent Clinical Inventory* (MACI; Millon, 1993) provides many of the benefits of the MMPI-A and a wider range of clinical and personality scales than the BSI. For youths who cannot read, the test is short enough (160 items) that examiners can read it to them (or use audiotaped presentation). Interpretations of MACI scores will be limited until norms for juvenile court samples are published. Other common tests used with delinquent youths are the *Child Behavior Checklist* (Achenbach, 1991a) and the *Personality Inventory for Children* (Lachar & Kline, 1994). These tests, however, tend to focus on behavior problems, which are usually less relevant than clinical symptoms for explaining functional deficits related to trial competence.

Examiners sometimes may wish to use measures of *cognitive abilities, intelligence,* and *achievement* in their competence evaluations of youths, especially when deficits in understanding or reasoning about trial-related matters have been observed. The wide range of instruments available in this category does not need description here. Those that are most likely to be of use will focus on the youth's fund of general information; ability to deal with abstract concepts, vocabulary, expressive and receptive language abilities; and attentional abilities. Unfortunately, there are few standardized tests of youths' abilities related directly to decisionmaking: for example, a youth's ability to come up with a range of possible choices in response to a problem, or to think of a range of consequences if a particular choice were made. Standardized research measures with objective scoring do exist to assess such abilities. But they tend to focus on specific problem situations: for example, choosing medical procedures, or choosing whether to waive or assert "Miranda rights" when questioned by police officers. What is not available is a clinically practical way to assess decisionmaking abilities of youths in the abstract or as applied specifically to decisions that must be made by defendants in the trial process.

Some youths may have cognitive capacities sufficient to understand and reason with information related to their trials yet may use poor judgment in arriving at decisions because of *immaturity in psychosocial development*. For example, some youths may have the capacity to think of consequences during decisionmaking but may not have developed an adult-like future time perspective that would allow them to weigh longer-range consequences when thinking about their choices. Others may not yet have developed the capacity to delay responding to problems long enough to use their decisionmaking abilities. Some may see problems from their own perspective only, without being able to see how the decision might influence others whom they care about. Theoretically, some adolescents may not yet have reached their own adult level of capacity within these areas of psychosocial development.

Although these psychosocial characteristics often can be inferred from clinical observation, their measurement would be helpful in determining whether a particular youth's development in these areas is "immature" in relation to his or her own peers, as well as in relation to adults. Unfortunately, currently there are no such instruments to recommend for use in clinical forensic evaluations of juveniles.

5.0   INTERPRETIVE ISSUES

Interpreting data from the evaluation first requires taking stock of the ways in which the youth has manifested *strengths and deficits in legally relevant functional abilities* during inquiry in the competence interview and examining the clinical data for potential *explanations for any deficits* that are observed in those functional abilities.   Second, the *significance of these deficits* must be considered in light of the demands of the youth's trial.   Third, courts will often ask the examiner to offer an opinion that the *evidence more strongly supports a finding of competence or incompetence* to proceed to trial.   Finally, if the youth appears incompetent, then the data must be examined to arrive at an opinion about the *prospects for rehabilitation* that will allow the youth to be brought to trial.

5.1   *Identifying Deficits and Their Causes*

5.11   Deficits in Understanding

Most youths who are over 13, are of average intelligence, and do not have serious cognitive or emotional disorders are likely to have little difficulty understanding (comprehending) the nature of their charges and their possible consequences. Similarly, they are likely be able to grasp in a general sense the roles and functions of various participants in the trial process. This is not to say that youths will understand all of these things when they come to the evaluation. Many younger adolescents may have little knowledge of the trial participants and the trial process, and at least some older adolescents may have gaps in their knowledge as well. In these cases, the issue is whether they are able to assimilate and comprehend such information when they are provided careful instruction that attempts to "educate" them to the things that are important for them to know.

There are many reasons that certain youths will not be able to benefit by an examiner's attempts to clarify the meanings of various trial-relevant concepts. The problem might be related to limited intellectual ability (e.g., mental retardation) in some cases. It may also be seen, however, in some youths with adequate intellectual capacity who have certain specific cognitive disabilities that interfere with learning, as well as youths who have attentional problems that interfere with the reception and assimilation of new information. Attentional problems may be specific (e.g., Attention-Deficit/Hyperactivity Disorder [ADHD]) or secondary to other psychiatric disorders (e.g., a psychosis in which internal and external stimuli compete for attention).

Remember that the mere fact that a youth can be given any of these diagnoses does not mean that the youth is unable to understand or learn what is needed to be competent to stand trial. Disorders are *not indicators* of deficits in understanding. Put another way, they *should not be used to infer* poor capacities to understand. Their role in the evaluation is to *explain the reasons for deficits which have been directly observed* by the examiner. Thus the fact that a youth can be diagnosed ADHD should not, by itself, be taken to mean that the youth is deficient in the capacity to understand or learn trial-relevant information.

Although the examples provided previously involve cognitive deficits, poor comprehension or learning may occur for noncognitive reasons as well. For example, one can imagine youths with Oppositional Defiant Disorder who might resist examiners' efforts to teach them relevant concepts—not because they could not learn them, but because they simply refuse to take part in the exercise.

5.12 Deficits Impairing the Development of a Defense

The development of the youth's defense is, of course, the job of the attorney. In many cases, however, the attorney's ability to fulfill this legal role is dependent to some degree on the capacities of the youth. Therefore, a part of the interpretation of the evaluation data should focus on the youth's deficits that might reduce the attorney's ability to represent the youth effectively.

One type of deficit that can interfere with the development of a defense is the youth's *inability to perceive the lawyer as an advocate.* Even if youths have a basic understanding of the intended advocacy role of defense counsel, some of them may not believe that counsel will provide that advocacy. In fact, past research has suggested that it is fairly common for youths not to expect that their attorneys will be of much help to them. For many youths, the notion of an adult who would defend them against other adults who seek to punish them is so novel that it is difficult for them to believe. In this light, suspiciousness about an adult who is claiming to take that role is understandable.

Yet it is not mere suspiciousness or mistrust that is at issue in juveniles' competence to stand trial. Many adult defendants are also mistrustful of their attorneys. And most skeptical adolescents and adults tend to respond to continuing efforts by their attorneys to win their confidence. The deficits that make a difference here are those that seem not to be easily remedied because their cause is rooted in some dysfunctional condition of the youth. For example

- The youth whose psychotic delusion that "everyone is trying to kill me" makes it impossible for him to trust his lawyer
- The traumatized youth who, because of extreme physical abuse by adults during her childhood, sullenly refuses even to talk to an adult who attempts any relationship with her
- The immature and fearful youth who, in response to the attorney's questions, seems only to be able to shrug his shoulders and say "I don't know"
- The oppositional youth who argues against any suggestion by the attorney, even when suggestions are made that accommodate to the youth's perspective

The attorney's ability to work collaboratively with a youth may be impaired not only by the youth's pathological mistrust but also by the youth's *passivity*. Although they may understand matters well enough, some immature youths may react to their jeopardy by denying its threat; they may defensively avoid the fear it creates by acting as though the legal process does not really matter. Others may be so depressed that they cannot focus on the process and the efforts of the attorney. Such reactions may result in a passive lack of involvement that reduces their input to the attorney, as well as their preparedness to make decisions in response to options that their attorney presents them.

Deficits in the *capacity to communicate with the attorney* are evident in several of the preceding examples. Other communication deficits may not be due to mistrust or immaturity, but to neuropsychological deficits. This is manifested primarily in the youth's difficulties in telling a coherent story or relating historical information in a manner that can be clearly interpreted. For example, the youth may seem unable to relate pieces of the events surrounding the alleged offense in chronological sequence or to provide important details about personal history. Sometimes this is due to very poor general intellectual functioning, deficits in memory, or chronic problems in expressive language abilities. The same psychological dysfunctions may reduce the capacity of the youth to testify in his or her own defense at trial, which in some legal cases is necessary for an adequate defense.

Sometimes it is important that the youth be able to *monitor and evaluate information* that arises in the process of the trial. For example, some issues that are important to the defense may not arise until witnesses are called. As they testify, there may be some aspects of their testimony that could be challenged only with the youth's own knowledge of facts that would contradict the witnesses. In these cases, the attorney is dependent upon the youth to track the proceedings, attend to what is being said, and recognize discrepancies between the witnesses' statements and the youth's knowledge of the situation about which the witnesses are testifying. Some youths with attentional deficits and with difficulties in processing information, or associating new information with previous knowledge, may have difficulty assisting their attorneys in this way.

5.13 Deficits for Making Important Decisions

There are certain decisions that attorneys cannot make for their clients. Only defendants can waive constitutional rights, such as the right to a jury trial and the right to plead guilty (i.e., to incriminate themselves by admitting to the offense with which they are charged). By extension, only the defendant can agree to accept a plea bargain, which usually involves pleading guilty to an offense after the prosecutor presents the possibility of a more favorable (less punitive) outcome than if the defendant pursued a not-guilty verdict. Youths' capacities for decisionmaking, therefore, are important. Indeed, most criminal cases never reach a formal trial in which evidence is heard regarding the possible guilt of the defendant; over 90% of them are concluded instead by defendants' decisions to waive the right to a trial by pleading guilty.

Evidence for deficits in decisionmaking abilities may arise in two broad ways in competence evaluations of adolescents and children. In some cases, youths who are given hypothetical problems and asked to process them aloud will manifest an *inability to manage the cognitive process.* For example, some youths' developmental immaturity or cognitive deficits do not allow them to think well in abstractions. They have difficulty imagining situations that do not yet exist. Intellectual deficits, as well as various mental disorders, may interfere with the youth's ability to consider more than one option at once or to consider multiple consequences of the various options even when they are explained to the youth.

In other cases, the cognitive aspects of the task may be mastered, but the youth manifests *poor judgment* as a consequence of mental disorder or developmental immaturity. For example, there is evidence that many preadolescents, adolescents with delayed cognitive development, and youths who are particularly impulsive have a tendency to focus on the positive and negative immediate consequences of a choice, at the expense of considering the eventual impact of longer-term potential consequences. In contrast, in some legal cases, the choices that youths make about their defense may literally affect them for the remainder of their lives. Other examples of judgments influenced by transient stages of development arise in the context of idealistic thinking that is characteristic of younger adolescents:

- The 13-year-old "wannabe," only peripherally involved in the gang offense with which he is charged, who refuses to talk about the involvement of the rest of the gang even when informed by his attorney that the others will be witnesses against him
- The 14-year-old who denies the pain of his father's chronic abuse by idolizing him, and therefore refusing to allow his attorney to raise his victimization as a mitigating factor in a trial on serious felony charges.

When interpreting these circumstances, it is important to remember that "poor judgment" is not determined simply by the fact that the defendant chooses what others would see as an ill-advised option. The decision will be suspect not simply because it is harmful to the defendant but because it is also clearly influenced by psychopathology or by characteristics of the youth that are in developmental transition.

5.2 *Interpreting the Significance of the Youth's Deficits*

Deficits in abilities to take the role of defendant are not equally important in all cases even though the deficits might be substantial. As noted earlier, the degree and nature of the youth's deficits need to be considered in light of the actual demands of the youth's own trial circumstances.

The discussion in 3-2.13 listed a number of ways in which youths' trial circumstances vary in the demands that they make on youths' capacities to participate in their trials. There is no formula for weighing these trial circumstances against the youth's degree of ability. One simply weights various deficits in a youth's abilities more or less heavily when the relevant demands for those abilities will be great or minimal.

For example, some trials require only minimal capacity on the part of the defendant. When the defendant's illegal behavior was observed and described by several independent passers-by, the attorney's ability to grasp what happened is not so dependent on the youth's report. Thus one would have less concern about deficits in the youth's ability to provide a coherent picture of the events surrounding the offense. In contrast, the youth's ability to reconstruct the events may be critical when the accuser is the parent of a 4-year-old alleged victim of the youth's alleged assault while baby-sitting the child in the parent's absence.

Similarly, some youths with monitoring and memory deficits due to an attentional disorder may be quite able to manage and participate in a brief trial process in juvenile court. Yet they may be completely unable to deal with lengthier proceedings—for example, a complex waiver hearing or a criminal court trial of several days duration—especially those trials that may involve distractions associated with public hearings and media attention.

Examiners should expect that in some cases they will not be able to engage in these comparisons between youths' abilities and specific trial demands with confidence or in detail. Often the request for a competence evaluation will occur fairly early in the legal process, soon after the youth is charged. Attorneys them-selves often will not be able to anticipate what a future trial process has in store. For example, I find that when attorneys are asked at that early stage whether the youth is likely to have to testify, typically they answer, "Possibly," or "I don't know yet." One strategy is to use available information to make inferences that rule out very unlikely demands (e.g., a complex trial process is not likely for a first-offender who is charged in juvenile court with a misdemeanor) and to consider others as quite probable (e.g., a high-stress waiver hearing is likely for a youth facing first-degree murder charges in a highly publicized case).

Some of the factors that need to be taken into account in considering the importance of a youth's deficits pertain not so much to legal circumstances but to the future social context in which the legal process will occur. For example, in a particular case, the examiner might infer from parents' past relationship with their child that they are likely to provide significant, positive support and assistance for the youth during the legal process. This could reduce the degree of concern one would otherwise have about the youth's deficits for thinking through important deci-sions. Conversely, if the examiner can foresee that additional social stress is likely to be placed on the youth in the near future— for example, that a grandparent with whom the youth has had a strong attachment is gravely ill and may die within a short time— this might heighten one's concern about the youth's already limited emotional ability to deal with matters pertaining to the trial.

5.3 *Making the Competence/Incompetence Decision*

Using the previous inferences to arrive at a judgment that the youth is competent or incompetent to stand trial will not be hard when youths show only slight deficits in relevant abilities. It is also not difficult when they manifest gross deficits that are related to serious mental disorders or significant developmental immaturity. Many cases between these extremes, however, will offer challenges. We will discuss the reasons for those challenges, and how to deal with them, in the next section on report writing and testimony (3-6.0).

At the time that the examiner is interpreting the data, it is not actually necessary to resolve all ambivalence concerning whether the youth should be considered competent or incompetent. The question may seem important in order to get to the final interpretive step: that is, deciding what remedial action if the court finds the youth incompetent. The remediation question, however, can be considered at this point without struggling to arrive at a competence/incompetence conclusion. As long as the examiner has identified significant functional deficits and their causes, the examiner can proceed on a conditional basis: "*If* these deficits were to result in a finding of incompetence, what could I recommend that would reduce their impact on the youth's participation as a defendant?"

5.4 *Deciding on Potential for Remediation*

We must remember that the doctrine of competence to stand trial was not developed to shield persons with mental illness or developmental disabilities from being put to trial. The purpose was to assure that when put to trial, they would not be unacceptably disadvantaged by their condition when participating in their defense. Given a finding of incompetence, therefore, remediation focuses on bringing defendants to competence so that they can be tried. This objective is presumed to hold for children and adolescents as well. When incompetence is due to immaturity, presumably the same principle will apply. The objective will be to remediate the deficits associated with immaturity so that the youth might be brought to trial.

Most states require that if remediation cannot be accomplished within a reasonable period of time, the charges must be dismissed. Presumably this also applies to youths in criminal or juvenile court although its application in juvenile court proceedings has not been explicitly addressed by lawmakers or courts in most states.

Recall that there are three questions for the examiner to address when youths' functional deficits seriously threaten their ability to participate in their trials:

- whether there is an intervention that could augment the youth's relevant abilities;
- if there is, the likelihood that the intervention could produce those changes; and

- the time that is likely to be required to bring about the necessary change.

5.41 Incompetence Due to Mental Disorder

When the youth's deficits for trial participation are related to a mental or emotional disorder, the examiner can draw from child clinical literature and experience to determine the nature of the necessary clinical intervention in light of the type of disorder. For example, if the deficits are related to delusional thinking as part of a psychotic condition, the examiner might recommend appropriate medication with a period of hospitalization to monitor its effects. Similarly, clinical knowledge must be applied to the specific case in order to arrive at an estimate concerning the likelihood that the youth will respond to the treatment and the general length of time that this is likely to require.

When making these judgments, the examiner should remember that the question of remediation of deficits related to competence to stand trial is not quite the same as the clinical question of treatment aimed at remission of the underlying disorder. In many cases, complete remission of the disorder will not be necessary, as long as treatment brings about a reduction in the severity of the critical symptoms that were responsible for incompetence. For example, treatment to reduce the intrusion of delusional ideas interfering with the defendant's perceptions of the trial process might not deal with some issues (e.g., social skills development) that would be necessary if one were preparing a patient to manage everyday problems in living in the community.

Often the examiner may be uncertain about the specific amount of time that will be required to bring about these changes. A highly accurate prediction about a specific date is not necessary; a general estimate will suffice. It may be helpful to think in terms of quarterly options: whether remediation is anticipated within 3, 6, 9, or 12 months or would require longer than a year.

5.42 Incompetence Due to Mental Retardation and Specific Cognitive Disabilities

When incapacities are due to mental retardation, it will be necessary in some cases to conclude that there is no intervention that is likely to augment the youth's abilities sufficiently to satisfy a competence standard in the foreseeable future. Disabilities other than mental retardation that have a significant effect on the assimilation or processing of information—for example, specific learning disabilities and attentional disorders—are less likely to be sole reasons for a finding of incompetence although they may contribute to an overall picture of incompetence (e.g., when their effects are compounded by those of other mental and emotional disorders). The likelihood of their remediation will vary across cases. When such disorders constitute the primary reason for doubting a youth's competence, the examiner should take careful steps to determine whether a change in external conditions might produce a remedy that does not require prolonged treatment intervention: for example, increasing the youth's social supports and assistance in the legal process, or making recommendations to modify the trial process to accommodate to the youth's disability.

5.43 Incompetence Due to Developmental Immaturity

Examples provided throughout this chapter have referred to a number of cases that do not involve mental disorder, mental retardation, or specific cognitive dysfunctions. They include, for example

- The 12-year-old who is so dependent and fearful that he cannot communicate with his attorney, make decisions that would be considered in any way independent, or tolerate the emotional impact of a trial process without being significantly traumatized.
- The 15-year-old who seems to be unable to appreciate the actual consequences of his first-degree murder charges—not because of mental retardation or psychotic distortions of reality but because of poor intellectual abilities together with a significant delay in his development of a capacity to think abstractly and in terms of long-range future consequences.
- The bright 16-year-old for whom the idealism and sense of invulnerability often seen in certain stages of adolescent psychosocial development is manifested in an extreme way, although short of being a "mental disorder," causing him to firmly reject a trial option that is clearly in his best interest.

119

As different as these cases appear, they are each an example of potential incompetence due to immaturity. For all of these youths, it can be presumed that the deficits in their abilities to participate in their defense are a consequence of their incomplete development. Put another way, if they had committed their offenses when they were several years older, the predictable developmental processes that would have occurred between now and then probably would have reduced the competence-related problems seen at their current stage of development.

What is the proper remedial prescription for youths whose trial-related deficits are due to their present developmental status as children or adolescents? In some cases, there may be no other logical response—from a clinical perspective—than to provide time for development to take its course. The examiner should recognize, however, that this recommendation is highly problematic. In the case of older children or young adolescents, this may mean a delay that is in no one's interests. If the court chooses to suspend the hearing "until the youth grows up," this means that both the state and the youth will suffer certain consequences of trial delay. In a small number of cases this may simply be unavoidable.

The number of cases for which this unsatisfying conclusion has to be reached, however, may be reduced further by a strategy that employs a basic principle emphasized throughout this chapter: It is not the defendant's mental disorder in general, but rather the defendant's trial-related deficits, that need to be changed. Similarly, with proper attention to this principle, examiners might often find ways to remediate trial-related deficits that are the consequence of a youth's current stage of incomplete maturation without having to conceptualize the remedy as simply allowing the youth to "mature." In some cases, clinical intervention might compensate for the difficulties produced by immaturity. Two case examples will help to illustrate this.

- A 15-year-old girl was charged with sexually molesting two younger children whom she had regularly baby-sat. The girl was almost totally deaf as a result of a serious infectious disease at about age five; she could speak so as to be understood with careful attention, could read lips fairly well, and could manage sign language, despite her low-average intellectual ability. She presented as psychosocially immature, very dependent, and acquiescent in relations with adults. The alleged offense seemed to arise in part from her immaturity; she typically interacted with the children as though there was little difference in age between them and herself.

The primary issue concerning competence to participate in her defense was her emotional lability arising out of her intense shame. In court, in her sessions with her attorney, and in the examination sessions, any mention of her offense or its possible consequences brought on a flood of emotion accompanied by wailing, moaning, and copious tears, with vehement explanations that while she had been bad, she was really a "good girl." Her reaction overcame any efforts by others to proceed with matters at hand, essentially making meaningful communication (or courtroom procedures) impossible.

Although this problem was due to psychosocial immaturity involving no clear mental disorder, a therapeutic remedy was found. The examiner noted that the girl seemed to be somewhat better able to control her emotional reaction during sessions in which she had been assisted by a signer whom she had known for many years. (Signers at other sessions had been people she did not know, having been appointed by the court.) Indeed, she was able to talk a bit about her feelings of shame. The examiner recommended that the court delay the trial for a month or two while the girl was provided counseling (accompanied by her signer-friend) to work through or desensitize her to the emotional impact of the accusation. In addition, it was recommended that she be allowed to have her own signer present—rather than the court-appointed signers—during attorney consultations and court hearings, in order to provide emotional support and comfort. These efforts were successful.

- In another case, a 16-year-old boy of superior intelligence was charged with murder and was facing a juvenile court hearing on his possible transfer to stand trial in criminal court. He had schizoid qualities, significant delays in psychosocial maturation, and no prior delinquencies or school behavior problems. The question of competence was school behavior problems. The question of competence was raised by his refusal to allow his attorney to present any evidence at the transfer hearing concerning a history of his family life, which had been particularly chaotic and reflected gross neglect by his parents. His attorney felt that an adequate defense (against transfer) could not be built without offering this information into evidence for the court to consider in weighing the issues of waiver to criminal court (see Chapter 6). The evaluation revealed that the youth had long dealt with his underlying anger at his parents by denying that their behavior reflected their lack of caring for him. His defense was compounded by an intense idealism that characterized his outlook on many things at this particular stage of his development. He claimed that he would rather go to prison for life than to reveal to an unsympathetic community intimate matters of the family history that would cause his parents pain. (Waiver hearings involving murder charges were open to the public in this state.)

The defendant is allowed to make this decision if it is clear that it is being made competently. The concern here was that the youth was making the decision under the influence of psychodynamic and developmental factors that, as he matured in later years, he eventually would regret—that in retrospect, he would see in a different light with the benefit of later maturation. While the issue was potentially important enough to question the youth's capacity to assist counsel in a defense, a competence judgment was never needed in this case. At the recommendation of the examiner, a series of meetings between the youth, one of the parents, and the attorney (in consultation with the examiner) eventually softened the youth's rigid refusal.

6.0   REPORTS AND TESTIMONY

6.1   *Contents of the Report*

Examples of competence to stand trial reports (for criminal courts) can be found in Melton et al. (1997) and Grisso (1988), and they offer a template that can be used for juvenile court cases as well. In addition, many states' forensic mental health systems have manuals describing their preferred style of reporting the results of a competence to stand trial evaluation. The following outline is an example:

- *Identification* of the youth and the charges
- Listing of *assessment methods* used
- Description of *what the youth was told* about the purpose of the evaluation
- *Social, clinical, and developmental history*
- *Mental status data*, including any psychological testing data
- *Competence data*: that is, data from the assessment of competence to stand trial abilities
- *Interpretation of the data*, including clinical or developmental explanations for any serious deficits in competence abilities
- *Interpretation of the relevance of any deficits*, in light of demands of the legal circumstances, and the examiner's *opinion about competence/incompetence* (if requested)
- *Recommendations for remediation* of deficits if youth is found incompetent

The social, clinical, and developmental history often will not need to be as extensive as might be found in psychiatric or psychological evaluations for many other clinical and treatment-planning purposes. The history should offer just those facts that are necessary in order to address the competence and remediation issues that arise later in the report. Some cases will require more details than others. The court should not be burdened with a dutiful and standardized recitation of clinical and developmental points that end up having little bearing on the case. Select the facts to be described based on their actual relevance.

In the history and the competence data section, the examiner should be careful not to describe what the youth tells the examiner about the alleged offense. Copies of reports of court-ordered competence to stand trial evaluations are provided not only to the defense but also to prosecuting attorneys. Thus there is reason for concern about self-incrimination. Even if law prohibits the use of the competence report in later hearings on guilt, some courts prefer (and some statutes require) that such statements not be made available pretrial except when the defendant has expressly waived the right to avoid self-incrimination.

(The fact that the defendant agreed to provide information for a court-ordered competence evaluation does not constitute the defendant's waiver of that right.)

Various sections are described in the preceding outline as including "data" or "interpretations." I recommend that the examiner write the data sections with particular attention to providing data *only* (no inferences or interpretations), and providing in those sections *all* of the data that will be needed for later sections on interpretations. The interpretation sections, therefore, should offer no new data; they should include inferences based on the data. In addition, the examiner should be careful not merely to provide inferences (e.g., "The youth is suffering from a mental disorder"), but also specifically to explain what data and clinical reasoning support the interpretation or opinion.

6.2 *Special Issues in Competence/Incompetence Judgments*

Earlier we noted that some clinicians prefer not to offer a bottom-line clinical opinion that the youth is "competent" or "incompetent." They argue that the competence-or-incompetence question requires that one determine the degree of deficit in abilities, relative to the demand of the situation, that would constitute "unfairness" if the defendant were required to participate in his or her defense. What is fair or unfair in a particular case cannot be defined clinically or operationally, for which reason the examiner has no clear guidance in making the judgment.

For examiners who do choose to state an opinion that the youth is "competent" or "incompetent" to stand trial, the judgment will not be so difficult in cases in which the youth is grossly impaired or manifests only very mild deficits relative to the average adult defendant. The judgment will be more difficult in nonextreme cases, however. This is especially so because courts have not yet provided even general guidance concerning how the *Dusky* standard is to be applied in adolescent cases.

For example, it is clear that in *criminal court,* deficits due to mental illness and mental retardation may result in incompetence to stand trial for adolescents just as they do for adults. As noted throughout this chapter, however, some adolescents have functional deficits due to developmental immaturity that are just as significant in reducing their ability to assist counsel in a defense as deficits that are related to mental disorder. Yet at this writing, there is no firm legal precedent for "incompetence due to developmental incapacity" when an adolescent with no significant mental illness is tried in criminal court. When examiners believe that a particular adolescent is incompetent to stand trial because of developmental deficits, they may have a solid logical foundation for their opinion but may be treading on uncertain legal ground.

The comparable problem in *juvenile court* is uncertainty about the general threshold to be applied. The abilities to be considered for competence to stand trial are the same in juvenile court and in criminal court—the abilities summarized in the *Dusky* standard. Yet the very fact that there is a separate system of juvenile justice suggests that the general *degree* of ability that is required for participation as a defendant in juvenile court may be lower than for participation in criminal court proceedings. This argument is based on a presumption that the juvenile court proceeding and its outcome have a rehabilitative rather than a solely punitive objective.

There are two problems with this presumption, however. First, courts have not yet explicitly determined that the degree of ability required for a defendant's participation in juvenile court is any different than in criminal court. Second, whether juvenile court proceedings can be said to have any different objectives than criminal court proceedings may or may not be true, depending on the particular juvenile court for which the examiner is performing the competence evaluation. Therefore, examiners have no clear guidance for applying the *Dusky* standard to decide whether the youth is competent or incompetent. Errors in requiring too much or too little ability to meet judicial expectations (and notions of fairness) are equally likely.

6.3 *Special Issues in Remediation Judgments*

Testimony that speaks generally to an incompetent juvenile's "need for psychiatric treatment" is not helpful to the court. As in many other aspects of the evaluation, the focus of remediation should be on symptoms impairing those specific abilities that, in this particular case, render the youth incompetent to participate in a defense. What will reduce those symptoms (as distinct from producing remission of the disorder)? How likely is it that the prescribed course of treatment will be able to do that, and within what period of time?

When making recommendations for inpatient mental health services to treat youths who are found incompetent, examiners should be aware of age jurisdictions and regulations in their state for treatment of youths in inpatient facilities. The mere fact that the incompetent youth is being tried in criminal (adult) court does not mean that the youth can be sent to forensic mental health units where remediation of competence is usually provided for criminal cases. Recommendations for an inpatient placement to treat a mental disorder related to incompetence should be consistent with the age limits for inpatient mental health treatment in one's state. For example, a 16-year-old being tried as an adult in criminal court but found incompetent might not be an adult for purposes of the state's age requirement for commitment to adult inpatient psychiatric facilities.

In conclusion, we have reviewed the legal purposes and standards for competence to stand trial, as well as the reason that the question of juveniles' ability to understand the trial process and assist counsel was rarely raised until recently. Addressing the clinical questions related to standards for competence to stand trial requires a consideration of the youth's cognitive and psychosocial development, the youth's mental status, and the demands of the youth's trial. Assessment methods were reviewed, including special instruments that evaluate functional abilities directly related to competence to stand trial.

Clinicians who perform competence to stand trial evaluations of juveniles should watch for new research literature on this topic to appear during the next 5 years. At the time this book was written, only a few relevant empirical studies were available. A number of studies are in progress, however. They are likely to shed better light on many of the issues raised in this chapter, for which discussions had to be based primarily on clinical experience and theory rather than guidance from empirical research.

Chapter 4

Assessing Risk of Harm
to Others

One of the most frequent questions posed to mental health professionals who perform evaluations for juvenile courts is a youth's potential for future assaultive behavior that may harm others. These assessments can be raised for many different purposes in various contexts:

- To assess the *need for secure pretrial detention*
- To assess risk of *harm to other youths during pretrial secure detention*
- To address the "public safety" standard in *juvenile court hearings on waiver* of a juvenile to criminal court for trial as an adult
- For youths adjudicated delinquent in juvenile court, to assist the court in determining the *degree of security needed during rehabilitation* (for the juvenile court "sentencing" or "disposition" hearing)
- After a period of commitment to a secure rehabilitation program, to assess *whether rehabilitative efforts have resulted in reduced risk of future harm* to others that would allow for placement in a less secure program
- To assess the *need to extend juvenile court custody* in states that allow extension of juvenile jurisdiction beyond the usual maximum age based on an assessment identifying continued risk of violence if released to the community

The scope of these assessments, and the specific procedures involved, will vary somewhat for these different contexts. This chapter provides a framework for risk of harm assessments that can be applied across these contexts. Chapter 6 uses the information in this chapter to address evaluations for the question of waiver of youths for trial in criminal court.

1.0   FRAMING THE ASSESSMENT QUESTION

There has been very little research on the accuracy of clinical prediction of violence with adolescents. We can learn much about how to approach these assessments, however, by taking some cues from the extensive research on this topic with adult populations (for reviews, see Borum, Swartz, & Swenson, 1996; Monahan, 1981; Otto, 1992). This research identifies serious limits to our ability to predict who will and will not engage in future violent acts. The same research, however, has taught us much about *why* our predictive abilities are limited—for example, the low base rates of violent behavior for certain populations (which nearly guarantees a substantial false-positive error) and our inability to identify unforeseeable circumstances that will arise to stimulate a person's violence. Knowing what contributes to our errors, we have learned much about ways to minimize them. The following guidelines for framing an assessment of future violence in delinquency evaluations have that aim.

1.1   *Use Risk Factors*

When clinicians do assessments of youths' violence potential, they should bring to the task a set of factors, or variables, that are known empirically to be related to future violence. Psychological theory, research, and clinical experience provide a number of factors that bear some relationship to future violence. None of them, alone or in combination, is powerful enough to produce actuarial or clinical predictions with great accuracy. Nevertheless, their relationships to violence at least make them relevant for the assessment task, and they provide structure that can keep the clinician from making errors due to a lack of systematic inquiry. Later we will review a set of factors that clinicians can use when addressing the question of youths' potential for future harm to others.

1.2   *Recognize the Importance of Social Context*

There is a strong tendency for clinicians and courts to frame the question of future violence as though it were answerable based on predispositions of the youth alone. This happens despite the fact that clinicians, and presumably courts, understand that the likelihood of future violence is in part a function of circumstances that people will encounter. This is true for youths with and without individual predispositions to harmful aggression. Assaultive behavior, like almost all other behaviors, is a function of interactions between a person's predispositions and environmental circumstances.

This simple axiom has many implications for assessments of the likelihood of future harm to others. Some social contexts stimulate or inhibit aggression for all youths, no matter what their predispositions. For example, the base rate of violent behavior is much lower in most secure, structured pretrial detention centers than in the hallways of an inner-city housing project. For a youth who has a behavioral tendency toward aggression, the likelihood of that behavior may depend on varying levels of chaos and stress in the household or environment in which he or she is living. Some youths who have a history of aggression may show that behavior only in one type of setting or social circumstance and never in any other circumstances. Some youths with very little predisposition to aggression may manifest it nevertheless in certain extraordinary circumstances.

An evaluation for future violence, therefore, should not be thought of as an evaluation of a youth. It is *an assessment of the likelihood of future harm, which requires an evaluation of a youth and that youth's future social context.*

Several clinical evaluation guidelines follow from this perspective. First, the *clinician's set of risk factors will not focus entirely on characteristics of the youth.* They must include some factors that describe the social contexts in which youths live and to which they react.

Second, *a clinical opinion about the likelihood of future harm must always be provided with reference to some social context.* It makes no sense, and is of little assistance to a court, to say that a youth "is likely to be violent in the future." For a given youth, clinicians should strive to describe the likelihood of harmful behavior in the specific setting or social circumstance that the youth will face.

Third, *clinicians often should form several opinions about a youth's prospects for future violence, corresponding to various future social contexts.* For example, the clinician might have one opinion about the likelihood of violence if the youth is returned home, another if the youth is placed in a group home, and a third about aggression if the youth is placed in a secure youth facility.

1.3 *Aim for Risk Estimates, Not Predictions*

As noted earlier, everything we know from research on clinical predictions of violent behavior suggests that there are important limits to our ability to identify who will or will not engage in violence in the future. Does this mean that clinicians should not offer opinions about future violence? Most experts in this area do not think so. It simply means that we should be offering our opinions in ways that better reflect the limits of our abilities.

One way to do this is to offer *risk estimates*, rather than predictions. In a risk estimate approach, one does not try to determine whether a youth *will or will not* engage in violent behavior in some future setting or circumstances. The clinician collects information about the youth on a set of risk factors, noting whether the degree of risk is increased or decreased by the information on each factor. After combining this information and weighing its clinical significance, the clinician tries to arrive at a conclusion about the degree of risk that the case poses *relative to some population* (e.g., relative to youths who come before the court in delinquency cases, or relative to youths in a particular detention or rehabilitation setting). The degree of risk in the case in question is then expressed as "high," "average," or "low" relative to that population. Other designations are also possible (e.g., "very high" or "somewhat above average").

In effect, the clinician is saying, "I do not know whether this youth will engage in violent behavior, but the risk that it may happen is (greater than, similar to, less than) the risk posed by youths in general in (the relevant setting)." In my experience, courts have found this type of opinion quite acceptable especially when I can tell them fairly clearly how I arrived at the opinion: that is, (a) why each factor is relevant, (b) the data for the youth on each factor, and (c) the reasoning I used to combine the data to reach my opinion. Were I to testify that the youth would or would not engage in violent behavior, in most cases I would have much greater difficulty defending my opinion against a good cross-examination that focused on the limits of clinical prediction that a person would or would not engage in harmful behavior in the future.

1.4 *Recognize Heterogeneity Among Delinquent Youths*

Youths who engage in delinquency do not constitute a "type." This is partly because illegal behaviors are so common in adolescence. In relation to their proportions of the population, adolescents are responsible for more illegal and violent acts than are adults. In some communities, over two-thirds of male youths will have a juvenile court record by the time they reach late adolescence. Because so many youths engage in delinquent behaviors, there are few "predictors" that do a good job of distinguishing which youths will engage in delinquencies and which will not.

Serious violent acts also are more common among adolescents than among adults. Moreover, they are committed by a wide variety of youths with differing backgrounds and personalities. Even juvenile murderers do not fit a particular profile. Some of them are predators who kill while committing rape or robbery, but others are youths who are defending themselves from gangs, boys who kill girlfriends and then themselves, and abused children who kill their parents (Cornell, E. Benedek, & D. Benedek, 1989; Ewing, 1990; Heide, 1992). Although youths who murder sometimes have extensive violent histories, they are just as likely to have no prior record of any delinquent behaviors at all.

Keep in mind that violence risk assessment with adolescents is not a search for a type of youth. It must be carried out with an expectation that an elevated risk of violence among youths whom one encounters in juvenile justice or mental health settings may be found among many types of youths for many different reasons.

1.5 *Delinquent and Violent Behavior Usually Desists after Adolescence*

One of the best documented and most important facts about illegal behavior by adolescents is that most youths discontinue their delinquent behavior as they approach adulthood (Gottfredson & Hirschi, 1990). Many reasons have been offered for the desistance of delinquency in late adolescence:

for example, the maturing of various psychosocial abilities related to decisionmaking, stability associated with marriage commitments, and the benefits of employment. Whatever the reasons, for youths who have committed violent behaviors by the age of 18, only about 2 or 3 out of 10 are arrested for violent acts in adulthood (Elliott et al., 1983; Elliott, Huizinga, & Morse, 1986). Most delinquent youths—even those who are violent during adolescence—do not present a substantial long-term risk of violence. Later we will examine what is known about differences between the majority of youths whose delinquency is limited to adolescence and the minority whose illegal and violent behaviors persist into adulthood.

These observations have several implications for clinicians' assessments of risk of future violence. First, clinicians should recognize the difference between short-term and long-term risk estimates. In some cases, *clinicians will find that they need to arrive at different opinions about the degree of risk for different time frames*: for example, one opinion about risk during the pretrial period, another opinion regarding the risk of violence during the remainder of the youth's adolescence, and yet a third opinion if the court wishes to know if the youth presents a substantial risk of continued violent behavior in adulthood. For some youths the level of risk will be the same in all of these time frames. But for others it may be quite different—for example, very high immediately after arrest, moderate to high while the youth is in rehabilitation programs following adjudication, yet relatively low as the youth attains adulthood (even independent of the effects of ensuing rehabilitation efforts).

The fact that most violent adolescents do not continue their violence in adulthood also suggests how we should begin our reasoning process when weighing various risk factors for future violence. Despite a youth's violent behavior in the past, and even if we believe that the youth presents a substantial *immediate* risk, we should begin with the hypothesis that the youth will not represent a substantial *long-range* risk of violence (i.e., upon reaching adulthood). Then we should reach the opposite conclusion only when factors in the case have carried the burden of proving it to us.

2.0 RISK FACTORS ASSOCIATED WITH FUTURE HARM TO OTHERS

As noted earlier, the key to assessment for risk of future violence among adolescents lies in using a meaningful set of risk factors. Research has demonstrated consistent relationships between a number of case characteristics and violent behavior among adolescents. The following factors have been selected for review because of those empirical relationships. There has been far less research on ways to use these factors to make risk estimates in individual cases. Therefore, the following comments concerning *how* to apply these factors are based primarily on theory and clinical experience. Nine critical factors will be reviewed in the following order:

- Past Behavior
- Substance Use
- Peers and Community
- Family Conflict and Aggression
- Social Stressors and Supports
- Personality Traits
- Mental Disorders
- Opportunity
- Future Residence

The discussion will not review risk factors associated with sex offenses. Risk assessment in those cases requires the use of a somewhat different set of factors, and their review is beyond the scope of this chapter. Guidance for assessing risk of future sex offending can be found in Barbaree, Hudson, and Seto (1993), Groth and Loredo (1981), Ross and Loss (1991), and Weinrott (1996). Be aware also that some of the generalizations described here probably do not apply equally to males and females. There has been little research on the correlates of violent behavior among female juvenile offenders. Moreover, my experience in evaluating young women who have committed violent delinquent acts has been too meager to provide competent guidance in assessing their future harmful aggression.

2.1 *Past Behavior*

Clinicians know the axiom, "Past behavior is the best predictor of future behavior." When applied to estimated risk of future violence in adolescent cases, this guideline is both correct and misleading. No assessment for this purpose would be complete without a review of the adolescent's past harmful aggression. Yet its presence or absence alone does not allow us to presume either greater or lesser future risk. One must examine several dimensions that constitute ways in which youths' past aggressive behaviors vary: their *chronicity, recency, frequency, severity,* and *context.*

2.11 Chronicity

A good deal of research now suggests a greater risk of harmful aggression and its continuance into adulthood for youths whose aggressive behavior predates their adolescence. In studies of self-reported delinquency, Elliott (1994) found that about 5 in 10 youths continued their violent behavior into adulthood if their first violent acts occurred prior to age 11, about 3 in 10 if the first violent behaviors occurred in preadolescence (ages 11-13), and only about 1 in 10 if their first violent behaviors occurred during adolescence.

Moffitt (1993) has called the early starters "life-course persistent" delinquents, in contrast to "adolescence limited" delinquents whose harmful aggression begins in adolescence and usually ends as they near adulthood. During adolescence, the nature of the aggressive acts of these two types of youths are not particularly distinguishable. Life-course persistent delinquents, however, are more likely to have been identified in the primary school years as disruptive and difficult, and they tend to have been younger at first arrest. They show less of a tendency to adapt to social circumstances so that their delinquency tends to occur across life situations (home, school, street), while adolescent limited delinquents respond more to opportunity and contingencies. (See also Loeber & Stouthamer-Loeber, 1998 for recent refinements in developmental pathways to violent behavior.)

The key message here for estimating risk of future violence is that if the youth is currently engaging in violent behaviors, the likelihood that these will continue into adulthood—and that they will be repeated in adolescence—is greater if the youth's earliest aggressive acts were identified before age 12 or 13.

2.12 Recency

The fact that a youth has engaged in violent behaviors in the past may have different implications for risk estimates depending on whether those behaviors have been recent or at some distant time in the past. For example, imagine an adolescent who was harmfully aggressive in childhood, but has engaged in no violent behaviors in the past few years, due perhaps to the effects of a change in family relations or adequate clinical attention. In other cases, periods of aggression may have arisen at a particular developmental stage in the youth's life but ended when those developmental tasks were resolved. If the youth's history of aggression shows harmful aggressive behavior some years ago but not recently, the earlier aggressive acts should not be given the usual weight when making estimates of the risk of future violence.

2.13 Frequency

Some youths who engage in violent behavior do it frequently, (e.g., fighting is part of their weekly routine). The violent acts of other youths occur only sporadically, with long latencies between events. Megargee (1971), for example, identified violent offenders whom he called "under-controlled" (impulsive, irritable, overly responsive to threat) and "over-controlled" (anxious, repressed, but angry). Assaultive behaviors of under-controlled offenders are troublesome for their frequency, while those of over-controlled offenders are of special concern because, although less frequent, they are less predictable, tend to be more explosive, and are therefore likely to be more harmful.

It is clear that risk is increased when recent harmful aggression has been frequent, as in the case of many under-controlled youths. The less predictable nature of aggression by over-controlled and angry youths presents greater difficulties for risk estimates. Other factors (e.g., see Mental Disorders, 4-2.7) typically must be considered together with this one when determining how to interpret the infrequent violence of over-controlled youths.

2.14 Severity

There is a tendency for society to believe that the greatest risk of repeated violence is among youths who have engaged in the most serious violent offenses. This may be a valid assumption for some types of offenses, especially rape and sexual assaults on younger children. For most violent offenses, however, there appears to be little relationship between the seriousness of past offenses and the likelihood of future violence. For example, Cornell et al. (1989) found that youths charged with murder had somewhat less violent histories than youths who were charged with nonlethal assaults. Youths who murder family members often have no delinquent history and, in follow-up studies, almost never engage in any future violent behavior (Cormier & Markus, 1980). Moreover, the difference between a nonlethal assault and a murder often is not a function of the intent or capacities of the youth, but a matter of chance. Society is understandably concerned about the likelihood of future violence for youths who have murdered, and courts may decide that even a low risk of future violence is too much in light of the seriousness of the youth's past offense. But empirically, a charge of murder—taken as a fact alone—does not necessarily elevate the likelihood of future violence substantially.

By the same token, the fact that a frequently delinquent youth has never engaged in an assaultive act does not necessarily mean that the youth is at low risk for future assaults. For example, imagine a youth who breaks into dozens of houses each month, and has been careful to do so only when he knows that no one is home. If he typically carries a weapon when he enters houses, there is a substantial risk, given the frequency of his behavior, that sooner or later he will encounter someone he does not expect and that violence will ensue.

2.15 Context

Clinicians must learn the specific circumstances and contexts in which a youth has engaged in violent behaviors in the past. Some youths have a history of aggressive behaviors only in certain types of settings or at certain times: for example, primarily in the winter when school is in session, or primarily in the summer when it is not; only at times when the family has been in turmoil about parental conflicts; or only in unstructured situations.

I once examined a youth in a murder case who had had nearly perfect attendance at school for several years, where he was never known to cause any disturbances. He would frequently get in fights, however, after school hours on the way home, usually when other youths were around to observe and reinforce his brutality to his victims. This youth exhibited model behavior while awaiting his trial in detention for several months. In other words, his harmful aggression seemed only to occur when he was not under the eye of adult authorities. This type of information can be helpful when the clinician is forming opinions about the nature of future situations in which a youth might present a higher or lower risk of violence.

Sometimes the contexts for youths' past aggression can be highly idiosyncratic. In one case of a 15-year-old who murdered his girlfriend, I found three major violent incidents in the youth's life. One involved a violent event at home, where he lived with his father and younger sister. The second was the murder, which occurred when he was with his girlfriend and his best male friend. The third was while he was awaiting trial in a secure detention facility and involved a conflict between himself, a boy with whom he had paired in detention, and their female counselor. Each context involved conflicting relationships between himself, another male, and a female. Given the absence of serious and harmful aggression in any other contexts, it was reasonable to incorporate the information into my description of the types of future situations in which this youth might present a high risk of harmful aggression even though the evaluation did not provide an explanation for the pattern.

2.2 *Substance Use*

Sociologists have shown that drugs have played an important part in the increase in arrests of adolescents for violent offenses in recent years. In a general sense, the use of substances by youths who have engaged in violent behaviors increases the risk of future violence. Yet the simple fact that a youth has or has not used substances is not all that the clinician should learn about this risk factor. Its relevance often lies especially in its relation to aggressive behavior for the given youth in question. In examining this relation in my evaluations of youths who use substances frequently, I have encountered harmfully aggressive youths whose violent behaviors

- *usually* occur at times that they *are* using substances, and *usually do not* occur when they are *not* using them (violence seems directly related to substance use for that youth)

- occur *whether or not* they are using substances at the time (their violence is not directly associated with substance use)
- *never* engage in violent behavior during times that they *are* using substances (their violence seems to be *negatively* related to substance use)

This variability in associations between substance use and harmful aggression from case to case suggests that automatically raising the risk estimate because the youth frequently uses substances is not necessarily the best way to use this factor. Instead, the clinician should explore the role that substance use has had, if any, in the youth's past aggression, then apply and weight the factor accordingly.

How the factor is weighted may depend on various aspects of the youth's substance use. Among these are frequency of substance use, the type of substance typically used and its amount, and times when substance use typically occurs (e.g., weekends, while in school, only at parties). Finally, substance use may have secondary effects on the likelihood of future violence. For example, a youth who has begun to sell drugs in order to maintain access to them is working in a milieu where he is more likely to encounter circumstances that stimulate a violent response.

2.3   *Peers and Community*

Youths who have engaged in harmful aggression and who associate with violent peer groups (whether they are organized gangs or less formal neighborhood groups) often present a high risk of future violence. Violent peer groups provide a social norm that encourages violence, increases the likelihood that youths will find themselves in situations that call for a violent response, and often provides greater access to weapons.

Although frequent contact with delinquent peer groups increases the risk of future violence, different degrees of weight might be attached to this factor based on individual circumstances. For example, many urban youths "hang out" during part of the day with youths who are known to be involved in violent gangs yet manage to avoid involvement in their delinquent activities. In certain inner-city neighborhoods, to completely avoid delinquent peer groups would require that one lead a life of social isolation. Many youths learn to keep one foot in their neighborhood culture and the other on a path that they hope will lead to better circumstances in the future adult world of work and marriage. In these neighborhoods, proximity and social involvement with youths who belong to gangs should not be interpreted by itself to suggest that the youth is at high risk for violent behavior. The nature of the youth's involvement—for example, evidence that the youth has begun to identify with the group and its harmful activities—is the more important point.

2.4 *Family Conflict and Aggression*

Family aggression and intrafamily conflicts contribute to a greater risk of future violence by youths in several ways for several different reasons:

- *Current family conflicts may add to present and future stress* for the youth, which in turn increases the likelihood of anger, irritability, and consequent aggressive responses to situations encountered both in and outside the home.
- Some youths have grown up in homes where *aggression between family members has been modeled as acceptable.* Youths who witness frequent family aggression have been raised to experience it as a typical way to deal with interpersonal conflicts. This can increase the likelihood that they will pattern their own behavior after this model as they develop through adolescence into adulthood.
- Youths who have been *victims of abuse and neglect by family members* are at greater risk of engaging in violent behaviors themselves in the future (Widom, 1989; Widom & Maxfield, 1996).
- *Some families may be characterized as antisocial,* supporting and even encouraging criminal activity as a way of life. Whether for biological, psychological, or sociological reasons, youths from these families often constitute a greater risk of manifesting harmful aggression in the future.

2.5 *Social Stressors and Supports*

Pending divorces of parents, illness that threatens the life of a family member and sudden economic reversals in a youth's family may place added stress on coping mechanisms and increase feelings of threat, insecurity, and loss. These, in turn, increase the risk of harmful aggression for youths with histories of aggressive behavior.

Clinicians, therefore, need to carefully explore potential sources of future stress when estimating violence risk. I was once consulted in a case involving a liability claim against a hospital emergency room after it discharged a 16-year-old boy who killed his girlfriend and himself within the following 24 hours. Despite evidence that he was in psychological distress and was acting dangerously (they had treated him for lacerations caused by driving his fist through a window during a fight), medical personnel did not question him about circumstances pertinent to future risk. Had they done so, they would have learned that in the last few days, his father had kicked him out of the house, he was living in his car, his mother (who was his emotional support) was in the hospital with a life-threatening illness, he had been kicked off the school football team, and his girlfriend had threatened to leave him.

Risk may be mitigated for youths whose life circumstances include significant social supports. An especially important consideration in many risk assessments is the quality of the youth's relations with parents and whether the parents appear to have the capacity to provide adequate control and structure to manage the youth's behavior during the time period in question. Youths often have formed significant attachments with aunts, uncles, or grandparents who can offer a stable source of comfort, assistance, or control. Clinicians in the community also can be sources of support if a youth has already developed a stable, enduring, therapeutic relationship with the clinician.

2.6 *Personality Traits*

Several personality characteristics have important implications for estimates of the risk of future violence among youths who have engaged in harmful aggression in the past. Chief among these are *anger, impulsivity,* and *lack of empathy*. When these traits appear to be characterological, they increase the risk of future violence. Before discussing them, however, it is important to note two difficulties in applying them in adolescent cases.

140

First, all three characteristics may be manifested as states rather than traits. The mere fact that during a clinical interview the youth appeared angry, said some things impulsively, and showed little sense of concern is not enough to conclude that these are "characteristic" of this youth. Some evidence is needed that what one has seen is typical of the youth. Second, anger, impulsivity, and deficient empathy are sometimes said to be "typical" of adolescence as a developmental stage. (Indeed, this is consistent with the higher base rate of illegal behaviors among adolescents than among adults.) This is important when one is making estimates of long-range risks of violence (e.g., whether the youth will be a continued risk as adults) because these characteristics tend to decrease for most adolescents as they mature into adulthood.

The clinician, therefore, needs to determine whether a youth is manifesting these characteristics as more enduring traits or as developmental phenomena associated with adolescence. The following discussions point out the developmental qualities of these characteristics, which may help the clinician to distinguish them from personality traits that have special significance for estimates of longer-range risk of violence.

2.61 Anger

Many youths are rebellious and sullen at various times in their adolescent development. Typically this is part of a temporary repertoire and is seen only in particular situations or with particular people (most often parents or other adult authorities). In contrast, some youths manifest more than the usual amount of anger across time, including the preadolescent years. They are more likely to be experienced as angry and irritable by adults and peers alike, across a variety of settings and situations.

Tendencies toward anger in either type of case may increase the risk of harmful aggression. However, the implications of the factor will be different for youths who are "developmentally angry" and those for whom anger and hostility are a more enduring trait. The latter cases offer the greater potential for long-term risk.

2.62 Impulsivity

Developmental research has provided much evidence that adolescents more often respond impulsively, take greater risks, and think less about long-range consequences of their actions than do adults (Arnett, 1992). A tendency for adolescents to perceive themselves as invulnerable, or less likely than others to suffer negative consequences, is noted repeatedly in developmental psychological theory. Therefore, the mere fact that a youth has engaged in some impulsive acts in the past is not sufficient to conclude that the youth is "impulsive" as a matter of enduring personality structure.

Some youths, however, manifest a more persistent pattern of impulsivity that elevates the risk of harmful behavior beyond that which is common to adolescents in general. For example, some youths have a long history of responding quickly to slight provocations. They engage in reckless behaviors independently, not merely when being encouraged by peers. They have a history of "sensation-seeking": looking for situations that will produce arousal through risk (Zuckerman, S. Eysenck, & H. Eysenck, 1978). These youths for whom impulsivity is characterological present a risk of future harmful behavior that exceeds the norm for adolescents.

2.63 Deficient Empathy

Perhaps no other risk factor is given as much weight by judges and juvenile justice personnel as a youth's apparent lack of remorse, empathy, or concern for past harmful behaviors. This factor may deserve the weight that they give it when there is evidence that deficient empathy is characterological for a given youth. This may be the case for some youths who are developing narcissistic personalities or who are manifesting early signs of psychopathy (Frick et al., 1994; Lynam, 1996). Uninhibited by the ability to experience or sense the pain that they inflict on others, the risk that they will do so in the future is increased.

Yet the mere fact that a youth appears to lack concern or remorse for a past harmful behavior is not necessarily a sign of narcissism, psychopathy, or an enduring, trait-like deficiency in empathy. Developmental psychologists have long identified egocentrism as a typical feature of adolescent development, during which youths have not yet developed a capacity to fully see the world as others see it. The capacity for empathy requires the development of the ability to think abstractly and hypothetically.

These abilities usually are developed by early adolescence, but for many youths it is delayed. For the latter, their apparent lack of empathy is not necessarily an enduring condition, and it should be given less weight for long-range estimates of future harmful aggression.

When applying this factor to delinquent youths, it is especially important to recognize that they sometimes fail to show remorse for their offenses for reasons that have little to do with their capacity for empathy. One of the most consistent clinical observations of youths who have killed their parents is their lack of affective response to their behavior (Cormier & Markus, 1980; Ewing, 1990; Heide, 1992). (This is also seen with some frequency in youths who have murdered persons other than their parents.) In interviews they present as detached from the experience, not sorrowful or remorseful. Follow up indicates that usually they do not lack the capacity for empathy, which manifests itself fully after time has distanced them from the event. Clinicians who treat these youths speculate that psychological denial and numbing of affect is at work during a period of time following the event in order to protect against decompensation that would occur if youths fully experienced the horror of their actions. Yet in those cases, the court may simply see a youth who appears cold, unconcerned, and without empathy that would deter further harmful aggression.

Just as a youth's apparent lack of affect does not necessarily signify a lack of capacity for remorse, dramatic displays of repentance do not necessarily provide reliable evidence that a youth is empathic or remorseful. Remorseful statements are frequent among delinquent youths whose lack of empathy is characterological.

2.7 *Mental Disorders*

We do not know whether youths with mental disorders are more likely to engage in violent behaviors than other youths. Among youths with past aggressive histories, however, the presence of some mental disorders does increase the risk of future aggression. Clinical experience and research identify several mental disorders that deserve special attention in this regard.

2.71 Depression

Youths with depressive disorders frequently display anger, irritability, and demandingness. Adolescents sometimes use angry retaliation to deal with low self-esteem associated with depression, especially if their poor self-image is related to early neglect. Fragile self-worth often leads them to over-react to criticisms or slights, making them appear irritable and touchy. It is important for the clinician to identify the underlying depression in such cases because courts and attorneys observing the youth may see merely an "angry child."

When youths with depressive disorders manifest these symptoms and have past histories of aggression, then their symptoms somewhat elevate the risk of future violence. The violence itself often is as likely to be toward themselves as toward others, and in some youths there is a thin line between suicidal and assaultive behavior tendencies (Holinger et al., 1994).

2.72 Attentional and Hyperactivity Disorders

There is considerable evidence that youths with attentional and hyperactivity disorders present an increased risk of harmful aggression (Barkley, 1990). There are three ways in which conditions such as Attention-Deficit/Hyperactivity Disorder (ADHD) come into play in estimating the risk of future aggression.

First, attention difficulties and hyperactivity themselves increase the likelihood that youths will react impulsively to threats or challenges. Their disruptive behavior in social situations also increases the chances that others will react negatively to them. In other words, their deficits in self-constraint often stimulate aggressive behaviors in others and cause them to be over-responsive to the aggressively stimulating behavior of others.

Second, symptoms of ADHD often are first identified in the preschool or early elementary school ages. Related deficits in self-constraint, therefore, often result in an early presentation of disruptive and aggressive behaviors that continue through childhood. As noted earlier in this chapter, risk of future violence among adolescents who have engaged in violent acts is greater when they have a pattern of aggression prior to the adolescent years.

Third, recent research has examined the overlap between ADHD adolescent populations and delinquent populations. Although most delinquent youths do not manifest ADHD symptoms, a substantial minority of ADHD adolescents—perhaps 40%—have delinquent histories. Based on accumulated research, theorists hypothesize that within this ADHD/delinquent overlap there may be a subtype of "fledgling psychopaths," youths who will enter adulthood as habitual offenders at high risk for harmful behaviors (Lynam, 1996). Clinicians should be careful, however, not to use ADHD itself as a "predictor" of psychopathy. At most, ADHD in adolescents with lengthy aggressive histories should alert the clinician to examine whether they are actually exhibiting the antisocial and unempathic characteristics associated with psychopathy.

2.73 Schizophrenia (Psychotic Disorders)

Schizophrenia rarely has its onset in childhood, only occasionally in adolescence, and usually between the ages of 18 and 35. When schizophrenia is present in adolescence, youths may report frightening hallucinations or delusional ideas with paranoid content, as well as thought disorganization. These symptoms can increase the risk of aggressive behavior because they contribute to a perception of others as threatening, as well as reducing impulse control in responding to perceived threat.

Some nonpsychotic adolescents report similar experiences and ideas. For example, youths with anxiety and trauma disorders sometimes report feelings or visual experiences that are bizarre and frightening. Some youths with extensive substance abuse histories also describe hallucinatory experiences and unusual feelings that are directly related to their substance abuse.

Clinicians who work with delinquent youths are also familiar with cases in which nonpsychotic youths experiment with strange ideas as a defense to deal with their psychic pain and feelings of alienation. They may have bizarre notions about the nature of the world (something between psychotic-like delusions and "dungeons and dragons" fantasies), frightening visions (a nonpsychotic delinquent youth I recently assessed saw human figures emerging from the wall of his segregation room in the detention center), and distorted beliefs about their identity (e.g., that they are evil or in league with the devil). Although frightening, these ideas offer some youths a way to concretize internal conflicts that are otherwise vague or to avoid the real and more painful aspects of their cognitive and emotional life. Sometimes the reactions that they produce in juvenile justice staff also provide social reinforcement that maintains this defense mechanism.

Distinguishing these cases from youths who are truly developing a psychotic disorder is sometimes difficult but is nevertheless important for making decisions about youths' placement, treatment, and prognosis. It may be less important, however, for estimating the risk of future violence among youths with aggressive histories. Whether youths' bizarre, violent, and frightening ideas are defense mechanisms or symptoms of a developing psychosis, they provide a cognitive context in which youths encounter everyday events. As such, they increase the likelihood that youths will react either by withdrawal or aggression. When their past history includes aggressive acts, data of this type increase the risk of future violence for both psychotic and nonpsychotic youths.

2.74 Trauma Disorders

Youths' reactions to witnessing traumatic events sometimes include symptoms that increase the risk of aggressive behavior. Relevant symptoms of Posttraumatic Stress Disorder include irritability and feelings of threat associated with recurrent recollections of the event. Some youths experience dissociative-like symptoms that keep them out of touch with their anger, thus reducing their ability to control their aggression. A sense of foreshortened future is found in some cases, including a feeling that one is unlikely to live long enough to reach adulthood. This can decrease the youth's motivation to avoid risks when dangerous situations arise, thus increasing the chance that the youth will become involved in situations that are harmful to others.

2.75 Brain Syndromes

Head trauma due to accidents, fights, or early abuse, and abnormal neurological development due to nutritional deficiencies or toxins, are fairly common in serious delinquent populations. Clinicians and researchers have observed an increased prevalence of brain dysfunctions in samples of youths who frequently display violent and disruptive behavior (Lewis et al., 1988). The research methods in these studies have been questioned, including their broad criteria for brain dysfunction. Nevertheless, it is well known that damage to certain brain structures increases impulsivity and angry responses to provoking stimuli or may impair judgment and self-constraint. When neurological examination suggests central nervous system abnormalities in youths with past aggressive behaviors, this factor should increase one's estimates of the risk of future aggression.

2.76   Treatment Factors

Although there are a number of factors that increase the risk of violence for youths with mental disorders, some of these factors may be mitigated if there is evidence that the youth's response to timely psychiatric and psychological interventions will reduce the risk. Records of past treatment efforts sometimes provide data with which to examine these factors. Evidence that the youth is likely to be compliant with relevant medications should be examined, as well as the likelihood of maintaining therapeutic contacts that have had some stabilizing influence in the youth's life in the past.

2.8   *Opportunity*

The risk of future violence may vary depending on circumstances external to the youth that influence the degree of opportunity for harmful violence to occur. These factors are important to consider not only for making risk estimates but also to identify ways in which the risk may be reduced by modifying the conditions that one identifies.

When a youth's harmful aggression has been targeted toward a particular person, risk of future violence may be reduced if the target is no longer available: for example, the targeted victim moves to another part of the country or has died. Many youths who kill their parents are at little risk of harming others in the future, partly because their anger was directed specifically toward their parents and no one else. Nevertheless, when the individual on whom the youth has focused is no longer available, one must consider whether "substitute" victims might be targeted in the future (e.g., other family members).

The ready availability of weapons increases the risk of violent behavior in some cases, especially the risk of lethality during aggressive acts. When employing this factor, remember that, in a sense, weapons are almost always available to anyone. Guns are easy to procure in most cities, and every kitchen has a knife. Therefore, not the general availability of weapons, but rather their *timely* availability, may be the important question—that is, the likelihood that weapons are "at hand" when anger and impulse are aroused. Examples include the availability of guns in the house in which the youth lives, or the fact that the youth typically hangs out with youths who are carrying guns.

2.9 *Future Residence*

Risk estimates may vary depending on where the youth is likely to be residing in the near future. Residential situations differ in their structure and the degree to which they offer an opportunity for violence. For example, in a specific case, the future risk estimate might be reduced if the youth is expected to be in a secure youth facility for the next few years, especially if the facility has a reputation for providing a high degree of structure and control. In contrast, a very different estimate might be reached if the youth is expected to be returning to the community from which he or she came prior to the current offense. Often a consideration of future residence will lead the clinician to offer several different estimates of risk, coinciding with the various possible residences in which the youth might be placed depending on the legal outcome of the case.

2.10 *Factors Suggesting Resiliency*

The body of research that has found relationships between these nine factors and harmful aggression has also begun to provide some clues for identifying youths who have overcome negative effects that would be suggested by their high-risk backgrounds. For example, Smith et al. (1995) sought to identify youths who did not engage in serious delinquencies despite the fact that they were in a high-risk group. That is, their families were relatively transient, poor, and abusive of the youth, and family members often experienced trouble with drugs and the law.

They found that youths in this group who did not engage in serious delinquency were more often committed to school, did well in school, intended to continue their education, were well attached to their parents, and associated with conventional peers who themselves were approved of by the youth's parents. A youth showing a few of these "resiliency factors" was only slightly less likely than other high-risk youths to avoid delinquency, while youths showing most of them had a much lower likelihood of serious or repeated delinquency. Future research will probably refine the clinician's ability to identify youths with high-risk profiles who turn out to be the exception to the rule.

3.0 OBTAINING DATA ON RISK FACTORS

3.1 *Risk Assessment Tasks*

The chapter began with a list of circumstances in which juvenile courts are in need of estimates of the risk of future violence. Those circumstances include three broad types of decisions: (a) to determine whether a youth is *in need of secure detention prior to trial*; (b) to determine whether the youth presents *too great a danger to be retained in the juvenile justice system* (relevant for the question of waiver to criminal court); and (c) for youths who are retained in the juvenile court and found delinquent, to decide about the *need for security during rehabilitation* after the youth has been found delinquent.

The process of assessment and the amount and types of data that the examiner will collect are likely to differ across these situations. Clinicians often have to form an opinion about *pretrial detention* in a relatively brief period of time, sometimes within a day or two after the youth's emergency detention at the time of arrest. This provides so little time for data collection that one would not expect the clinician to employ the full range of data sources that are discussed later in this section. Efficiency will often dictate that the clinician must work with limited data, relying primarily on past juvenile records, a brief interview, and perhaps a structured screening device, while foregoing psychological testing and a comprehensive developmental workup.

Risk assessments for *hearings on waiver to criminal court*, on the other hand, tend to focus on longer-range estimates of future violence, especially whether the youth is likely to continue to be a danger to the community during the remainder of adolescence and early adulthood. The legal decision that the waiver evaluation addresses can have far-reaching implications for the youth's future because waiver to criminal court places the youth at jeopardy of lengthy sentences and, in some states, the death penalty. In these "high stakes" cases, clinicians typically should perform comprehensive risk assessments that use many sources of data from among the options discussed next.

Risk assessments to assist courts in deciding on *secure rehabilitation options* for youths who are found delinquent in juvenile court will vary in their demands. But typically they should involve more extensive data collection than the "screening" processes that are used for making decisions about immediate pretrial detention.

3.2 *Records and Third-Party Information*

Rap sheets provide a necessary starting point for identifying a youth's past violent behaviors. Yet they almost never provide satisfactory information for clinical purposes. At most they identify the seriousness of the youth's past charges. Often they do not address chronicity because the violent behaviors of youths when they are in the primary school years rarely result in arrests or any other juvenile court referral. Their information related to recency and frequency of harmful aggression tends to be incomplete because youths often engage in violent behaviors that are never detected or recorded by police or the courts.

Rap sheets provide no information on the context for youths' past offenses. *Law enforcement officers' reports* of arrests, investigations, and interviews with witnesses and victims do begin to identify the context. Yet good police reports focus on a behavioral account of the critical event, not its social and psychological antecedents.

Records from various agencies often provide useful data related not only to dimensions of past violent behaviors of the youth but also the full range of other risk factors. For comprehensive risk assessments, one should consider the availability and possible usefulness of the following types of records (in addition to police documents):

- *School disciplinary documents*, for all grades and schools in the youth's history
- *Documents from juvenile justice facilities and programs* that have worked with the youth in the past (sometimes they include daily, weekly, and/or monthly summaries of behavior and progress)
- Admission and discharge *summaries from psychiatric hospitals* or outpatient mental health agencies where the youth has received services

Typically the clinician may be able to obtain more fine-tuned information about past violent behaviors, and information related to all of the other risk factors, through interviews with parents, teachers, people who have worked with the youth in prior juvenile justice contacts, and the youth. In one recent case involving the question of waiver to criminal court, my investigation of the youth's past aggressive behaviors involved interviews with primary school teachers, written narratives from school records documenting the reasons for school suspensions in primary and junior high school, interviews with the youths' parents, lengthy discussions with personnel in a juvenile justice facility who had worked with the youth during an earlier commitment, a probation officer who had daily contact with the youth in the weeks prior to his present murder charge, and a neighborhood youth worker who observed the boy almost daily while working with groups of youths on the street in an inner-city housing development.

Obtaining observations from many people about a youth's day-to-day behaviors in various settings often produces a wealth of information that can be cross-referenced for consistencies and combined to produce a rich perspective on chronicity, recency, frequency, and context of aggressive behaviors. Typically it also provides examples of situations in which the youth is *less* likely to engage in harmful aggression.

3.3 *Youth Interviews*

Youths are sometimes reluctant to discuss past delinquencies and assaultive behaviors. Even when they do, the clinician must anticipate the possibility that they will distort or minimize the events, just as adult defendants often do. It is often helpful, therefore, to complete some of the data collection through documents and third parties before interviewing the youth so that one can guide the interview in directions that would not be revealed by the youth's self-report. Having said this, it is important to note that some youths reveal *more* than was learned from other sources, especially about their associations with other delinquent youths and even the extent of their substance use.

In addition to examining past aggressive acts, the clinician should explore with the youth the event associated with the present charges. This process should treat the offense as an event that occurred in the broader social context of the youth's life. Thus the discussion may begin at a point several days prior to the event, including exploration of what was happening in the youth's life at that time—any other critical events, thoughts, and perceptions in the preceding days and hours. The youth should then be encouraged to recall the circumstances of the alleged offense chronologically in some detail, and the clinician should probe for information related to relevant risk factors.

In risk assessments that are done prior to a youth's trial on a serious charge, clinicians working for the court may be prohibited in some jurisdictions from talking to the youth about events related to the current alleged offense. This is a legal precaution against self-incrimination in the context of a non-privileged communication. Unfortunately (from a clinical perspective), this deprives the examiner of important information related to some of the risk factors that might not be available from other sources: for example, the youth's feelings about the offense (e.g., remorse), the social context in which the offense occurred, or ways in which symptoms of mental disorder might have been related to the offense. In these cases, the evaluation certainly should not be declined and need not be considered incomplete. But clinicians often will have to limit their opinions accordingly. This might require explaining to the court how the unavailability of certain types of relevant data compromises their degree of certainty or (in some cases) does not allow them to form a clinical opinion about certain questions.

3.4 *Psychological Testing*

There are no psychological tests that assess specifically the risk of future violence among youths. When psychological tests are used in risk assessments, typically they include measures of personality and mental disorder, two of the factors we have discussed earlier. The *Minnesota Multiphasic Personality Inventory-Adolescents* (Butcher et al., 1992) and the *Millon Adolescent Clinical Inventory* (Millon, 1993) provide two, well-validated multidimensional methods. The *Child Behavior Checklist* (Achenbach, 1991a, 1991b, 1991c) (for parents, teachers, and youth self-report) offers a way to identify youths whose problems are exhibited in "externalized" and "internalized" ways, dimensions that are sometimes useful in conceptualizing their harmful aggression (although the two types do not signify different likelihoods of future violence). Recently the *Psychopathy Checklist* (Hare, 1991) has been used with adolescents (Frick et al., 1994), especially to differentiate youths who may be developing psychopathic characteristics from other youths who, although antisocial, do not show the deficiencies in social attachments or empathy that are part of the psychopathic personality.

3.5 *Screening Devices*

Juvenile justice agencies in some states have developed their own checklists and brief screening devices to guide their decisions about youths' risk of future violence. Many of these were collected, reprinted, and reviewed by Wiebush et al. (1995). In most cases their validity is not known. But they do encourage the use of a consistent set of risk factors, and they allow the user to assign objective ratings based on those factors.

For some of the risk screening devices, ratings are summed to produce a score and criteria are provided that translate the score into a level of risk or a type of placement within the state's juvenile justice system. These devices may be useful for clinicians to examine if they are asked to develop screening methods for their own juvenile courts. They may also be useful when making rapid decisions about pretrial detention. In general, however, they do not guide the clinician to make the finer discriminations (e.g., dimensions of past violent behavior) that have been described earlier in this chapter.

3.6 *Learning about Social Contexts*

A full understanding of the conditions under which a youth is or is not likely to engage in violent behavior sometimes requires knowing the social settings in which past violent behavior has been more and less frequent. This, in turn, may require that the clinician learn about the conditions and contingencies in those settings. For example, if a youth has often been disruptive in one juvenile facility but rarely was aggressive in another, the clinician may wish to learn about the nature of their programs from their facility staff to determine whether program differences might provide clues to the conditions in which the risk of future violence for this youth might be higher or lower.

4.0 FORMING AND REPORTING OPINIONS

Decisions about youths' *detention prior to trial* typically focus on the safety of the public and of the youth while the case is being adjudicated. Opinions about risk associated with a court's decision regarding detention should take into consideration the relevant time frame. Most states allow overnight emergency detention of youths and a decision in the next day or two as to whether the youth presents a sufficient risk to be detained further. Many states require a more formal hearing within a week or two to determine the need for longer-range detention which, if the youth is awaiting trial on serious charges, may last up to several months. Clinical opinions related to the first decision need only weigh the risk factors as they currently exist (e.g., the youth's present psychological state and current conditions at home as they relate to the likelihood that parents can provide adequate supervision). Clinical opinions related to continued, longer-range pretrial detention must consider the wider range of circumstances that might arise during that time as they relate to the risk of further aggression.

Clinical opinions about a youth's *disposition and placement after adjudication* require a consideration of degrees of risk that would be posed in each of a variety of settings. Typically courts have several basic options for placements: for example, physically secure facilities (locked and strictly segregated from the community), various levels of "staff-secure" facilities (e.g., group homes in the community, with staff restricting the movement of youths outside the house to certain places and at certain times), and nonsecure settings such as the youth's own home or a foster home. Often the clinician will be expected to describe the degree of risk that the youth would pose in each of these types of placements. The matter of safety of the public and the youth also will focus on a longer time frame, often a year or two. Clinicians have little reason for confidence in their ability to predict situational factors that might influence the youth's aggression and self-control more than a year in the future. Moreover, the youth's future risk of violent behavior will depend in part on whether the youth changes during that time as a consequence of maturation, rehabilitative efforts, and a host of other possible factors that often cannot be known at the time of adjudication.

Clinical opinions related to courts' decisions about *waiver to criminal court* require a consideration of the likelihood that the youth (a) will be a danger to others if retained in the juvenile system and (b) will continue to be a danger to society as an adult after the juvenile rehabilitation system must relinquish custody. These are two different questions that will require at least two separate clinical opinions about violence risk. The latter question about long-term risk (i.e., risk of violence in adulthood) requires that the risk estimate must include an opinion about the likelihood that the youth would respond to rehabilitative efforts in the years that remain for the juvenile justice system's jurisdiction. Assessments for this latter purpose are discussed in Chapters 5 and 6.

When reporting the results of a risk assessment, clinicians should avoid "blanket" statements about a youth's potential for violent behavior. Frequently I make it a point to inform the court, early in the report or in testimony, that I have not one but two or three clinical opinions about risk. I am referring, of course, to separate risk statements for (a) different social contexts (e.g., home

155

vs. facility placement) or (b) different time frames (e.g., in the next year vs. in adulthood). I then frame the opinions as "if . . . then" statements. For example, "If the youth were to be placed in a staff-secure group home, then he would present a moderate risk of harm to others in the community," or "If the youth is placed in a secure facility, then he will present a very low likelihood of harm to other youths or to staff."

In conclusion, when clinicians are asked to make "predictions" about youths' future violent behavior, the approach described in this chapter encourages

- the use of *risk factors* that bear some relationships to violent behavior
- recognition of the importance of *social context*
- making *risk estimates* rather than predictions that the youth will or will not engage in violent acts
- recognizing that there is no single type of youth who commits violent acts
- remembering that delinquent behavior desists after adolescence for many youths

We reviewed risk factors with known relationships to future harmful aggression among youths (although their application to female juvenile offenders is uncertain), and discussed ways to obtain the necessary data.

As noted at the beginning of this chapter, there has been very little research to guide our assessments of risk of future violence among adolescents or to demonstrate our ability to estimate risks accurately. In the future, research using the risk factors reviewed in this chapter (and other factors if necessary) may provide actuarial base rates of violent behavior for youths. That information will place clinicians' risk estimates on a much more firm foundation.

Until actuarial base rates are available, however, risk estimates will have to be based on systematic clinical logic that uses the risk factors described in this chapter. Reports and testimony about these estimates *must provide a complete description of the data and logic on which they are based.* The court should be given enough information to decide the weight to be given to the evidence and our opinions and should provide attorneys with sufficient information to challenge any of the clinician's assumptions. If the job is done systematically, using multiple sources of data to attend to the full range of risk factors, complete disclosure of the clinician's logic is far more convincing and helpful to the court than an unsupported recitation of one's conclusions.

Chapter 5

Rehabilitation Evaluations

Since the beginning of the juvenile justice system, mental health professionals have advised juvenile courts on a case-by-case basis regarding "what to do" with delinquent youths to meet the juvenile court's rehabilitative mandate. There are a number of different kinds of evaluations focusing on youths' rehabilitation, corresponding to different points of intervention by the juvenile justice system. Although each type of evaluation is called by different names, I have placed them together in this chapter because they share certain conceptual and procedural features.

The chapter begins with a review of types of rehabilitation evaluations, rehabilitation options of the juvenile justice system, and the evaluation process (1.0). This chapter then examines several specific parts of rehabilitation evaluations and their implications for the examiner's task (2.0 through 5.0). Readers who are especially interested in evaluations for waiver of youths to criminal court (Chapter 6) should read the present chapter first. One part of the waiver evaluation pertains to a youth's rehabilitation potential, which is the focus of this chapter. Chapter 6 then demonstrates how this is integrated with other information in waiver evaluations.

1.0 PERSPECTIVE ON REHABILITATION EVALUATIONS

1.1 *Types of Evaluations*

There are several situations in which juvenile courts ask for evaluations regarding the rehabilitation of delinquent youths;

these vary in their demands and specific questions. They include evaluations for (a) *waiver* to criminal court, (b) *disposition* for juveniles found delinquent, and (c) what I will call *progress and outcome* evaluations to assess the course of rehabilitation.

1.11 Waiver Evaluations

In many states, prosecutors can request a judicial decision to waive its jurisdiction over a juvenile who is alleged to have committed certain offenses (and/or who has a particular offense history), allowing for trial in criminal court rather than juvenile court. The specific criteria involved in a court's waiver decisions and the process of waiver evaluations are described in Chapter 6. Part of the legal question in these cases is whether the juvenile would be *amenable to rehabilitation* if the youth were found delinquent and provided rehabilitative services in the juvenile justice system. The question of amenability thus requires an inquiry into the prospects for rehabilitation of the youth, focusing on the youth's treatability and the juvenile system's resources. These are pretrial evaluations, of course, because the question of waiver must be decided before the case can move to adjudication in either juvenile or criminal court.

1.12 Disposition Evaluations

After a youth is adjudicated delinquent, the court must hold a separate hearing to decide what will be done as a consequence of the adjudication (what the disposition of the case will be). Options generally include some form of probation with community services, or commitment to the custody of the state's youth authority. Commitment, in turn, may result in placements at home (with various services and requirements), in residential facilities in the community, in special nonsecure programs such as "camps" or "ranches," or in secure facilities with various forms of education, rehabilitation, and/or clinical services. Courts may also decide to refer youths to programs operated by a state's mental health system (e.g., inpatient psychiatric facilities) when their clinical needs cannot be met in programs for delinquent youths within the juvenile justice system.

Disposition evaluations provide courts with information to determine the types of services and degree of security that are needed for a particular youth. Some states require that disposition evaluations may not be conducted until after adjudication. This is to avoid the possibility that self-incriminating information that could arise in the assessment will not make its way into the adjudication process. Most states, however, allow the evaluations to be performed prior to the delinquency hearing so that the results will be available to the court without delay immediately after the youth is found delinquent.

1.13   Progress and Outcome Evaluations

Youth authorities will sometimes request evaluations to assess the progress of rehabilitation efforts. For example, courts or juvenile facilities may be required to document decisions to move a youth from a more secure to less secure placement as a step in the youth's rehabilitation process or to transfer the youth from a juvenile justice program to a psychiatric facility in the state's mental health system. Examiners often will be asked to provide evaluations of youths' progress or of new developments regarding the youth's needs, in order to assist courts in these decisions.

Some states provide an option for the extension of juvenile court custody beyond the usual maximum age. Typically this requires a court hearing to decide whether extension is important for public safety and/or whether progress suggests that the extension would serve to complete the rehabilitation process. Laws limit such extensions, however, so that they may not occur beyond some further maximum age. The examiner's task is to assess rehabilitation progress thus far, often to assess the risk of harm if custody is not extended, and to determine any potential benefit of further rehabilitative efforts.

1.2   *Legal Concepts Influencing the Rehabilitation Objective*

As noted in Chapter 1, rehabilitation was one of the primary objectives of a separate system of juvenile justice. It was reasoned that adolescents did not yet have the characteristics that they would have as adults. Thus proper interventions during adolescence had a chance to shape youths in a way that would reduce the likelihood of their recidivism and the development of longer-term criminal character.

Notice that embedded within this rehabilitation objective is another, ultimate objective to protect society from a youth's future criminal behavior. Rehabilitation efforts were expected to do this in two ways: first, by removing youths from the community for rehabilitative intervention if this was necessary for society's immediate protection and, second, by changing youths so that the likelihood of harm would be reduced when the youth was returned to the community.

How the rehabilitation objective is implemented in the juvenile justice system is influenced by several legal concepts one must consider when performing rehabilitation evaluations: (a) *jurisdictional age*; (b) the *definition of delinquency*; (c) *amenability to rehabilitation*; (d) *least restrictive alternative*, and (e) *offense-based sentencing*.

1.21 Jurisdictional Age

Each state has established a maximum age for juvenile court jurisdiction (i.e., an age below which charges are filed in juvenile court) and a maximum age at which juvenile justice authorities lose custody of youths who have been adjudicated delinquent and are in juvenile rehabilitation programs. (In some states the maximum ages are different for these two purposes.) Maximum jurisdictional age is typically 16, 17, or 18. Some states allow extention of the system's custody of a youth who has been adjudicated delinquent, often into the twenties. This is important to consider in any rehabilitation evaluation because the youth's current age and the system's maximum age of jurisdiction define the amount of time that is allowed for achieving the system's rehabilitative goals for a given youth.

1.22 Delinquency

A youth may be found delinquent and placed in the custody of a state's youth authority for rehabilitation only if the youth has committed an act that would be a crime if committed by an adult. Until recent decades, youths could be found delinquent not only for those behaviors but also for others that were illegal only because of youths' status as minors. The most common "status offenses" are truancy, running away from home, and being "unruly" (habitually disobeying parents). Legal reforms eventually set these behaviors apart so that they could not result in a finding of delinquency. This limited the juvenile court's discretion in arriving at rehabilitative options for "status offenders," in that they could not be sent to certain types of secure placements or other rehabilitation programs that were provided for youths who were found delinquent.

1.23 Amenability to Rehabilitation

Juvenile law and policy have always assumed that some youths are "not fit and proper subjects" (a phrase used in many statutes) for rehabilitation within the system. Therefore, juvenile courts have long had the option to waive their jurisdiction over certain juvenile cases, allowing prosecutors to file charges against the youth in criminal court.

The term "mature" was often used to describe youths who, although of adolescent age, could be remanded to criminal court for trial and punishment as though they were adults. As discussed in Chapter 6, the concept of the "mature juvenile" who was not amenable to rehabilitation was never very specifically defined. In practice, it meant that

- the youth's character was a "mismatch" with juvenile rehabilitation programs, in the sense that the programs *could not provide sufficient security* to protect the public (or other youths in custody) from the risk of the youth's harmful aggression; and/or
- that the youth had a pattern of adult-like criminal character and conduct that was *unlikely to be altered* by rehabilitation efforts provided to most delinquent youths.

Youths deemed inappropriate for juvenile justice placement were construed as no longer malleable—in effect, prematurely mature—and their presence in juvenile programs was considered fruitless and likely to impede a program's work with other youths.

Thus the juvenile justice system did not intend to meet the needs of every delinquent youth. Some few would be beyond the reach of rehabilitation, and they needed to be identified. This gave rise to the need for rehabilitation evaluations that would assist courts to determine which youths were unlikely to benefit from rehabilitation provided in juvenile correctional programs.

1.24 Least Restrictive Alternative

In the last few decades, most states have acknowledged (by statute or case law) that juvenile courts are allowed to deprive delinquent youths of liberty only to the extent necessary in order to promote their rehabilitation and to protect the public. This concept, called "least restrictive alternative," has discouraged routine commitments to secure juvenile facilities. Where applicable, it requires that a youth must be placed in community-based programs or nonsecure facilities unless it is shown that greater security is needed. As a general rule, this concept should influence clinicians' reasoning and recommendations as well. They should recommend the least restrictive alternative that will provide necessary rehabilitation services and adequate public protection.

1.25 Offense-Based Sentencing

Juvenile courts and their rehabilitation programs originally were given wide discretion regarding the places and lengths of time that youths could be held in custody within the jurisdictional age limit. Juvenile courts typically sent youths to training schools, for example, for indefinite periods of time. Moreover, youths with relatively minor delinquencies often would be in custody as long as (sometimes longer than) youths with major offenses. This was because the system was expected to focus not on the nature of the youth's offense but on the youth's rehabilitation needs.

Many of these dispositional practices and presumptions still exist in some states. In recent years, however, many states' laws have reduced this discretion, requiring courts to "sentence" youths uniformly based on the nature of their offense. Although youths may still receive rehabilitation services wherever they serve their juvenile sentences, the time that they are in custody will sometimes be based on a state's statutory requirement, not on the basis of the youth's individual needs or rehabilitation progress alone.

1.3 *Resources of the System*

Recommendations to juvenile courts for rehabilitation interventions must be made with a realistic view of the resources of the juvenile justice system. Society does not provide juvenile justice systems unlimited resources for the rehabilitation of delinquent youths. It is not helpful for clinicians to make routine recommendations for "individual psychotherapy" or comprehensive neurological examinations that the system cannot provide on a routine basis. To a large extent, *rehabilitation evaluations are attempts to match the needs of a youth with the resources that are reasonably available within the juvenile justice system* and to assist the court in using resources efficiently so that they are available to those youths who are most in need of them.

Clinicians, therefore, should be thoroughly familiar with the resources of their juvenile justice systems. This should include the range of services available for youths on probation; the various types of open and secure residential facilities available for placement of youths; and special programs such as boot camps, outward bound programs, and special placement options that may be available for youths with serious mental disorders or special developmental disabilities. Clinicians should periodically update their knowledge of these programs, which may change in their focus, quality, staff, or resident composition across time.

Although most states' rehabilitation resources are seriously limited, appellate legal decisions in some states have held that the juvenile justice system cannot use these deficiencies in services as an excuse to avoid providing special services that a youth actually needs. In these states, the absence of a program for youths who are both seriously delinquent and seriously mentally ill cannot be the basis for deciding that a youth cannot be rehabilitated in the juvenile justice system merely because the system does not have a program to do it. For example, the state might be required to purchase relevant services from another state that does have such a program. Recommendations for out-of-state placements, however, typically require very strong arguments regarding the exceptional need in order to overcome concerns about the financial cost.

1.4 *A Structure for Rehabilitation Evaluations*

Although there are several kinds of rehabilitation evaluations that clinicians are asked to provide, all of them have certain characteristics in common. A simple structure for all such evaluations is represented by the four following assessment questions:

- *What are the youth's important characteristics?* The evaluation should describe the youth, including the youth's personality and medical, family, academic, and delinquent history.
- *What needs to change?* The evaluation should provide an understanding of the youth's character and needs as they relate to past offenses, as well as a description of the ways in which the youth and the youth's environment would need to be modified in order to reduce the likelihood of recidivism.
- *What modes of intervention could be applied toward the rehabilitation objective?* The evaluation should describe interventions that are available and are known to have some relation to the preceding rehabilitation objectives for this particular youth, with attention to employing the least restrictive alternative.
- *What is the likelihood of change, given the relevant interventions?* The evaluation should describe the likelihood that rehabilitation objectives could be met given the nature of the youth, the interventions described earlier, and the time available within the jurisdictional age limits of the juvenile justice system.

When I perform rehabilitation evaluations, I typically use these four elements as an outline for my report.

How much information will be collected for each of these four elements will vary for different types of rehabilitation evaluations. The following sections of the chapter devoted to each of these four elements discuss the full range of information that might be included, recognizing that the actual amount of information in specific evaluations will vary from case to case. The first section on "describing youths" (2.0) represents virtually all of the data collected during the rehabilitation evaluation. Therefore, data collection methods will be discussed in this section. The other three elements (discussed in 3.0 to 5.0) consist of inferences and opinions that the clinician must make based on the data obtained for the description of the youth.

2.0 DESCRIBING YOUTHS: WHAT ARE THE YOUTH'S IMPORTANT CHARACTERISTICS?

A helpful rehabilitation evaluation is based on a meaningful conceptualization of the youth, providing the court a fundamental understanding of the youth and the youth's social circumstances. There is no single way to describe youths; different cases will call for different approaches. Yet it is helpful to have a set of descriptive topics that will be used consistently across cases, then to vary the focus or detail of information on those topics in response to unique features of the individual case.

The following discussion describes a set of content areas for use in describing youths in rehabilitation evaluations. There is no particular significance to the order in which they are presented here; clinicians will have their own ways of organizing their descriptions based on their own clinical experience. Each subsection comments on the topic area and ways in which it can be structured and offers suggestions for methods to obtain the information necessary to describe the youth's characteristics in that topic area.

2.1 *Health and Medical History*

The juvenile justice system is responsible for providing medical treatment for important illnesses that the youth may have and for being aware of risks related to chronic medical problems (e.g., epileptic disorders, allergies). The examiner, therefore, should obtain information from medical records or parents and the youth regarding past illnesses and general medical history, including medications.

It is very important to inquire about any past injuries (from birth to present), especially head injuries and their sequelae. Head injuries that appear to have resulted in brain trauma, especially unconsciousness for more than a few minutes, should signal the need for more detailed inquiry because this is known to increase the risk of problems in impulse control, anger, and aggression.

Special attention should be given to records (as well as family members' and youths' descriptions) of previous psychiatric treatment for mental disorders, developmental disabilities, and substance use and dependency. Many delinquent youths have had past contact with mental health centers and inpatient psychiatric facilities. The clinician should obtain records from those treatment contacts whenever it is feasible, especially to learn about other psychiatric and psychological evaluations in the past, diagnoses, treatment provided, outcome, and any medications that were prescribed. If these contacts have been numerous, it is especially helpful to organize them chronologically for purposes of examining the course of the disorder and the process of medical intervention.

Youths themselves are often the best source of information regarding current physiological phenomena that may have medical significance. Examples include headaches, somatic complaints, sleeping patterns, and past and present eating habits.

2.2 *Family and Social Background*

Most clinicians are aware of the many ways in which a family's history may influence a youth's current needs, provide explanations for the development of delinquent behavior, and help identify treatment objectives. Moreover, rehabilitation of youths frequently requires attention to needs of the family as well as resources the family can bring to the rehabilitation process. Some youths are highly unlikely to change without significant change in the family. In other cases, families may have strengths that can further the youth's rehabilitation.

Information that will help to identify the familial context for a youth's development generally requires interviews with a family member (or several family members) as well as the youth. Without trying to offer an exhaustive list, there are certain fundamental matters of family history that almost always warrant inquiry:

- Family constellation during early childhood, including changes historically (e.g., divorces, separations, deaths)
- Stability, resilience, and parental efforts to meet the youth's needs in early childhood
- Chaos, criminal behavior, neglect, and/or abuse in the family history
- Significant attachments of the youth during childhood
- Loss of parental affection/contact and other significant losses
- Current sources of strength and support within the family

It is often helpful to organize these observations chronologically, in order to identify their potential significance in relation to the youth's behavior and development at particular times in childhood. When interviewing the youth, the clinician will also want to obtain the youth's reflections on family historical events and relationships. Often the importance of family background lies not only in the nature of family events and characteristics but also in their significance (or insignificance) as perceived by the youth.

Prior to adolescence, the most important social relationships outside the nuclear and extended family tend to be with other authority figures, such as teachers. From around age 11 or 12, however, peer relationships become an increasingly important part of youths' social lives independent of their families and require special attention in understanding youths' development. Interview inquiries should explore the nature of early-teen friendships, especially in terms of groups and gangs that may have played a role in the development of delinquent behavior.

Few instruments provide norms for dimensions of family life or family relations in the assessment of delinquent youths. One that has demonstrated considerable value, however, is the *Family Environment Scale* (R. Moos & B. Moos, 1986). This paper-and-pencil instrument (true/false responses) is administered to as many family members as is feasible, and scores on the various descriptive dimensions can be calculated for individuals, the family as a whole, or separate scores for parents and children. Scores represent the family members' perceptions of the family on

10 dimensions that are well defined and often meaningful in describing and explaining the family milieu (e.g., Cohesion, Conflict, Independence, Organization, Control).

The *Parent-Child Relationship Inventory* (Gerard, 1994), taken by parents, is a self-report questionnaire that measures seven features of parenting, including such variables as Parental Support, Involvement, Communication, and Limit Setting. Initial reliability and validity data are promising. For peer relations, several instruments described later in 5-2.42 (e.g., the *Child Behavior Checklist*) have items that identify the nature of peers with whom the youth socializes, as well as adjustment to peer groups.

2.3 *Academic and Intellectual Functioning*

Virtually all descriptions of youths must include some information about general intelligence and aptitudes because of their importance in identifying the youth's cognitive resources and educational needs. Some delinquent youths are seriously deficient in intellectual capacities either because of mental retardation or inadequate educational histories.

School records and teachers' observations are sometimes good sources of this information. School records often provide the results of formal intellectual and achievement testing at various points in the youth's school career. Primary school test results can be helpful in estimating a youth's intellectual potential. This is because they often predate the emergence in early adolescence of poorer academic motivation and cumulative effects of disruptions in education that result in performance in adolescence that is below the youth's potential intellectual baseline. Reviews of academic records should also attempt to identify potential strengths on which rehabilitation efforts could capitalize.

The youth's history of academic performance often provides important information about motivation as well. Many youths' chronological records of school performance mirror the negative impact of adverse historical events at home or in social groups. Downturns in formal test results across time sometimes allow one to locate the time (and the parallel events in the youth's family/social life) at which performance began to deteriorate.

School records often contain material documenting school misbehaviors, suspensions, and expulsions, including teachers' observations and evaluations of youths' behavior. These records can help to determine how early a youth's disruptive and aggressive behavior began and how it developed across childhood and into the adolescent years. Occasionally they also identify interventions or situations that temporarily reversed the course of delinquent behavior for this particular youth, offering clues to potential rehabilitation strategies.

Clinicians may use a variety of tests for describing youths' intellectual abilities and levels of academic achievement. Frequently used tests of intellectual functioning include the *Wechsler Intelligence Scale for Children-III* (Wechsler, 1991) and the *Wechsler Adult Intelligence Scale-Revised* for older adolescents (Wechsler, 1981). The *Peabody Picture Vocabulary Test-Revised* (L. Dunn & L. M. Dunn, 1981) is sometimes useful for measuring verbal intellectual capacity in youths with verbal expressive problems.

To address questions of academic performance and placement in educational programs, specialized achievement tests sometimes are more useful than general intelligence tests. Achievement tests often used in assessments of delinquent youths include the *Wide Range Achievement Test-Revised* (S. Jastak et al., 1984), the *Kaufman Test of Educational Achievement* (A. Kaufman & N. Kaufman, 1985), and the *Peabody Individual Achievement Test-Revised* (Markwardt, 1989). When using these tests, remember that test norms for academic grade levels associated with various levels of performance are based on national norms and might not accurately reflect local norms.

Many clinicians may wish to refer some youths to other testing specialists when they strongly suspect neurological deficits or specific learning and perceptual disabilities. Methods such as the *Halstead-Reitan Neuropsychological Test Battery for Older Children* (Reitan & Wolfson, 1985), for example, require specialized equipment and training to administer and interpret the battery. Other tests are best administered and interpreted by psychologists specialized in educational assessment if the clinician is not specifically trained in their interpretation: for example, the *Woodcock-Johnson Psycho-Educational Battery* (Woodcock et al., 1989).

2.4 *Personality Description*

Descriptions of psychosocial traits and behavioral predisposi-tions usually are clearer when the clinician uses some systematic structure for reporting them. There are two broad ways to do this: descriptions that are based on *general theories of personality and development* and descriptions based on *typologies* especially devised for use with delinquent youths.

2.41 Personality and Developmental Descriptions

General theories of personality sometimes provide a helpful framework for describing significant, enduring characteristics of youths relevant for understanding their delinquent behavior. Psychodynamic theories identify significant conflicts inferred from the youth's development and current presentation. They also assist in organizing one's description of maladaptive (and delinquent) behaviors in terms of a particular style of coping or defense that the youth typically employs in reaction to conflicts in current social circumstances. Cognitive behavioral theories also provide structure for describing youths' perceptions, presumptions, attributions, personal scripts, and behavioral predispositions.

Some clinicians use *developmental theories*, such as those of Piaget, Erikson, and Kohlberg, to organize parts of their descrip-tions of personality. These theories identify stage-related changes in normal child and adolescent development, and they provide the opportunity to describe youths in terms of adequate, delayed, or abnormal development of particular cognitive and psychosocial characteristics.

Comprehensive measures of personality often provide useful information for these descriptions. The *Minnesota Multiphasic Personality Inventory-Adolescent* (MMPI-A; Butcher et al., 1992) provides scores not only on the 10 clinical scales that form the primary basis for the test but also on a number of adjunct scales that describe personality traits and behavior tendencies. The *Basic Personality Inventory* (Jackson, 1995) is less well known; it employs only about half as many items as the MMPI-A, provides scores on 12 personality characteristics that are relevant for describing adolescents, and offers norms for samples of delinquent youths. The *Millon Adolescent Personality Inventory* (Millon et al., 1982) and the newer *Millon Adolescent Clinical Inventory* (Millon, 1993) yield scores on several personality styles as well as the youth's expressed concerns (e.g., Peer Security, Family Rapport, Personal Esteem).

These instruments typically require a reading ability in the 5th to 7th grade range. Clinicians will often encounter youths in the juvenile justice system who cannot read well enough to take the tests on their own and to whom the items must be read by the examiner (or presented with an audiotape). Because these tests are somewhat lengthy, clinicians must take special care to identify youths whose motivation or attention might wane during the testing process, thereby jeopardizing the validity of the results.

2.42 Typology Descriptions

A number of conceptual systems are available for grouping or categorizing delinquent youths into "types." Many of the delinquent typologies were developed in the hope that the needs of particular types of youths could be matched with particular types of rehabilitation programs, thus providing a basis for placing youths in programs that would maximize the likelihood of rehabilitation success. Unfortunately, research on matching types of youths with particular types of programs has met with only limited success. Nevertheless, several of the typologies themselves have proven useful for descriptive purposes and for anticipating youths' behavioral tendencies during rehabilitation.

In association with a program of research by the California Youth Authority in the 1960s and 1970s, Warren (1976) developed a classification system called *Interpersonal Maturity Level (I-Level)*. It is theoretically anchored in conceptual assumptions about the sequence of development of more primitive to more mature levels of perception, cognition, and interpersonal behavior. Each level has two or more subtypes:

- *I-Level 2*: Asocial (Asocial Passive, Asocial Aggressive)
- *I-Level 3*: Conformist (Immature Conformist, Cultural Conformist, Manipulator)
- *I-Level 4:* Neurotic (Neurotic Acting-Out, Neurotic Anxious, Cultural Identifier, Situational-Emotional Reaction)

In general, rehabilitation programs that were expected to be more successful for the various types were relatively authority-based and structured for I-Level 2, contingency-based reinforcement systems ("behavior modification") and peer sanctions for I-Level 3, and programs relying on more abstract and "clinical" methods (e.g., transactional analysis) for I-Level 4. Classification was aided in the original project by a semistructured interview schedule (Warren, 1966), but it has not been developed in sufficient detail and is difficult to obtain because the interview was never published. However, I-Level classification can be based on the *Jesness Inventory* (Jesness & Wedge, 1984, 1985), a paper-and-pencil self-report measure.

Dating from the same time period, the *Quay typology* (Quay, 1964, 1966) for classifying delinquent youths has undergone revisions across two decades (Quay, 1987). The latest types included in the Quay system are

- Conduct Disorder
- Socialized Aggression
- Attention Problems–Immaturity
- Anxiety-Withdrawal
- Psychotic Behavior
- Motor Tension Excess

To aid classification, the *Revised Behavior Problem Checklist* (Quay & Peterson, 1987) is given to an adult who is sufficiently acquainted with the youth (e.g., parent, teacher, someone who has worked with the youth clinically) to be able to check those items of behavior that are typical of the youth. Scores on the *Checklist* then allow the clinician to classify the youth according to the Quay types.

Achenbach developed three instruments for use in describing youths on several dimensions that are clustered within two primary types: youths whose difficulties are *"internalized"* (e.g., anxious, inhibited) and those whose problems are *"externalized"* (e.g., impulsive, acting out). The three instruments use different sources of information but all provide scores on the same dimensions. They include the *Child Behavior Checklist* (Achenbach, 1991a; completed by parents), the *Child Behavior Checklist–Teacher Report Form* (Achenbach, 1991b), and the *Child Behavior Checklist–Youth Self-Report* (Achenbach, 1991c).

Informants describe the youth on about 100 items referring to behaviors and attitudes of the youth.

Clinicians evaluating youthful offenders have sometimes used *Megargee's MMPI-based classification method for offenders* (Megargee, 1984; Megargee & Bohn, 1979). The method was originally developed for use with adult offenders, describing them according to 10 offender types associated theoretically and empirically with different levels and types of risk as well as suggested rehabilitation programming. Its use with adolescents, however, has been questioned (for a review of the issues, see Zager, 1988). Moreover, there has been no attempt as yet to adapt the system to the new adolescent version of the MMPI (the MMPI-A).

Finally, mention should be made of recent applications of the *Psychopathy Checklist-Revised* (PCL-R; Hare, 1991) in the evaluation of youths. Originally developed for assessing adults, the PCL-R uses an interview format and record reviews to rate individuals on a variety of traits and behaviors that are consistent with psychopathic personality. Application of the PCL-R to delinquent adolescent samples suggests that it may be useful in identifying youths who fail to form attachments to others, lack feelings of remorse or guilt about their antisocial behaviors, and manifest other signs of early development of psychopathic characteristics (Brandt et al., 1997; Forth, Hart, & Hare, 1990; Frick et al., 1994). As a typological descriptor, youths who could be identified as having psychopathic characteristics would represent a subgroup with theoretically poor prognosis for success in most rehabilitation programs. At this writing, however, there has not been sufficient research to determine the validity of the use of the PCL-R (or the formal concept of psychopathy) with adolescents.

2.5 *Clinical Diagnostic Description*

When delinquent youths manifest symptoms of mental disorders or emotional disturbance, their identification is important to ensure that their need for clinical services is taken into account in decisions about the youth's rehabilitation. This does not necessarily mean that they will need treatment in psychiatric programs. But it often indicates that the juvenile justice system may have to provide special services to such youths if it is to meet its rehabilitation objectives.

Research on the prevalence of various mental disorders in delinquent populations is quite incomplete (see 1-4.3), with estimates varying substantially across studies (due primarily to sample and method differences) (Otto et al., 1992). It is clear, however, that special attention should be given to the potential for mood disorders (especially depression), anxiety disorders, Posttraumatic Stress Disorder, Attention-Deficit/Hyperactivity Disorder, substance use disorders, and (less often) psychotic disorders.

A large proportion of youths in the juvenile justice system will also meet criteria for a diagnosis of Conduct Disorder. This diagnosis alone, however, usually is of very limited value in describing youths, their needs, and their rehabilitation. Because so many delinquent youths meet criteria for Conduct Disorder, it fails to distinguish anything particularly different about the youth in question compared to the majority of other youths seen by the juvenile justice system. In addition, the diagnosis has only limited value for identifying a youth's needs because the criteria for Conduct Disorder simply indicate that the youth has engaged repeatedly in a variety of illegal, disruptive, or antisocial behaviors. Attaching a diagnostic label to these behaviors, which themselves are often already obvious without clinical evaluation, does not explain the behaviors and does not offer a conceptual link to any particular approach to rehabilitation. Moreover, as discussed in Chapter 1, the label tends to provide superficial satisfaction that the problem has been "identified" (whereas in fact many youths with Conduct Disorders manifest other clinical disorders), and there is a tendency for lay persons to identify Conduct Disorder as a precursor for adult Antisocial Personality Disorder (whereas Conduct Disorder typically remits in late adolescence, with only a minority of such youths progressing to Antisocial Personality Disorder in adulthood).

One value of Conduct Disorder as a diagnostic descriptor is the *DSM-IV* identification of two subtypes: Childhood-Onset Type and Adolescent-Onset Type. As discussed in Chapter 4, the latter type is less likely to persist in delinquency through adolescence or to continue into adulthood as Antisocial Personality Disorder.

Identifying youths' mental and emotional disorders is aided by reviews of any past records of a youth's contacts with psychiatric hospitals or mental health centers of which parents and the youth are aware. Often, however, delinquent youths' mental disorders have gone undiagnosed and untreated throughout childhood. The clinician's identification of possible disorders during the evaluation often is the first formal diagnosis of disorder for many delinquent youths. Thus clinicians must engage in careful exploration of the possibility of mental disorders using diagnostic interviews, clinical observations, and psychological testing when it is necessary.

There are now a number of structured interview methods for assessing psychopathology in adolescents. Among them are the *Affective Disorders and Schizophrenia for School-Age Children* (K-SADS; Ambrosini, 1992), the *Diagnostic Interview Schedule for Children* (DISC; National Institute of Mental Health, 1991), and the *Diagnostic Interview for Children and Adolescents-Revised–Adolescent Version* (DICA-R-A; Reich, Shayka, & Taibleson, 1991; Shaffer et al., 1993). (For a good review of these interview schedules, see Rogers, 1995.)

Comprehensive assessment of youths' clinical conditions generally will include one or more of the major paper-and-pencil tests designed for this task that have been cited earlier: for example, the *Minnesota Multiphasic Personality Inventory-Adolescent (MMPI-A)*, the *Millon Adolescent Clinical Inventory (MACI)*, the *Child Behavior Checklist,* or the *Behavior Problem Checklist.* Archer (1992) and McCann (1998) provide excellent reviews of the use of the MMPI-A in assessing adolescent psychopathology. Reviews of research and clinical use for the MACI can be found in McCann (1997, 1998) and McCann and Dyer (1996).

A number of instruments are also available for use in identifying the nature and seriousness of specific disorders (i.e., they focus on single disorders rather than the range of disorders) about which a clinician may be concerned on the basis of the initial clinical interview and record review. Examples include paper-and-pencil or interview screening instruments for depression and other affective disorders (Barrera & Garrison-Jones, 1988; Weinberg & Emslie, 1988), suicide potential (Reynolds, 1991), Posttraumatic Stress Disorder (Blake et al., 1990; Fletcher, 1996; Nader, 1997), substance use disorders (Tarter, 1990), and Attention-Deficit/Hyperactivity Disorder (DuPaul et al., 1997).

2.6   *Delinquent Behaviors and Legal History*

The examiner should identify all of the major incidents of school misbehavior during the youth's primary and secondary school years, as well as all events resulting in arrests (regardless of whether they were adjudicated). In addition, the examiner should try to understand the incidents in their social context and as they were perceived by the youth. This becomes important when the examiner develops hypotheses about the youth's motivation for misbehaviors and the relation between the youth's personality and offenses (see 5-3.0).

Primary sources of information for describing this aspect of the youth's history include school documents as well as law enforcement and juvenile court records of arrests, charges, court hearings, adjudications, and prior commitments to the state's youth authority. Often these records do not provide information about the social context in which the youth's misbehaviors occurred. That type of information should be sought in interviews with parents, juvenile authorities who may be familiar with the past incidents (e.g., teachers, probation officers, attorneys), and the youth.

Sometimes the youth will have considerable insight into causes and motivations for his or her illegal behaviors that are not revealed in records or interviews with third parties. Not everything that youths say about these incidents can be taken at face value, of course. Even so, their explanations and manner of describing their past offenses often reveal their own cognitive and emotional style of coping as well as their own degree of insight into their behavior. Discussions of past offenses also provide an opportunity to explore whether the youth experiences remorse for past offenses, which in general suggests somewhat better potential for rehabilitation. As noted in Chapter 4, however, "remorse" is a particularly difficult concept to assess. Some youths may be inhibited from expressing it even when they experience it, and others who do not experience it at all may express it extremely in an attempt to manipulate the clinician's impressions.

2.7   *Responses to Past Rehabilitation Efforts*

People often have exerted great effort to change a youth's behavior in the past. Parents have tried various forms of "discipline," schools have placed the youth in special programs, and/or the youth has already been in programs of rehabilitation managed by the juvenile court and juvenile authorities. The course of these attempts to modify the youth's behavior should be described, as well as their effects on the youth's behavior. Courts often use this information to gauge the likelihood that future rehabilitation efforts will or will not be worthwhile, and it can provide clinicians with clues to the types of interventions that may be more or less likely to meet with success in the future.

Lack of previous success, however, does not necessarily translate into a prediction of unlikely success in the future. For example, when exploring earlier rehabilitation efforts, the clinician should take into account the youth's developmental status and social context at the time of the previous intervention. The fact that a particular intervention did not work (or did work) for a given youth at a given point in the youth's development does not necessarily mean that the same type of intervention would not work again when applied within another developmental and social context in the youth's life.

In addition, one should obtain details of the past intervention. For example, it is not adequate to report that the youth was "on intensive probation for 6 months" and "failed to respond" as evidenced by a subsequent arrest. This could have one meaning if the youth's probation included daily face-to-face contact by a community case worker every day during that period and quite another meaning if the youth simply received a couple of telephone calls a week from the probation officer. Evaluating the nature of the intervention might also require knowing something about how the probation officer used the time with the youth. Did a typical encounter involve discussing with the youth the choices he was going to make that day and the conflicts he was having with the guy on the next block, or merely checking to see that the youth was in school?

Similarly, the mere fact that youths were "treated" for periods of time in particular residential rehabilitation facilities does not provide enough information to weigh the significance of their success or failure after being released from those settings. What services did the youth actually receive in the facility? How expertly were the services provided? What were the events within the facility at that time that constituted the social context for the intervention? What were the actual conditions of supervision after the youth left the facility, and how did those conditions actually play out? Were there any extraordinary stressors that the youth faced upon release from the facility, possibly sabotaging what otherwise could have been a more successful community re-entry?

Information of this type requires going beyond official statements of past rehabilitation attempts that are provided in juvenile court probation office summaries. One may need to contact programs that have worked with the youth, obtain their more detailed "monthly summaries" of the youth's progress in the program, and talk to staff who worked directly with the youth.

While examining these past intervention efforts, the clinician should look for things that "went right" as well as things that "did not work." Even when past interventions have been ultimately unsuccessful (i.e., the youth was a repeat offender after intervention), program staff often are able to describe periods of time during the rehabilitation process when "things were going okay" or "he was headed in the right direction." These observations should be explored in detail for the specific program conditions that existed at the time because they might reveal clues for prescribing future interventions that have the potential for a better outcome.

2.8   *Risk of Harm*

The clinician's description of the youth should include a summary of factors that are related to the likelihood of harm to others. The factors to take into consideration have been described in detail in Chapter 4. Data for most of these factors will have been obtained in the course of interviewing and testing to provide the description of the youth in the various domains related to the previous subsections. During the evaluation process, however, the clinician should determine whether all of the factors have been covered and whether additional inquiry is needed to obtain information that might not have arisen in the course of collecting data for the general description of the youth.

A special subsection of the report should describe these risk factors as they apply to the youth in question. The purpose of this subsection of the report is not to state an opinion about risk of harm but simply to bring together in one place—for the convenience of the reader—the relevant pieces of information that have already been provided in various parts of the foregoing description of the youth's history and personality.

2.9 *Comment on Reporting One's Description of the Youth*

When writing the portion of the report that describes the youth, the clinician should consider following a few general rules that will maximize the clarity of the description:

- *Be educative.* Recognize that the purpose of the description is to help readers (the court, probation officers, attorneys) to understand who this youth is and what the youth's background has been. This means describing things simply, chronologically when possible, and in terms that are easy for anyone to understand.
- *Be databased.* Recognize that a major purpose of this section is to provide historical data, a personality description, and a familial/social context that lays the foundation for your later inferences about rehabilitation. While laying that foundation, this section of the report *should not offer opinions or inferences* about the major questions that the rehabilitation evaluation is intended to address. That comes later.
- *Be complete.* "Complete" means that this section contains *all* the data and basic description of the youth that you will need to support your inferences and opinions that will follow in the remaining sections of the report.
- *Be concise.* "Concise" means two things. First, you should provide *no more* information than is needed to support your later inferences. Report only those aspects of the youth's history and personality that are truly relevant for the objective of the report and omit irrelevant details. When you read your first draft for revisions, test every piece of information against this criterion: "Does the reader have to know this in order to understand my opinions that I'll offer later?" Being "concise" also means using no more words than are necessary to make

an observation. Nothing obscures meaning more than over-extended explanations and needless repetition.

3.0 DESCRIBING REHABILITATION OBJECTIVES: WHAT NEEDS TO CHANGE?

Having described the youth and the youth's history and social circumstances, the examiner must then form a "theory" about the relation between this picture of the youth and the youth's delinquency. This theory becomes the logical basis for identifying *what needs to be changed* in order to meet the juvenile justice system's objectives to provide for the welfare of the youth and promote public safety, both of which are furthered by pursuing the goal of reducing the likelihood of future offending.

The "theory" does not have to be a comprehensive formulation of the youth's personality. It merely has to explain the youth's offending. *What is it about this youth, and this youth's social circumstances, that best explains his or her past offenses, and therefore identifies those things that must change in order to reduce the likelihood of future offending?* This explanation will not simply repeat the information in the previous "description" section. It will transform, synthesize, frame, and simplify the information in a way that makes it useful for identifying the targets for rehabilitation— "what needs to change"—therefore providing a bridge to the later task (5-4.0) of prescribing an intervention.

The explanation must be relatively clear and simple, but the clinician's own logical process for getting there sometimes will be quite complex. Moreover, clinicians differ in their theoretical and attitudinal approaches to forming their explanations about a given youth's misbehavior. A treatise on this process and on clinicians' different approaches to this task is well beyond the scope of this chapter (and probably beyond my own capacities in any forum). Yet there are some basic considerations that may help clinicians to frame what they are doing when they engage in this explanatory phase of the evaluation. The following discussion is "atheoretical," in the sense that much of it can be fitted to psychodynamic as well as cognitive, behaviorist, and social theoretical positions that clinicians may use as a function of their training and professional preferences.

3.1   *Two Broad Theories of Delinquency*

Examining the wide range of theories for delinquency in criminological and clinical literature, one finds that at the broadest level they can be classified as two types: those that focus on *character* and those that focus on *social circumstances.*

Theories that focus on *character* attribute basic causal importance to conditions of the youth that are seen as relatively enduring and endogenous. Theories that emphasize biological and neurological factors are in this category, as well as theories that postulate the importance of early social influences in the development of personality traits and clinical conditions that the youth brings to adolescence (or that are transformed into delinquency-prone traits upon entry into adolescence).

Theories that focus on *social circumstance* attend more closely to the social conditions of youths in explaining their current delinquency. In criminological literature, they are more consistent with the theoretical notion that most delinquent youths "drift" into delinquency rather than being destined for it by their character. The explanatory emphasis is on social and economic conditions that may reinforce behavior that is contrary to the norms expressed in law and social convention, as well as the absence of countervailing forces (in society, community, or family) that would direct youths in a more conventional and prosocial course of development. These theories vary widely across disciplines, from Marxist and social control theories in criminology to developmental explanations associated with modern society's extended "delay" of adult status during adolescence, to which many adolescents react in illegal ways that provide them a sense of accomplishment (e.g., see Moffitt, 1993).

For clinicians, the importance of these two broad ways of explaining delinquency is not their relative validity. Neither is more right than the other. It is the recognition that (a) some cases by their nature will "fit" better into one or the other of these two ways of framing an explanation for the youth's delinquency (discussed below in 5-3.2), and that nevertheless, (b) *both* notions are important in explaining any individual case (5-3.3).

3.2   *Fitting Cases to Theoretical Explanations*

Earlier we examined two typologies that clinicians have long used to differentiate youths engaged in delinquent activities: the I-Level typology and the Quay typology (see 5-2.42). Although they were developed by different researchers observing different samples of youths, they manifest certain interesting similarities. For example, both identify a class of youths whose delinquency is related to *faulty development or character traits* that are antisocial ("asocial," "conduct disorder"). They also include a class whose delinquency seems closely tied to *conformity to the norms of delinquent peer cultures* ("conformist," "socialized aggressive"). And both have classes for youths whose delinquency seems related to *clinical conditions* ("neurotic," "anxious-withdrawn," "psychotic").

In the process of sifting through the relevant information that they have obtained for describing a youth, clinicians who use these typologies will begin to identify the case with one of these categories. Some cases will fit better with an explanation of delinquent behavior that emphasizes endogenous, "character-like" conditions such as personality traits, mental and emotional disorders, and developmental disabilities (corresponding to the "asocial" and "clinical" classifications in the typologies). Other cases will fit better with explanations that focus on environmental and social conditions attending the development of the youth's disruptive or delinquent behavior, especially cases in which preadolescent behavior was not particularly problematic.

3.3 *The Importance of Integrated Explanations*

Having recognized that some cases will lend themselves better to one or the other type of explanation, it is equally important to realize that virtually every case will require an explanation for the youth's delinquency that draws from both perspectives. Serious mental disorder may be the *primary* feature in explaining one youth's violent acts. Yet a careful inspection of violent incidents in the youth's history might reveal that the timing for their occurrence was related to particular events in the family's history of interactions. Another youth's delinquency may be explained *primarily* as an early-adolescent rebellion against a new stepfather who decided to rule with an iron hand, as well as the reinforcement provided by a set of delinquent peers. Yet the youth's characteristic anger and low self-esteem (having developed throughout earlier childhood as the result of the absence of a father) would also be relevant as part of the explanation for the youth's behavior.

A more familiar way of saying what is being observed here is to remind us that behavior is a function of what the *person* brings to a situation and the particular *social conditions* and contingencies presented by the situation. An explanation containing one and not the other is incomplete.

3.4   *Identifying What Needs to Change*

Providing an explanation for a youth's past delinquent behavior does not automatically translate into an identification of what needs to change in order to prevent such behavior in the future. Sometimes problems have multiple causes, and changing one or two will not be enough. Other times the problem is relatively circumscribed, but there might be several types of changes that would deal with it.

For example, in the case briefly noted earlier, an adolescent with low self-esteem (due to problems in early childhood relationships with parents) acts out with other delinquent youths as he reaches adolescence and acquires a new stepfather who is rather tyrannical. What needs to change?

- A change in the stepfather's understanding and behavior, and possibly the mother's insight into the situation, might alter the relationship with the youth and reduce the friction that increases his anger and acting out.
- A change in the youth's self-esteem and understanding of his problem might increase his resilience and his ability to cope with his stepfather's over-control.
- A change in the youth's peer relationships might reduce the social influence of peers who provide him the opportunity to express his anger in antisocial ways.

In other words, often we can imagine several types of changes that might reach our objective. This should not be viewed as a frustration but rather as a condition to be desired. As in so many cases, there probably is no "right" thing to change in this case. Imagining several things that could profitably change provides us a variety of hypothetical pathways to reduced recidivism and allows us the option of dealing with the situation by multiple interventions rather than selecting among them. It also allows us to have alternatives from which to choose if one or more of the approaches turns out not to be feasible.

Certainly some ways of changing the youth's likelihood of future delinquency will be more feasible than others. To state the options, as we have done in the preceding example, says nothing about whether the services are available to implement such changes. This is addressed later in the section on developing an intervention plan (5-4.0). It also says nothing about resistance that may be encountered by pursuing certain options: for example, whether the parents are amenable to participation in the youth's rehabilitation or whether the youth is more or less likely to respond to any of these options. That is addressed in the section on estimates of the likelihood of successful rehabilitation (5-5.0).

It is important to recognize that some things may be identified for change even when they are not part of the clinician's causal model for a given youth. In addition to preventing further delinquency, the juvenile justice system's mandate includes meeting the basic needs of youths in its custody. Some youths have basic medical and educational needs that should receive attention on humanitarian and legal grounds, regardless of whether they have a direct conceptual link to youths' past or future delinquent behaviors.

Conversely, not all of a youth's needs, deficiencies, or troublesome attitudes need to be changed in order to meet the objectives of the juvenile justice system. For example, when considering whether rehabilitation within the juvenile justice system is likely to "succeed" (whether a youth is "amenable to rehabilitation"—see Chapter 6), it is usually not relevant to raise issues of political ideology or sexual orientation unless they are so closely related to the youth's delinquency that they represent a serious threat of physical harm to the public. Even then the question of "need for change" in these areas is likely to be controversial because of conflicts between our interests in the protection of society and the preservation of individual freedom.

4.0 DESCRIBING A REHABILITATION PLAN: WHAT INTERVENTIONS ARE RELEVANT AND AVAILABLE?

The third element of the rehabilitation evaluation involves *the selection and description of interventions that make sense.* The clinician seeks the best match between available intervention alternatives and those things that have been identified as in need of change, as well as the level of security that is suggested by the risk of harm to others.

4.1 *Available Interventions*

States vary considerably in the types of interventions and placements that are available to the juvenile court. It is very important for the examiner to attain an intimate familiarity with all intervention options available in a state's juvenile justice system as well as their current functions and services.

One way to organize one's thinking about rehabilitation intervention options is to think in terms of (a) *placement options* and (b) *services.*

In general, most states have the following range of *placement options,* which are listed here in order of increasingly restrictive placements (i.e., increasing control and decreasing freedom):

- Placement *at home* with any of a variety of probation and counseling services
- Placement in the community in a *group or foster home* setting, with educational and health services provided by the community
- Placement in *residential treatment programs in the community,* in which counseling and/or mental health services may be provided within the program, which is itself structured but within an open (community-based) facility
- Placement in *residential, nonsecure rehabilitation programs outside the community,* such as forestry camps, ranches, farms, and some "boot camps"
- Placement in a *secure juvenile facility* separated from the community (such facilities may range from large "training schools" to smaller facilities with more intensive and individualized rehabilitation and treatment services)

- *Hospitalization in a psychiatric facility* (typically operated by a state's mental health department rather than its juvenile justice system) or in specialized medical programs such as drug rehabilitation centers

The other way of organizing one's thinking about interventions is by types of *services*:

- *Medical and physical rehabilitation* services (related to special medical and dental problems, vision and hearing problems, and maintenance medical issues concerning such chronic conditions as allergies and respiratory problems)
- *Psychopharmacological* services (involving prescription and clinical maintenance of medication for mental and emotional disorders)
- *Educational* services (including general and special educational programs)
- *Vocational* services (including work skills and specific vocational training)
- *Contingency-based milieu* services (any system that provides incentives, rewards, and disincentives on the basis of target behaviors and progress toward behavioral and attitudinal objectives, within the context of daily activities in the placement setting)
- *Individual and group psychotherapeutic* services (including psychological counseling, more intensive psychotherapy, and psychotherapies focused on special problems such as substance use and sexual offenses)
- *Family therapy* services (ranging from parent counseling to intensive conjoint family therapy involving the parents, youth, and other family members)

In theory, any of these services could be provided in any of the placement options described earlier. This is often not the case, of course, in reality. Some training schools, for example, may be quite limited in the range and types of psychotherapeutic services, vocational services, and even educational services that they provide. Even nonclinical placements, however, should have a way to provide psychopharmacological services and to monitor a youth's medications (e.g., coverage by a visiting psychiatrist and monitoring by a program nurse).

4.2 *Reasoning about Placement and Service Recommendations*

The process of arriving at an intervention recommendation involves selecting the most relevant of these placement and service options. As a clinical matter, the *placement* recommendation often will need to take into consideration (a) the level of security and control that is needed to protect the youth and society based on the clinician's estimate of the future risk of harm and (b) whether certain placements do or do not have particular services that are considered critical for the youth's rehabilitation. In some cases, more restrictive placements are therapeutic in addition to providing necessary security. For example, some youths need to be removed from the chaos of the family and community in order to reduce the pressure of extraordinary interpersonal conflicts. For these youths, the structure and safety of a relatively restrictive setting are sometimes experienced as a relief, providing them a period of time to regroup and stabilize in a social environment that is nonthreatening (relative to their communities), despite its deprivations of freedom.

The *services* that a youth needs will be determined on the basis of the clinician's logic regarding that which needs to change and a process of matching the youth with services that are most likely to be successful in meeting rehabilitation objectives. Where those services are located may then have some influence on the placement that is recommended. For example, a youth with a serious mental disorder may be in need of intensive psychiatric services that can only be provided in facilities operated by the state's mental health system rather than in programs of the juvenile justice system. Similarly, certain types of special education may only be available in a limited number of the state's juvenile justice facilities.

While recent research has demonstrated the value of some types of rehabilitation programs for delinquent youths in general (e.g., Lipsey, 1992; Tate, Reppucci, & Mulvey, 1995), research has not provided much guidance in matching types of youths with types of rehabilitation programs. Generally the clinician must reason about such matters based more on theory and personal knowledge of local programs than on research-validated information. Youths with very limited cognitive and abstract abilities, for example, probably are not the best candidates for a program that employs an insight-oriented psychotherapeutic approach. They are likely to do better in structured, relationship-oriented, and behavior modification programs. Youths of many types may benefit from group therapies, depending on the nature of the groups themselves. Some youths may be in need of groups that improve social communication skills, while others may need groups that seek to exert peer pressure to modify attitudes and behavior. The value of family therapy is well validated, but whether it is recommended might depend on the degree to which the family plays a critical role in producing or maintaining the youth's delinquency, as well as the availability and willingness of parents to participate in therapy.

The considerations involved in recommending particular services, therefore, are quite complex, not formulaic, and often supported more by clinical experience and theory than by research evidence about matching types of youths with types of services.

Whenever possible, the rehabilitation plan presented by the clinician should be framed as a *process* that anticipates special needs that are likely to arise as the rehabilitation progresses. For example, when the plan includes placement in a secure facility separated from the youth's community, the youth will eventually need to be "transitioned" back into the community when sufficient progress has been made in the facility's program. Sometimes the nature of that transition can be anticipated: for example, the probable need for an increased level or type of probation services in light of the fact that the youth had failed during a previous transition process.

Having arrived at a recommendation for services and placement, one must recognize that courts' ultimate decisions about placements sometimes will not conform to the clinician's judgment. Judicial concerns related to broader justice system objectives will sometimes take precedence over clinical recommendations. For example, for certain very serious offenses, some courts will almost invariably require a secure placement that severely restricts the youth's freedom. This decision may be made quite apart from any rehabilitative logic, based simply on a mandate to provide punishment and to ensure a period of maximum incapacitation.

Nevertheless, *the clinician's role is to make recommendations based on a rehabilitative and public safety logic. The degree to which a placement should satisfy society's desire for punishment or retribution is not a clinical question.* It is outside clinicians' domain as mental health experts and should not be factored into their placement recommendations. The court can then do its own calculus in weighing the relative values of rehabilitation and retribution. In some cases involving very serious offenses, some clinicians may be able to anticipate that the court's decision to place the youth in a high security facility is almost a foregone conclusion. When this is the case, clinicians may still recommend other placements if they seem preferable from a rehabilitative perspective. But they should be prepared to describe what services the youth will need if the youth is placed in the more restrictive placement that one anticipates the court will choose.

Finally, the clinician should be prepared to explain not only the rationale for the recommended placement and services but also the reasons why other alternatives were considered less appropriate. It is also wise to have given some thought to "second best" options, in the event that unforeseen circumstances come to light in the course of the disposition hearing that would rule out the clinician's original recommendation.

5.0   DESCRIBING PROBABLE OUTCOMES: WHAT IS THE LIKELIHOOD OF CHANGE?

Finally, the clinician should describe *the likelihood that rehabilitation objectives can be met, given the interventions that have been recommended, the nature of the youth, and the youth's social and legal circumstances.* This element of the evaluation typically is not so critical for disposition hearings, while it is very important for evaluations regarding waiver to criminal court and the youth's "amenability to rehabilitation." For this reason, Chapter 6 (on waiver) describes this fourth element as it applies to waiver evaluations, while brief comments for other rehabilitation evaluations are offered here.

We have no evidence regarding the accuracy of clinicians' estimates about the likelihood that rehabilitation objectives will be met by the placements and services that they recommend in delinquency cases. Moreover, to my knowledge, no systematic ways of making these judgments have been provided in professional literature. A few points can be offered, however, to provide some structure for this judgment.

First, the clinician should have in mind—and be able to provide to the court—some definition for "successful rehabilitation" that is guiding the clinician's opinion. What "successful outcome" does the clinician have in mind when offering the opinion that a rehabilitation is or is not likely to be successful? Several definitions are possible:

- a substantial reduction in the risk of future harm to others
- a substantial reduction in the likelihood that delinquencies will be repeated
- the ability to adapt to normal demands of family/school/ community
- specific changes in personality and clinical characteristics

Whatever the definition, it should be explicit so that the court does not presume some other meaning.

Second, clinicians should be very careful in their descriptions of the likelihood of successful change. Their reports are likely to be read later by staff in juvenile justice programs in which youths are placed. Comments that offer pessimistic estimates of the likelihood of successful rehabilitation can be self-fulfilling if they create an expectation of failure among rehabilitation staff. Reservations about the prospects for change, therefore, should always be coupled with suggestions to staff that might increase the prospects.

Finally, progress in any rehabilitation intervention is sometimes enhanced or decreased by circumstances external to the youth. If one can anticipate strong family support—or the family's interference in the rehabilitation process—this may be important to consider in estimating the prospects for rehabilitation. When one knows that there are going to be potentially stressful events in the near future (e.g., the impending death of a youth's grand-mother who is seriously ill and was a primary caregiver), one can anticipate that this will place added demands on a youth that are likely to detract from, complicate, or prolong the progress of reha-bilitation.

Other external factors include the quality of the programs that will provide the recommended services. Factors such as recent staff turnover or setbacks in funding sometimes warrant an adjust-ment in one's optimism about a course of rehabilitation. Clinicians should be cautious, however, about developing their own rigid stereotypes of programs, which can be avoided by stay-ing in touch periodically with developments in the state's various placement options.

6.0 APPLYING THE FOUR ELEMENTS OF A REHABILITATION EVALUATION

The chapter has outlined four main elements in a rehabilita-tion evaluation:

- A working description of the youth's *history and salient cogni-tive, personality, and clinical characteristics*, including esti-mates of the *risk of harm by the youth*
- Opinions, and their support, that *explain the youth's delin-quency*, providing a focus for rehabilitative intervention
- Opinions, and their support, for a *placement, set of services*, and *rehabilitation process* that focus on changing the factors that are related to the youth's delinquency, while assuring public safety during the rehabilitation process
- An opinion, and its support, regarding the *likelihood that the recommended rehabilitation plan will succeed* in substantially reducing the risk of future offending

Recall that the first section of the chapter identified three legal circumstances in which rehabilitation evaluations are employed. How the four elements will be accomplished will differ somewhat for these various types of evaluations.

Rehabilitation evaluations for *dispositional hearings* are the most frequent request. The amount of information collected in these cases typically varies with the seriousness of the offense or the degree to which probation officers (who also collect information related to dispositional recommendations) are in need of assistance to address the dispositional questions. When the youth has been adjudicated in the past, often there is substantial historical and personality information already available from a previous evaluation.

Evaluations to assess *progress and outcome* of a rehabilitation plan that has already been implemented often do not require as much emphasis on the youth's developmental history, which will already have been documented in many cases. Most of the clinician's history-gathering efforts will focus on obtaining a detailed, chronological account of exactly how various services were provided to the youth since the rehabilitation effort began and the youth's response throughout that period. Recommendations for further interventions typically focus on changes in services in the current placement or a plan for services involved in transitioning the youth from the present placement to a new one (e.g., from a secure facility to placement with family or a community residential program).

The tasks involved in evaluations for hearings on *waiver to criminal court* are similar to those involved in dispositional hearings, except that the final element pertaining to the likelihood of successful rehabilitation takes on a much more critical function. In the evaluation for a disposition hearing, the opinion simply provides the court an indication of the length of intervention and intensity of services that are likely to be needed. In the evaluation for a waiver hearing, however, the clinician's opinion about the prospects of rehabilitation is related to the critical legal question for waiver: Can the youth be rehabilitated in the juvenile justice system, or are the prospects so diminished that the youth should be waived to criminal court for trial? The special nature of rehabilitation opinions and risk of violence opinions in waiver hearings is discussed in Chapter 6.

Chapter 6

Evaluations for Waiver to Criminal Court

Most states allow juvenile court judges to decide that in certain cases they will not try a youth in juvenile court but instead will waive the juvenile court's jurisdiction over the case. "Waiver" by the juvenile court allows the prosecutor to file charges against the youth in criminal court. The case is then processed according to criminal law that applies in the trial and sentencing of adults.

In some states, waiver hearings are required for youths above a certain age when they are alleged to have committed certain serious offenses, while other states allow prosecutors to decide whether they want to petition for a waiver hearing. When the court plans to hold a hearing to decide whether to waive jurisdiction, the court, the prosecutor, or the defense may request a special evaluation by a mental health professional to address certain questions relevant to the waiver criteria.

This chapter describes the purpose, nature, and legal process of waiver, as well as the critical legal questions that are relevant for framing the forensic evaluation for waiver hearings. The two main evaluation questions in waiver have already been discussed in Chapters 4 and 5: risk of harm to others and the likelihood that the youth can be successfully rehabilitated in the juvenile justice system. In this chapter, therefore, we will refer often to what was discussed in Chapters 4 and 5 as those matters apply to waiver evaluations.

Although the term *waiver* is used here to identify the judicial process for sending youths to criminal court for trial, various states use other terms to identify the same process: for example, *bindover* (apparently referring to the process by which a juvenile is "bound over" to criminal court jurisdiction), *fitness* (which refers to a conclusion that the youth is "not a fit and proper subject" for the custody of the juvenile justice system), and *certification* (referring to the court's "certification" of the youth for criminal court trial).

The term *transfer* has historically had the same meaning, but in the present chapter it will refer to a broader class of mechanisms, of which waiver is but one type, by which youths may be sent to criminal court for trial. Whereas waiver identifies a process that requires a *judicial decision* to waive jurisdiction, there are other legal mechanisms that send juvenile cases to criminal court "automatically" on the basis of certain objective criteria that do not involve a waiver hearing, a waiver evaluation, or a judicial decision. We will examine these additional transfer options in the next section.

1.0   THE CONCEPT AND PURPOSE OF WAIVER

Waiver has been a legal option for juvenile courts since their beginning early in the twentieth century. As described in Chapter 1, the juvenile court was developed on the presumption that adolescence was a developmental stage during which delinquent youths could be reformed. Thus they were not to be held accountable for their offenses in the manner prescribed by law for adults. The objective of the juvenile court would be rehabilitation, not simply punishment and retribution. Yet it was recognized that some youths might not be *amenable to rehabilitation* because, despite their young age, they might already be "mature" in the criminally sophisticated sense. Early juvenile law allowed juvenile court judges the discretion to waive jurisdiction over cases that they considered "unfit," or a bad match, for the rehabilitative objectives and services of the juvenile justice system. Those youths were sent to criminal court for trial and, if found guilty, for sentencing as an adult.

Almost all states allow waiver for certain types of cases based on a juvenile court judge's decision—that is, *judicial waiver*. Recent national trends in juvenile law, however, have resulted in two other ways in which youths may be sent to criminal court for trial. More than half of the states now provide for transfer by *statutory exclusion*. In these states, cases involving youths above a certain age (often 13 or 14) who are charged with very serious offenses (often murder and other major assaultive offenses) are automatically outside the jurisdiction of the juvenile court. The charge is originally filed in criminal court without the need for a juvenile court's decision on the matter. The other transfer mechanism that has been adopted recently by some states is called *prosecutor direct file*. This gives prosecutors the discretion to file charges against youths in juvenile or in criminal court for certain types of offenses. According to data provided by Torbet et al. (1996) for the Office of Juvenile Justice and Delinquency Prevention

- all but three states provide for judicial waiver by juvenile courts
- about three-quarters of the states have statutory exclusion for the most serious offenses, in addition to allowing judicial waiver for a broader range of offenses
- about 20% of the states allow prosecutor direct file
- five states allow all three types of transfer: judicial waiver, statutory exclusion, and prosecutor direct file

The ages and offenses specified in state statutes for statutory exclusion and prosecutor direct file vary considerable from one state to another (for state-by-state descriptions of transfer statutes, see Heilbrun et al., 1997; Torbet et al., 1996). Where multiple mechanisms are provided for transferring youths to criminal court, typically the nonwaiver mechanisms are restricted to more serious offenses, while waiver is allowed for a wider range of offenses.

In some states, criminal courts receiving transferred youths by statutory exclusion or prosecutor direct file have the option to transfer them to juvenile court. This process, sometimes called "reverse transfer" or "decertification," requires a pretrial hearing in criminal court that is somewhat like a waiver hearing. It allows the criminal court judge to waive jurisdiction and remand to juvenile court a youth who is considered immature and more appropriately handled in the juvenile justice system.

Waiver to criminal court requires that judges determine on a case-by-case basis whether youths meet certain legal standards that control the waiver decision. Those legal standards refer to a variety of characteristics of the youth that may have implications for public safety and the youth's rehabilitation. Therefore, judges traditionally have looked to mental health professionals to supply critical information that they need in order to weigh the arguments for or against the youth's waiver. Before examining the relevant legal standards (in 6-2.0 below), it is worthwhile to reflect on various purposes that transfer or waiver traditionally have been expected to serve in the juvenile justice system.

First, transfer has been considered important for the *welfare of other delinquent youths* in the juvenile justice system. Programs designed for the rehabilitation of the average delinquent adolescent might be less effective in managing the minority of youths who are more sophisticated and "hardened" in crime. Therefore, their presence in juvenile rehabilitation programs could be disruptive, thereby decreasing program effectiveness for the majority of youths. Youths who are antisocial in "adult-like" ways might also threaten the safety of more immature delinquent youths in juvenile correctional facilities.

Second, transfer has been seen as an important mechanism for serving interests in *public safety*. All states have an upper age limit of juvenile court jurisdiction (usually the 16th, 17th, or 18th birthday), after which the juvenile justice system must relinquish its custody and supervision of the juvenile. Very high-risk youths who have not been rehabilitated by that time might present a significant danger to others when they return to the community without supervision. Therefore, early in the processing of a delinquency case, the juvenile courts must be concerned about certain youths who have a very poor prospect of responding to the system's rehabilitative programs if they are tried in juvenile court and committed to the custody of the juvenile system. This concern is even greater for youths who are already near the upper jurisdictional age at the time that their cases are heard; the time remaining for juvenile court custody may be too short to expect any meaningful rehabilitative changes. Transfer, therefore, has served the purpose of reducing these risks to society.

Finally, transfer often has been supported by policy that promotes *punishment* for juvenile offenders. Especially in the present decade, many lawmakers have come to believe that adolescents who committed serious violent offenses need to experience tougher consequences for their crimes. Serious youthful offenders—especially those with repeated convictions for violent offenses—were not considered deserving of a juvenile justice system based on a rehabilitative objective or of sentencing practices that allowed them to avoid the punitive consequences that adults would face for the same crimes. These same beliefs have led to serious proposals for abolishing altogether a special system of justice for juveniles. While this extreme reform has not gained significant support, transfer to criminal court for increasing numbers of youths has come to serve similar purposes.

From the forensic examiner's perspective, the first two purposes described previously raise evaluation questions about a youth's potential for future harm to other youths or to the public, and the prospects for a youth's rehabilitation. These are matters about which a mental health professional might be able to form professional opinions. In contrast, the third purpose raises a question further removed from the clinical realm: whether the youth deserves to be punished like an adult. That question lingers, at least covertly, in almost all waiver hearings involving very serious violent offenses. Nevertheless, as will be shown in the next section, the waiver standards of most states do not instruct judges to waive juveniles based on a judgment that they "deserve" harsher punishment. Neither should clinicians approach their evaluations with this purpose in mind.

2.0   FROM LEGAL STANDARDS
TO EVALUATION OBJECTIVES

The waiver process always requires a hearing at which facts are entered into evidence bearing on the legal standards that must be met for the court to waive jurisdiction. The legal standards for waiver vary somewhat from one state to another, but most of them follow a consistent structure. They include (a) a set of threshold fact conditions that must be met and (b) another set of standards that requires judicial discretion to determine whether they have been met. Often the threshold facts state that the youth must be of a certain *age*, be charged with a certain *level of offense*, and/or have a specific *history of prior offenses* (e.g., has a prior juvenile conviction that resulted in a commitment to the state's youth commission). *Probable cause* to believe that the youth might have committed the alleged offense also is frequently required. When prosecutors petition the court for waiver, these are the facts that they must first establish.

Once these threshold facts have been acknowledged, the proceeding focuses on one or more legal standards pertaining to other characteristics of the youth. These legal standards arose in modern law in the U.S. Supreme Court case of *Kent v. United States* (1966) (6-2.1). This caused most states to develop statutory definitions that identified two main legal standards (6-2.2): the "danger" standard and the "amenability to rehabilitation" standard.

2.1 *Kent v. U.S.*

Standards for transfer were exceptionally vague prior to the 1960s, and judges were given wide discretionary latitude in deciding which youths to waive to criminal court. Then in *Kent v. U.S.* (1966), the U.S. Supreme Court addressed the constitutional rights of youths in juvenile court hearings on waiver to criminal court. The Court determined that youths in waiver hearings have the right to be represented by legal counsel, to avoid self-incrimination, and to confront and cross-examine opposing witnesses. The Court also recommended (but did not require) the use of a set of factors that judges could consider when weighing the issue of waiver. The following is a paraphrase of those factors:

- Seriousness of the offense charged, as related to community protection
- Whether the offense was committed in a violent, premeditated, or willful manner
- Whether the offense was against persons
- Prosecutive merit of the case
- Desirability of trial in criminal court because case involves adult associates
- Sophistication and maturity of the youth
- Previous history of the youth
- Prospects for (a) adequate protection of the public and (b) likelihood of reasonable rehabilitation "by procedures, services, and facilities currently available to the juvenile court"

The list is provided here for historical reasons. Some states adopted the list, including it in their statutes in the form that the Court provided. Nevertheless, *I do not recommend the Kent list as a guide for clinicians' waiver evaluations or as an outline for waiver evaluation reports.* Some of the *Kent* factors pertain simply to legal and administrative issues that are unrelated to clinical or psychological concepts (e.g., prosecutive merit of the case, desirability of trial with adult cohorts). Others (such as seriousness of alleged offense and the manner in which it was committed) are simply a few factors among many that clinicians would take into account in addressing other factors in the list (e.g., "adequate protection of the public") that are superordinate.

The "sophistication and maturity" factor has appeared in many states' waiver standards. Apparently these terms referred to "sophistication in crime" and to having a criminal attitude and pattern of behavior that had "matured" to an extent that offered discouraging prospects for rehabilitation. As such, they bear little relationship to the more general concept of "maturity" as it is used in developmental psychology.

The last factor in the *Kent* list had the greatest impact on states' waiver standards. Within a few years after *Kent v. U.S.*, almost all states had legislated the "danger" (or "protection") standard and the "amenability to rehabilitation" standard to which the Supreme Court had referred at the end of its list. Most states required that both standards be applied. Even in states in which one or the other was formally adopted, most courts interpreted waiver to require an inquiry into both issues. These are the real focus points in waiver evaluations.

2.2 *Danger to Others and Amenability to Rehabilitation*

The *"Danger" standard* requires that youths cannot be waived to criminal court unless they present a serious risk of harm to others. Most states' statutes do not define the standard beyond a brief phrase that identifies it, such as "protection of the community," "danger to public," or "public safety." Sometimes statutes will include modifiers to indicate the degree of danger that must exist (e.g., "significant," "substantial," or "imminent") although precisely what these terms mean in any given case is left to clinical judgment and judicial discretion.

The judge's task in addressing this standard is a good deal more complex than the various "danger" phrases imply. For example, courts often must consider the prospects of harm to others in a variety of possible contexts. At one time or another, judges in waiver cases have asked for my opinion about youths' potential harm to others in the following ways:

- "Are other youths in our juvenile facilities, or the staff in these facilities, going to be safe with this youth there?"
- "What is the danger to the public if this young man runs from a juvenile facility? And what's the likelihood that he'll try to escape?"
- "Is this the kind of youth who is going to continue to terrorize the community when he becomes an adult?"

In other words, there is no single "danger" question, but many that are related to different places and times in the future. The forensic examiner who is truly helpful to the court will try to address them, not to merely characterize the youth as "dangerous" or "not dangerous." Later we will identify those questions more specifically, as well as their meaning for evaluations.

The *"Amenability" standard* also appears in various forms in different states, including such phrases as "not amenable to reha-bilitation" or "is not a fit and proper subject" for juvenile custody. Notice that the *Kent v. U.S.* reference to this standard qualifies the preceding phrase, referring specifically to the potential for rehabilitation within the resources "available to the juvenile court." Most states have retained similar wording.

The Amenability standard, therefore, does not ask whether the youth's condition is modifiable *in general*. It asks whether it is reasonable to expect *the state's system of rehabilitation for delinquent youths* to be able to bring about necessary change with this partic-ular youth. This requires a consideration of

- The *characteristics of the youth* and the youth's social circum-stances,
- The *state's rehabilitation methods* (including those that reasonably may be purchased elsewhere if they do not exist within the state), and

- the *time available* to the juvenile system to try to accomplish the rehabilitative goal.

Note that the question about rehabilitation as it relates to waiver does not ask whether the youth can be dealt with more appropriately in the criminal justice system. The statutes of most states do not instruct judges to determine whether the youth is more suited to programs designed for adult offenders or whether the youth is more likely to be deterred from future offending by criminal court sanctions. Similarly, the clinician is not asked to compare the juvenile and criminal systems as alternatives but rather to determine the degree to which the juvenile justice system is likely to achieve rehabilitative objectives.

Exactly what rehabilitative goal is involved in the decision about amenability usually is not specified by statute or case law. It is reasonable to presume that the juvenile justice system's purpose for rehabilitation of delinquent youths is not focused generally on augmenting the psychological well-being of the youth. While this may be a desirable, intended, and sometimes achievable goal of rehabilitation, the ultimate purpose for rehabilitation in the juvenile justice system is best seen as twofold:

- To reduce the future risk of harm to the public posed by the youth, and
- To reduce the likelihood of an adult criminal career.

The "Danger" and "Amenability" standards, therefore, are closely related. *Current* risk of violence may influence the course of rehabilitation. It can potentially increase or decrease the likelihood of its success and sometimes will dictate where and how a rehabilitation plan can be implemented. In turn, estimates of *longer-range* future risk of harm to others must include a judgment about the likelihood that rehabilitation will reduce the risk. Therefore, both standards exist because of a concern for risk of harm to the public; judgments about one of them are often related to judgments about the other.

2.3 *Factors to be Weighed*

Statutes do not instruct judges concerning the specific facts that will justify a decision to waive jurisdiction on the basis of

Danger and Amenability standards. No particular fact or set of facts is dispositive of the waiver decision. Statutes simply require judges to take into consideration any information that might be relevant for judging the degree of danger and rehabilitation potential and to explain how they arrived at their opinions about waiver (i.e., their opinions about Danger and Amenability) on the basis of those facts.

Some statutes provide a list of factors (e.g., the *Kent* factors) that the court must consider. Others describe broad classes of data that the judge should obtain. For example, Massachusetts for many years required judges to consider

> "the nature, circumstances, and seriousness of the alleged offense; the child's court and delinquency record; the child's age and maturity; the family, school and social history of the child; the success or lack of success of any past treatment efforts of the child; the nature of services available through the juvenile justice system." (M.G.L. ch. 119, s.61a, 1995)

Most statutes that provide these lists indicate that they are not meant to be exclusive. Courts are free to consider any other information that they believe is relevant to the Danger and Amenability questions. Examiners should also be aware that some judges have developed their own lists of factors that they consider in waiver cases. When these are provided to the examiner, the report of the waiver evaluation should include information related to these factors as well as the ones that are specified in statutes. It is worth mentioning that statutes do not prohibit clinicians from including in their evaluations and reports various types of information or factors that go beyond those that are mentioned in statutes and by judges. Other factors may be used when the clinician believes that they are relevant to the Danger and Amenability questions.

2.4 *Evaluating Danger and Amenability*

Addressing the Danger standard in waiver evaluations requires using the same concepts, data collection guidelines, and clinical logic that were described in Chapter 4 for assessing the risk of future violence. Similarly, addressing the Amenability standard requires the same evaluation process that was described in Chapter 5 for rehabilitation evaluations. Therefore, the nature of these essential evaluation methods need not be repeated in this chapter. The following sections focus primarily on the performance of these two types of evaluations in light of special demands of waiver hearings.

3.0 THE LEGAL CONTEXT FOR WAIVER EVALUATIONS

There are several legal circumstances surrounding waiver hearings that have important implications for waiver evaluations. Clinicians should be aware of these circumstances so that they can adjust their evaluation procedures accordingly.

3.1 *Intensity and Demands of the Legal Process*

From the perspective of youths and youth advocates, waiver hearings are among the most significant events in juvenile courts because of the serious potential consequences of such hearings. At the very least, waiver to criminal court means that a youth's case will become public (in contrast to the confidentiality of most juvenile court proceedings) and that conviction will be on the youth's criminal record. At worst, waiver may result in criminal court conviction and sentencing that includes very long periods of incarceration or the death penalty. The youth also is in danger of losing the rehabilitative benefits that might have been available had the case remained in juvenile court.

The "real" significance of waiver has been debated considerably in the research literature. In some states, youths whose offenses are of only moderate seriousness may actually receive less punitive sentences in criminal court than in juvenile court. This can happen because, in many states, the amount of time in custody in the juvenile system is not particularly related to the seriousness of one's offense. Therefore, much more time may be spent in custody in the juvenile system for minor offenses that would not result in lengthy sentences in the criminal justice system. In addition, as first-time and "under-aged" offenders, youths have sometimes been treated leniently by criminal court judges or juries. For the most serious offenses, however, there is little doubt that youths typically are in jeopardy of receiving far more severe sentences in criminal court than in juvenile court.

The potentially severe outcome of waiver suggests that the proceedings require the highest standard of practice on the part of attorneys, judges, and mental health examiners. In some states this is widely recognized. For example, juvenile court waiver hearings in Massachusetts for youths charged with very serious offenses often have taken several months to accomplish, with attorneys logging as many contact hours with youths as would be typical for important criminal trials, and the waiver hearings themselves lasting several days. In one waiver hearing for a youth charged with murder, 3 full days were required for direct and cross-examination of my testimony alone, as well as 2 days of testimony from other examiners. The experts' evaluations themselves were as comprehensive and meticulous as one would expect for a proceeding with this magnitude of preparation by all parties.

Yet there appears to be great variation across states in the quality and nature of waiver hearings. In many states, the waiver hearing is a more modest procedure, while still being well argued and complete. At the opposite extreme, I am told that in some states, attorneys have their first contacts with youths they are representing in the moments just before the waiver hearing, which itself may take only 10 to 20 minutes (including the mental health examiner's testimony).

3.2 *The Right to Avoid Self-Incrimination*

Waiver hearings and waiver evaluations are, of course, pretrial events. Juvenile defendants have the right to avoid making self-incriminating statements. In most states, even if the youth does admit to the offense in a waiver proceeding or evaluation, the statement cannot be used as evidence when the case comes to trial (in juvenile or in criminal court) except in extraordinary and specific legal circumstances (described below). In some cases it may actually be to the youth's advantage—from a defense perspective—to discuss the offense openly with the clinician performing the waiver evaluation. This might be so, for example, if the way the offense occurred or the youth's motivations at the time of the offense provide information that could be interpreted to diminish the seriousness of future risk of harm or to augment the likelihood for successful rehabilitation. It is not uncommon, therefore, for defense attorneys to advise youthful defendants to be open with waiver examiners about the alleged offense.

In other cases, however, defense attorneys may advise youths to say nothing about the offense. They may believe that information the youth would offer about the event could increase the likelihood of waiver. Or they may believe that even though the youth's statements are protected from use at a later trial, they could provide a background and context for prosecutors' investigations in their later preparation for a trial. Moreover, in many jurisdictions there *are* certain conditions under which prosecutors might be able to enter in evidence at a later trial certain statements made by the youth at the waiver hearing. This could happen if the defendant says something at trial (or a clinician reports a statement by the youth) that is contrary to something that the defendant said in the waiver hearing. Prosecutors may then try to enter the conflicting waiver statement into evidence in an effort to impeach the defendant's current testimony. Finally, in some states juvenile waiver hearings in cases involving murder or other serious crimes are open to the public and press. This raises the possibility that prospective jurors at a later trial may have been exposed to a defendant's self-incriminating statements made in the waiver hearing as reported by the clinician who performed the waiver evaluation, even if the information is inadmissible as evidence at the trial itself.

Some defense attorneys, therefore, advise youths not to talk about the alleged offense during the waiver evaluation. In addition, some states have laws that routinely prohibit examiners from asking youths questions about the offense when performing an evaluation for a waiver hearing. Even when laws are silent on the matter, some judges themselves will order clinicians to refrain from inquiry about the offense. In some cases, therefore, the examiner will be asked to form opinions about risk of future harm to others and the youth's amenability to rehabilitation without the benefit of having talked to the youth about the alleged offense. We will discuss the implications of this in 6-4.1.

3.3 *Implications of Lengthy Waiver Procedures*

The waiver hearing constitutes an additional event between arrest and trial that is not present in most delinquency cases. Sometimes that event—from the time that a waiver hearing is requested until it is completed—can delay the overall legal process by several months. (It has been known in some cases to add a year or more to the pretrial process.) The delay typically is produced by attorney preparations and motions, mental health professionals' evaluations, and a crowded juvenile court docket that is further strained whenever any cases require more than the ordinary pretrial processing.

In cases involving major crimes, youths typically are being held during the pretrial period in a secure detention facility. Lengthy waiver proceedings mean a longer time in detention prior to trial, and this can have several implications for examiners and their evaluations. For example, sometimes the delay produces a very long period of time between the examiner's evaluation and the waiver hearing at which the evaluation will be presented. In the interim, events in the youth's life and in the detention facility's program may have produced changes in the youth's condition that would make a difference in the examiner's opinions about risk of harm and amenability to rehabilitation. These changes may be improvements, as when a youth manifests a very positive response and substantial gains in the detention center's educational program, or they may represent deterioration in the form of disruptive and threatening behavior. In either case, they are data that the clinician should have prior to the waiver hearing.

When there is a delay of more than 2 or 3 months between the waiver evaluation and the hearing, the clinician should schedule a "checkup" interview with the youth and detention staff to determine whether any important changes have occurred. Even when the delay is shorter, a telephone inquiry to detention staff is recommended just prior to the waiver hearing.

3.4 *Malingering and Dissimulation*

The prospects and consequences of waiver to criminal court provide motivation for some youths to attempt to deceive the clinician with regard to conditions that the youth believes might be important for avoiding waiver. In later sections we will discuss how this might influence youths to deny their involvement in the alleged offense. In addition, although it is relatively infrequent, some youths try to influence the clinician's perceptions of their clinical status in ways that they hope will reduce the likelihood of waiver.

This can take two forms. First, some youths may believe that they are less likely to be waived to criminal court if they are perceived as seriously mentally ill and therefore in need of clinical treatment rather than punishment. Similarly, they may believe that they will be perceived as less responsible for their alleged offense if their involvement in the offense was in part due to mental disorder and that this might have a "positive" effect on a judge's discretionary decision about waiver. Thus they may try to feign symptoms of mental disorder or exaggerate symptoms that they actually experience.

Second, some youths may believe that they are less likely to be waived to criminal court if they *do not* appear to be mentally ill. If they understand that part of the issue of waiver is whether the youth "is amenable to rehabilitation," they may believe that they will appear more responsive to rehabilitation if they present a picture of themselves that suggests "normalcy" or "mental health." This can motivate some youths to dissimulate, that is, to hide their emotional or social conflicts and suppress their reporting of negative affect.

McCann (1998) has extensively reviewed the various definitions and theories for malingering and deception in adolescents, as well as interview strategies and structured methods for identifying when adolescents might be feigning or suppressing symptoms of mental disorder. The *Minnesota Multiphasic Personality Inventory-Adolescents* (Butcher et al., 1992) and the *Millon Adolescent Clinical Inventory* (Millon, 1993) have special indicators that can alert the clinician to the possibility of symptom exaggeration or suppression. In addition, Rogers, Bagby, and Dickens (1992) have developed the *Structured Interview of Reported Symptoms* (SIRS), an interview schedule that provides scores to represent many "signs" suggesting an increased probability of malingering. The SIRS has shown promise in identifying malingering among 14- to 17-year-olds (Rogers, Hinds, & Sewell, 1996).

4.0 SPECIAL ISSUES IN WAIVER ASSESSMENTS OF RISK OF HARM TO OTHERS

The process of collecting data and making inferences about youths' risk of future violence was described in Chapter 4. We discussed the fact that several estimates of risk might be necessary, related to various contexts: the risk if the youth were in the community without interventions, risk during rehabilitation if the youth were to receive services of the juvenile justice system, and the likelihood that the youth would present a danger to others in adulthood. Any of these questions might be asked in waiver hearings, and the data collection and inferential process for the clinician in waiver cases is much as it was described in Chapter 4. Certain circumstances of waiver hearings, however, raise special difficulties in implementing those procedures when judging risk of future violence.

4.1 *The Dilemma of the Alleged Offense*

In Chapter 4 we noted that one important factor to explore in making estimates of risk of future violence is the circumstances of the offenses that a youth has committed. The degree to which past behavior predicts future behavior often depends on how, with whom, and for what reasons the past behavior occurred. In many forensic evaluations of juveniles charged with violent offenses, the examiner will discuss with the youth the specific events leading up to the latest offense and explore the youth's motivations and intentions. The examiner will also try to discover the social context in which the offense occurred, what impact that might have had on the youth's actions, and how the youth now feels about the offense and his or her responsibility for it.

In waiver evaluations, however, this information sometimes is not available. This can happen for several reasons, all of which are consequences of the fact that waiver evaluations and hearings are pretrial events.

One reason was discussed earlier in 6-3.2. Defense attorneys and courts sometimes insist that examiners may not talk to the youth about the alleged offense because the youth's statements might produce incriminating information that could influence a later trial. Some defense attorneys are also concerned that if youths are instructed to talk to examiners about the offense, the youth might admit to certain facts or motivations that are actually not true. This can happen if the youth is frightened and wishes to provide any type of information that might tend to "satisfy" the questioner.

In other cases, information about the alleged offense might not be available from the youth because the youth denies having done the offense. At the pretrial stage, a youth may deny the offense for many reasons (Barnum, 1990). For example

- The youth actually did not commit the offense
- Although there is substantial evidence that the youth committed the offense, the youth is psychologically defended against accepting the fact (e.g., due to psychological denial, repression, or cognitive distortion)
- The youth recognizes having committed the offense but denies it in order to avoid the embarrassment or shame of admitting it
- The youth believes that the act, although committed, does not constitute an offense (e.g., a claim of self-defense)
- The youth is fully aware of having committed the offense but wishes to avoid conviction

Even if youths do talk about the offense at the waiver evaluation, examiners must recognize that the information might contain self-serving inaccuracies or distortions that would be less likely to occur if the youth were being interviewed after having been found guilty of the offense.

When judges weigh the question of risk of future violence in waiver cases, they typically must base their answer in part on a *presumption* that the youth committed the offense. For purposes of the waiver hearing, the judge is not asked to determine whether the youth is guilty. Yet judges cannot ignore the implications for future risk of harm if it were true that the youth did engage in the offense. Therefore, in my experience, I most often hear judges framing the question this way: "Let's presume he did it. What does that say, if anything, about his dangerousness in the future?"

How can clinicians weigh the significance of a violent offense for the prospect of future violence when they cannot learn from the youth whether the offense occurred or, if it did, how it occurred, in what social circumstances, and with what thoughts and motivations? I have discussed this dilemma with other examiners and attorneys, who have raised a few suggestions.

First, in some cases the alleged offense is one that the youth has engaged in repeatedly in the past. Moreover, sometimes information is available on how the youth committed those offenses in the past, with what motivations and states of mind, and in what circumstances. When this is so, one strategy is to use this information to make inferences about how the present alleged offense might have occurred. Clinicians should clearly state the limits on their confidence in inferences based on this method, depending on the specifics of the case in question.

Second, in some cases relatives or friends might be able to describe characteristics of the youth on the day of the alleged offense, such as emotional states, intoxication, or behavior suggesting mental disorder. These observations certainly do not allow one to infer that the youth engaged in the offense. If the youth's guilt is raised as a hypothetical presumption at the waiver hearing, however, the examiner might sometimes be able to use the preceding type of information to make inferences about the conditions under which the youth might (hypothetically) have committed the offense.

Finally, in some cases there are witnesses to the alleged offense who can describe the behavior, circumstances, verbalizations, and emotions of the perpetrator (even if they cannot identify who committed the offense). Sometimes physical evidence at the scene of the crime suggests certain motives and degrees of planfulness. Observations of these types can sometimes be used to make inferences about the state of mind, motivations, or intentions of the perpetrator at the time of the offense.

Having made these suggestions, I must acknowledge that the inferential road from these observations to one's testimony is fraught with hazards. I have occasionally used these strategies, but in every instance I have found it necessary to inform the court that my level of confidence in the conclusions was not great. I suggest that the clinician use the following set of "rules" to communicate the limits of testimony based on these indirect lines of reasoning:

- The inferences usually offer interpretations that are merely *possible*; they only reach a higher level of certainty in unusual cases.
- In most cases, *different reasonable conclusions could be reached with the same data.*
- If the youth actually committed the offense, and *were the youth to tell me* about thoughts and feelings at the time, how it happened, and under what circumstances, it is possible that *I might reach different opinions* about the significance of the offense for estimating risk of future violence.
- Estimates of the youth's risk of future violence typically *should rely more heavily on factors with known validity* (e.g., history, past behavior, personality, etc.) than on inferences about the alleged offense.

4.2 *The Dilemma of Long-Range* *Estimates of Risk of Violence*

For a few years, Massachusetts had an unusual law pertaining to youths who were found guilty of murder in juvenile court. Juvenile courts were required to give youths 20-year sentences for first-degree murder, to be served in the juvenile justice system until they reached 18, with the rest of the time to be served in adult correctional facilities. I once testified in a waiver hearing in which the youth, charged with murder, faced this penalty if tried and convicted in the juvenile justice system and faced probable life without parole if waived and found guilty in criminal court. In the hearing, the judge posed the following question: "Doctor, tell me this, if this young man is tried in juvenile court and given the mandatory 20 years—he's 15 now, so he'd be about 35 when he re-enters the community—would he be a danger to society when he gets out?"

I think that the judge did not really believe that I could answer this question. Indeed, I suspect that she recognized the impossibility of any meaningful answer. Given the legal context, however, the question had to be asked. The judge was required to determine the likely risk to society if the juvenile were to be tried in juvenile court and given a disposition reserved for juveniles, and that is exactly what the inquiry was about. What rendered the question unanswerable was the legislature's decision to require that juvenile courts give sentences that punished youths until they were nearly middle-aged.

In fact, I found an answer, and the judge found it intriguing. I said that I could not make such a prediction for this youth specifically. Crime statistics, however, have shown that even men with extensive criminal careers (including violent crimes) have a much reduced likelihood to continue violent offending after about age 30.

Although this situation was unusual, the request to make other types of long-range risk estimates in waiver hearings is not. In fact, it is required in almost every waiver hearing. The court must determine whether juvenile justice interventions are likely to reduce the risk of violence by the time that the court must relinquish its custody of the youth, which often will be several years in the future.

All clinicians are aware that longer-range predictions of any behavior are more subject to error than shorter-range predictions. This is partly because there are so many possible intervening variables during the extended time period that might influence an increase or decrease in risk but which cannot be anticipated. When urged to provide an estimate, the only strategy of which I am aware is

- To develop a complete inquiry into a youth's current level of risk,
- Presume that the youth would receive the rehabilitation services that you are recommending if the youth were to remain in the juvenile justice system, and
- Take into account whatever other events can be anticipated between now and the more distant time for which an estimate is desired.

In large part, therefore, a long-range estimate of risk of violence in a waiver hearing is closely tied to one's expectancies about the degree to which the rehabilitation plan will be successful or unsuccessful in achieving its objectives. The factors used in forming one's opinion about likelihood of rehabilitation (see 6-5.0 below) must be clearly identified to the court as well, because the degree of confidence the court can have in the future risk estimate depends on those factors' strengths and limitations. Overall, long-range estimates of risk can be made with substantial confidence in only a minority of cases and with modest confidence at best in most cases. They should not be attempted at all in cases that allow for no more than mere speculation.

5.0 SPECIAL ISSUES IN WAIVER ASSESSMENTS OF AMENABILITY TO REHABILITATION

Chapter 5 described the fourth (final) element of rehabilitation evaluations as a statement about the likelihood that the recommended rehabilitation plan would be successful. This element also was noted as being especially important in waiver evaluations because it directly addresses the question of amenability to rehabilitation, a primary legal question for waiver proceedings.

Therefore, the clinician's process for estimating the likelihood of rehabilitation success in waiver hearings needs to be described in greater detail than was provided in Chapter 5. The following discussion offers some structure for the task but no formula for arriving at one's conclusion. We will consider the following definitions and factors: *defining rehabilitation* (5.1), *defining time limitations* (5.2), general *characteristics of youths* that are relevant for judging responsiveness to intervention (5.3), and factors related to the *community and the juvenile justice system's services* (5.4).

5.1 *Defining the Rehabilitation Objective*

In waiver hearings, the court will want to know whether the rehabilitation plan that the clinician has outlined is likely to be successful. To provide a meaningful opinion, the clinician must have a working definition of "successful rehabilitation." We noted in Chapter 5 that various definitions are possible. The important point is that the clinician should have one that is carefully considered and easily communicated.

The definition that I have found most useful is to consider rehabilitative efforts "successful" when they produce a *substantial reduction in the likelihood of recidivism or of serious harm to others in the future* (i.e., during the remainder of adolescence and early adulthood). This definition is consistent with the primary objective of the juvenile justice system. In the future, whether the goal has been achieved can be assessed by evaluating the degree of progress within the various components of this particular youth's rehabilitation plan.

5.2 *Defining Time Limitations*

In waiver cases, the court will be concerned about the likelihood of successful rehabilitation within the time that the juvenile court can have jurisdiction over the youth. The maximum jurisdictional age for youth authority custody is different in various states, ranging from 15 to 18 for general purposes. It extends up to 21 or 25 in some states, however, in special circumstances that allow for extension of jurisdiction or that provide by law for special sentences in cases involving serious violent offenses. In any case, whenever that age is attained, the court will be required to release the youth to the community while discontinuing probation assistance and all other juvenile justice services.

When youths are only a year or two away from the maximum jurisdictional age at the time of a waiver hearing, this may be one of the most important concerns of the court in determining whether the youth should be waived to criminal court. This can be especially problematic when the rehabilitation plan includes services in a secure placement. In those cases, the clinician's estimate of the likelihood of success within the available time must usually allow for a period of 3 to 6 months to "transition" the youth from the facility to the community. If the youth in the waiver hearing is only a year or so away from the maximum age, this leaves very little time for services in a future secure facility to have a positive effect.

These circumstances can produce frustrating "bottom-line" opinions in cases involving older adolescents. Clinicians sometimes will find it necessary to testify that the youth *could* be successfully rehabilitated with the services described but that the limited time remaining for the system to provide the services makes success unlikely.

5.3   *Youth Characteristics Relevant for Judging Responsiveness to Intervention*

When formulating a recommendation, the clinician has selected placements and services that seem most likely to fit with the character and needs of the youth in question. To say that one has achieved the best logical fit, however, is not necessarily a statement about one's expectations for successful rehabilitation. The best may not be good enough. The clinician's degree of optimism that the plan will succeed may be high, moderate, low, or uncertain, depending in part on certain characteristics of the youth or the youth's history and social circumstances. (This depends also on the anticipated quality of services that the youth will be provided, which is discussed in 6-5.4).

Individual characteristics of youths associated with more or less successful treatment will vary depending on the type of intervention. That source of variation will already have been taken into account when the clinician selected particular services as more or less appropriate for the youth in question. In addition, there are some characteristics of individuals associated with better or poorer prognosis for rehabilitation that can be said to apply generally across types of interventions. The first two of these three characteristics to be discussed below will be familiar to clinicians as features of individuals who have psychopathic personality structures or who are diagnosed as Narcissistic Personality Disorder in clinical contexts. *When these diagnoses or their implications are mentioned in following discussions, they should not be confused with the diagnosis of Conduct Disorder.* Empirically, only a minority of youths with Conduct Disorder manifest the characteristics described below. Moreover, only a minority of them develop Psychopathy (as defined by Hare, 1991) or Narcissistic and Antisocial Personality Disorders (as defined in *DSM-IV*) in adulthood. (See 1-4.3.)

5.31   Discomfort

Psychological change is motivated by a person's psychological discomfort. Typically, change is more likely to occur when individuals experience discomfort and dissatisfaction regarding their relations with others. The discomfort itself may be experienced and labeled in many ways that involve negative affect (e.g., anger, fear, anxiety, low self-esteem, or unhappiness). Any of these types of discomfort may themselves be conditions that are troublesome and have been part of the reason for others' concerns about the youth. Although they are often considered undesirable and the source of much of the youth's misbehavior, they can also produce the tension that is needed to promote change. *Their presence, therefore, should not necessarily be construed as reducing the likelihood of successful rehabilitation.* In fact, they frequently offer a source of dissatisfaction that can be used to mobilize change in behavior that will result in amelioration of the discomfort.

In contrast, some youths experience little enduring discomfort. Or they only experience discomfort that arises not from psychological or interpersonal conflicts but from what they perceive as the world's failure to satisfy their own impulses and self-interests. This narcissistic discomfort, rooted in a desire to gain personal satisfaction without concern about the consequences for others, often leads to manipulative behaviors that undermine therapeutic interventions, in that such youths seek to circumvent the personal changes that the intervention strives to promote. This is not to say that change is impossible with all youths manifesting this characteristic. But it is rendered more difficult, requiring a specialized, intensive, and lengthy process that makes success much more questionable.

In their judgments about a youth's likely response to rehabilitation efforts, courts attend closely to the degree to which a youth's discomfort about the offense indicates a sense of *remorse.* Judges often presume that rehabilitation is unlikely to be successful unless the youth acknowledges wrongdoing ("takes responsibility" for the offense) and feels sufficiently guilty about the offense to experience psychological discomfort.

Although a good argument can be made for this assertion, it is not easily translated in a way that can make "remorsefulness" a reliable factor for predicting a youth's response to rehabilitation. For example, youths with narcissistic and psychopathic tendencies often are quite capable of appearing to be remorseful, showing all the outward signs of guilt and repentance for the offense without actually experiencing any of the underlying feelings that would motivate change. In contrast, youths whose behavior does not suggest any remorse at the time of a pretrial evaluation often have strong feelings of guilt and shame that are being consciously or less consciously repressed. This sometimes happens in order to maintain psychological defenses in the face of the threat of decompensation, destruction of fragile self-esteem, or fear of social rejection.

Sometimes clinicians can identify this underlying discomfort despite the youth's lack of external manifestations of it. Often the discomfort will be more apparent only after the youth has gained some distance from the event and is in a therapeutic setting in which it is relatively more safe to reveal these feelings.

Given these considerations, neither courts nor clinicians should make presumptions about "feelings of guilt" or "remorsefulness" (or capacity to feel remorse) based simply on the presence or absence of youths' verbal and affective expressions of remorse. When a clinician has an opinion on the matter, it should be based on inferences made in light of other data: for example, a youth's expressions of remorse in situations wherein there was no particular potential for manipulative gains, or data from psychological tests that might reveal the presence or absence of the capacity for underlying feelings of shame and social rejection for one's antisocial behavior.

5.32   Potential for Adult Attachments

Many types of rehabilitative interventions tend to rely on the development of a *relationship between a helper and the person who is being helped*. This is no less true for interventions that focus on discipline, behavior modification, and cognitive restructuring than for interventions that rely more explicitly on the therapeutic relationship as a tool in dynamic counseling and psychotherapy. In the rehabilitation of youthful offenders, the youth's *capacity to form an attachment with an adult* becomes an important tool for the success of any intervention, and the absence of this potential jeopardizes the likelihood of successful rehabilitation.

In referring to "the capacity for adult attachments," I mean that the youth *shows evidence (or in the past has shown evidence) of caring about an adult's approval or disapproval, or being concerned about whether an adult cares about the youth*. Stated another way, youths have the capacity for attachments to adults when they can perceive adults as making a difference in their own identity and the way they feel about themselves.

Some youths show this potential by trustful responses to adults or by at least showing a sort of curiosity about adults' relation to them, even in the pretrial evaluation session. Sometimes it is identified in their psychological test results: for example, in recurrent positive or dependent themes about adult-child relationships in their Thematic Apperception Test stories or in scores on scales that measure dependency and seeking the approval of others. In contrast, youths who have developed narcissistic and psychopathic traits tend to express either marked disinterest in adults or an extreme but relatively superficial interest when this will satisfy the youth's own desire for some personal gain that is relatively unrelated to the relationship.

One of the difficulties in assessing a youth's capacity for forming adult attachments is that the assessment is occurring in the context of an adversarial process that makes the youth's present relations with adults hard to read. In many cases, therefore, the potential or its relative absence must be inferred from the youth's past relationships with adults. *The capacity is suggested when one can identify any adult in the youth's past life with whom the youth has had a trusting relationship, in whom the youth has experienced an interest, for whom the youth has expressed affection, or from whom the youth appears to have sought approval by engaging in socialized behaviors that the adult supported.*

In looking for evidence that a youth has ever had an attachment with adults in the past, one should explore possibilities that extend beyond the immediate family. Examples in my own cases (all of which involved murder charges) have included

- uncles and aunts who did not have primary responsibility for the youths' upbringing,
- an elderly man down the street who used to sit and talk with the youth on his front porch in the evenings after the youth had mowed his lawn,
- a teacher in the school's woodworking shop,
- the mother of a friend,
- a football coach who took special interest in the youth because of his potential, and

- a 12-year-old boy's search for his father—a lonely, fruitless, city-wide odyssey of several months—with whom he fantasized a future positive relationship despite the absence of any relationship at all in the past.

The potential often *cannot* be inferred directly from the youth's *present* way of relating to adults. The social and developmental contexts of youths' lives at the time that clinicians are evaluating them are often fraught with conflicts with authority, so that during the evaluation they may manifest only negative reactions to all adults currently in their lives. *But it is important to realize that the source of their negative reactions often is their desire for acceptance.* Anger, rejection of adults' attention and concern, and rebelliousness may all be signs that the youth is anticipating rejection by adults (often because of the youth's poor self-esteem or because adults' past reactions to the youth have reinforced this expectancy). In that context, the anger and rebelliousness are themselves indications that, in a more fundamental sense, the youth cares about adults' evaluations and wishes that they were favorable.

Current negative reactions to adults, therefore, are not necessarily signs that a youth cannot form positive attachments with adults. Such reactions may even be strong evidence that the potential is there and can be mobilized under the right circumstances to further the objectives of a rehabilitation plan.

5.33 Chronicity

In general, troublesome personality traits and clinical conditions that have a long history present a greater challenge for rehabilitative interventions than do psychological conditions that have developed more recently or are more reactive to current circumstances. This is relevant for making estimates of the likelihood of successful rehabilitation in juvenile justice programs.

Chapter 4 included a discussion of the relation between early or late onset of aggressive behavior and the risk of future violence. Youths whose disruptive and aggressive behaviors began several years prior to adolescence tend to have a greater rate of recidivism than youths whose aggression and delinquency have their onset during adolescence. Moreover, the former are at higher risk of aggressive and illegal acts when they reach adulthood. In contrast, youths whose delinquency developed during adolescence are more likely to be "adolescent-limited," desisting as a natural course of cognitive or social development during the transition from adolescence to the adult years. Therefore, *the prospects for successful rehabilitation (substantial reduction in the likelihood of recidivism), or the time that may be required to accomplish it, are likely to be related to the chronicity of the characteristics that have been targeted for change in the rehabilitation plan.*

Similarly, clinical and psychological conditions related to a youth's delinquency that have very early roots may be more difficult to modify. Everyone who has worked with delinquent youths has encountered cases in which the youth's earliest relationship with parents in infancy was so damaging that there seems simply to be no foundation for developing a relationship in which the youth expects anything other than pain. Similarly, some psychiatric conditions developing early in childhood never receive attention by parents, teachers, or mental health professionals. In these cases, problems often have become multiple and complex as youths have carried their conditions through several cognitive and psychosocial developmental stages, making increasingly maladaptive adjustments to new demands at every turn. Inevitably their conditions present a less optimistic prospect for rehabilitation within a reasonable time period.

Although these generalities about chronicity are sound, one should always be looking for reasons why a particular case might be an exception to the general rule. Resilience sometimes is found among youths whose chronic conditions normally require a realistic pessimism about the likelihood of rehabilitation (4-2.1).

5.4 *Community and Justice System Factors*

Prospects for successful rehabilitation are influenced not only by characteristics of the youth, but also by factors in the youth's future environment that may enhance or impair the progress of rehabilitation. Generally these can be described as social support and stress factors related to *community and family* and factors related to the *services of the juvenile justice system.*

5.41 Community Supports and Stressors

The degree of support that family members and others in the youth's community are likely to provide during the rehabilitation process can have both direct and indirect implications for the progress of rehabilitation. As a general rule, family members' encouragement and continued interest in the youth can have an indirect positive influence on the youth's progress and may be important more directly if the family is willing to be actively involved in rehabilitation activities themselves.

Yet there are exceptions. Family members' involvement in their children's lives can sometimes impede rehabilitation progress. This can happen, for example, if the family itself is highly enmeshed, is in conflict but denies the need for intervention, or actively supports the youth's maladaptive behaviors (sometimes contributing to the youth's resistance to the system's therapeutic efforts). Clinicians should not presume that a family's strong interest in their child is automatically a positive factor for rehabilitation. The quality of the parent-child relationship must also be taken into account.

Sometimes one can anticipate sources of future stress for the youth in events that will be happening in the family or community. Examples in my own cases have included

- a grandmother who was extremely important to the youth and held the extended family together, but who was expected to die within the next half-year;
- a mother who, during the youth's trial process, took up residence with a man who was known to have been physically abusive to women in the past; and
- a girlfriend who was currently a source of support for the youth during the trial process, but who was eventually going to have to deal with conflicts between her loyalty to the youth and her friendship with a peer group, one of whose members the youth had killed.

When sources of stress like these can be anticipated, they need to be considered in making judgments about the course of rehabilitation and the time it might take. Whether the youth will be undergoing rehabilitative interventions in the community or in a secure facility, such events place added burdens on the youth and may impair the accomplishment of rehabilitative gains or lengthen the time that is needed to attain them.

5.42 Quality of Rehabilitation Services

Rehabilitation services of all types vary in quality. A state's overall juvenile rehabilitation system may go through periods of time when it functions very well and other times when it operates poorly (e.g., given insufficient funds or low morale). In any system, some programs typically function better than others. Moreover, an individual program can vary in quality at different times in its history, due to changes in funding, staff, or administrative leadership and philosophy.

It seems unfair for a youth's "amenability to rehabilitation" to be judged in part on the basis of the quality of available services. In an ideal world, the services are always adequate, and any pessimistic judgments about a youth's prospects are based solely on the characteristics of the youth. Yet from an empirical and realistic perspective, it is quite clear that the likelihood of successful rehabilitation is not merely a function of a youth's characteristics. It is equally influenced by the quality of services that are provided.

There is a sense in which the clinician must take the system as it is, making estimates of the prospects for rehabilitation within the limits of the system that will be providing the services. Yet there are times—and the clinician should look for them—when clinicians should push the system to find the services that are necessary to maximize the likelihood of youths' rehabilitation. For example, imagine a youth with clinical depression who needs maintenance medication yet does not need hospitalization. Imagine further that there is a particular juvenile facility that would meet all of the youth's needs except for medication because the facility has not been provided a budget for a psychiatrist's services. In my opinion, it is within the examiner's role to recommend that the juvenile justice facility be asked to arrange for a consulting psychiatrist to follow the youth at the facility, with daily monitoring of medication provided by the program's nurse.

When it is reasonable from a program perspective—and will make a real difference in the likelihood of successful rehabilitation—similar recommendations for currently nonexistent services could be made with regard to special types of vocational, educational, and psychotherapy services. Similarly, many states have recognized the juvenile court's obligation to consider out-of-state placement and purchase of services when youths have good prospects for responding to types of programs that the state's juvenile system currently does not have. The clinician must be aware, however, that courts will not always see these recommendations as feasible, and the clinician must be prepared in those instances to offer "second-best" recommendations.

6.0 THE FUTURE OF WAIVER TO CRIMINAL COURT

As described earlier in this chapter, most states in recent years have developed laws that transfer youths to criminal court "automatically" on the basis of age and the level of offense that is charged, without the need for a judicial decision about waiver. As a consequence, waiver evaluations might be needed less often in the future than during most of the juvenile court's history. When youths do come before the court in judicial waiver proceedings, they will probably be younger or charged with less serious offenses than in past years; other forms of transfer that do not require judicial decisions typically are now applied with older youths and those who are charged with serious offenses. As a consequence, while many more youths are being transferred to criminal court by nonjudicial mechanisms, it is possible that a smaller percentage of waiver hearings will result in waiver than was true before recent juvenile justice reforms.

Although the future juvenile court may require fewer waiver evaluations than in the past, something like them will probably be needed with far greater frequency in a different legal context. When youths are transferred to criminal court by statutory exclusion or prosecutor direct file, many states now provide for a hearing at which the court must determine whether to proceed to trial or to waive criminal court jurisdiction and remand the youth to juvenile court. These requirements are fairly new in most states, and there is no broad consensus concerning the criteria and procedures for these "reverse waiver evaluations." Certainly they will address the suitability of the youth for criminal court prosecution, but more legal development of the concept and experience with these evaluations will be required before specific guidelines can be offered.

Finally, it is likely that waiver evaluations will increasingly be coupled with evaluations of youths' competence to stand trial. As discussed in Chapter 3, recent increases in the transfer of younger juveniles to criminal court have created a heightened awareness of youths' potential incapacities to participate meaningfully in their defense. Youths that are not likely to meet the criminal justice system's criteria for competence to stand trial ought not to be waived to criminal court. This may eventually cause more states to require competence evaluations in waiver hearings or to stimulate defense attorneys to request competence evaluations more routinely when challenging waiver to criminal court.

Chapter 7

Professional and Ethical Practice

C linicians who perform evaluations in delinquency cases need to know "how business gets done" in this special legal context and how they can get it done ethically. This chapter offers information and suggestions that can help clinicians avoid pitfalls they often encounter in doing evaluations for use in juvenile courts and discusses ways to satisfy professional and ethical obligations in the course of their work.

The fundamental authority for ethical practice in any setting, of course, is the general ethical guidelines that are sanctioned by the organization associated with one's profession (American Psychological Association, 1992; American Psychiatric Association, 1995). In addition, forensic groups within psychology and psychiatry have published guidelines for ethical practice in forensic work: the *Specialty Guidelines for Forensic Psychologists* (Committee on Ethical Guidelines for Forensic Psychologists, 1991), and the *AAPL Ethical Guidelines for the Practice of Forensic Psychiatry* (American Academy of Psychiatry and the Law, 1995). These specialty guidelines are consistent with the general ethical principles for one's profession, but they interpret them in light of the special circumstances that arise when psychology or psychiatry is applied in legal settings with forensic populations.

Although the forensic specialty guidelines are helpful when performing a wide variety of forensic evaluations, they do not spell out how the guidelines might apply in delinquency cases. This chapter, therefore, discusses some of the professional and ethical concerns that frequently arise specifically in delinquency cases and describes ways to deal with them that are consistent with the forensic specialty guidelines for ethical practice.

1.0 THE CONTRACTUAL RELATIONSHIP

Clinicians perform evaluations in delinquency cases in the context of either of two broad contractual relationships: as a member of a *court clinic service* or on a *case-by-case contractual basis*. These relationships are important to understand because they constitute an essential background for examining ethical issues that arise in practice.

1.1 *Types of Contracts*

A *court clinic service* is any individual or group of practitioners responsible for meeting the daily evaluation needs of a juvenile court. As discussed in Chapter 1, some court clinics are within the organizational structure of the juvenile court so that the clinicians are employees of the court. In other cases, the court clinic is a private practice group with a contract to meet whatever evaluation needs arise for the juvenile court on a continuing day-to-day basis. In either case, the court clinic's offices may be in the same building as the juvenile court or may be located in office space outside yet nearby it. The functions and obligations of professionals in these two arrangements are exactly the same. The differences are primarily administrative and with regard to the nature of the financial arrangement.

Professionals providing *case-by-case contractual services* are private practitioners who accept or decline referrals for evaluations in delinquency cases as they arise. They have no continuing contractual obligation to provide evaluations for any party. Their referrals may come from defense attorneys, prosecutors, or the juvenile court. In some communities, all of a court's delinquency evaluations are performed by one or more private practitioners, sometimes chosen on a case-by-case basis from a court list of professionals in the community. (In addition, some court clinics use a mixed model in which they perform some evaluations themselves and contract with private practitioners for other evaluations on a case-by-case basis.) These professionals may be on the court list by prior agreement with the court, and perhaps they have had to meet certain qualifications to be included on the list. But they accept cases as the need arises and as their time allows, rather than having an ongoing contract that obligates them to meet the court's needs.

1.2 *Who "Owns" the Evaluation*

The funds to pay for a delinquency evaluation may come from various sources. Court clinics, of course, are funded through juvenile court or other government budgets related to child services, and case-by-case contractors may also be paid directly by the court. In some cases, defense attorneys may pay for an evaluation with the private resources of the defendant although this is fairly rare. More often, case-by-case contractors who take referrals from defense counsel will be paid from a separate budget (often managed by the state court administrative offices) that is set aside to provide funds for legal services to indigent defendants. In the latter cases, the juvenile court usually must authorize the evaluation and the use of the state's funds for indigent cases at the request of the defendant.

The mere fact that a juvenile court orders the evaluation, or that the state pays for it, does not necessarily mean that the evaluation "belongs" to the state. The court may be requesting (and providing the funding for) the evaluation to assist the court itself, or it may be authorizing defense counsel's request for an evaluation in order to prepare a defense.

If the court's referral for an evaluation is made at the request of youth's counsel in order to prepare a defense, the evaluation ordinarily "belongs" to defense counsel and the defendant in the sense that the results are privileged and typically cannot be revealed to the court or other parties without defense counsel's approval. (Clinicians should consult their local juvenile court, however, to determine whether there may be unusual exceptions in their own jurisdiction.) A juvenile court's request for an evaluation to assist the court itself, however, is not privileged in that all information obtained may legally be revealed to the court without violating the defendant's rights. Some of the implications of this will be discussed in a later section.

2.0 CONSIDERING THE REFERRAL

Meeting professional and ethical obligations begins with the first contact from the juvenile court or parties in the case who raise the question of an evaluation. Deciding whether to accept the referral, and whether the person making the referral actually wishes to contract with the clinician, requires that the clinician and referral source share some information and clarify the potential relationship. Typically these matters are routinized in referrals from juvenile courts to court clinics because of their ongoing contractual relationship. Many of the following considerations, therefore, are more relevant for professionals performing evaluations for courts or attorneys on a case-by-case contractual basis.

2.1 *Understanding the Referral Question*

The clinician must obtain a clear view of the reason for the referral. The inquiry should go beyond the attorney's request for "a disposition evaluation" or "an evaluation of competence to stand trial." The clinician and attorney should discuss the *legal and clinical questions* associated with that type of evaluation and *the reason that the need for an evaluation has arisen in this particular case.*

Concerning the *legal and clinical questions,* often it is helpful to briefly mention in conversation with the attorney the legal concepts that the clinician understands as underlying the broad type of evaluation requested. This often clarifies the purpose of the evaluation and assures a mutual understanding of the relevant issues. For example, some mention of the "voluntary, knowing, and intelligent" components for "capacity to waive Miranda rights" may reveal that the defense attorney has no doubt that the youth was capable of understanding the Miranda warnings but that defense intends to question only the voluntariness of the waiver in light of the youth's very dependent and acquiescent manner. This gives the clinician a better grasp of what this particular Miranda waiver evaluation might require.

Sometimes an attorney requesting a particular type of evaluation will label it in a way that might be misinterpreted. For example, I once received a request to perform an "insanity evaluation" on a youth. I briefly commented to the attorney that this meant to me that I would be examining the youth's ability to have appreciated wrongfulness at the time of the offense and his ability to have conformed his conduct to the requirement of law (i.e., the main issues in an "insanity defense" or a question of criminal responsibility, which is very rare as a question in juvenile court).

The attorney then indicated that this was not at all what he was looking for. He wanted to know whether the youth was so mentally ill that he could not understand what was going on right now in his trial. In other words, the attorney wanted a competence to stand trial evaluation but used the term "insanity" in a more general way rather than in its specific legal sense.

In other instances, briefly discussing the concepts to be assessed can ensure that the clinician is properly informed about the law. If the clinician is taking a referral from a neighboring state, for example, the clinician might find that the legal issues are controlled by somewhat different definitions than in his or her own state.

The clinician should also inquire about the *reason that a request for an evaluation has arisen in this particular case.* For example, what suggested to the attorney that the youth might have deficits in abilities related to competence to stand trial? Typically this will elicit information about the case that can help the clinician identify clinical issues that are likely to arise and whether those issues are within the clinician's areas of expertise. For example, in a referral for an evaluation related to waiver to criminal court, the attorney might indicate that the question of amenability will focus on the conditions under which the offense occurred—specifically, whether it appeared to be coldly premeditated or whether several psychiatric medications together with an illegal substance that the youth was taking at the time might have influenced his behavior. If the clinician has little special expertise in psychopharmacology, should the referral be accepted?

2.2 *Assessing One's Competence*

Clinicians should take stock of their competence to accept various referrals for forensic evaluations. Competence is a legal question as well as a professional judgment based on notions of ethical practice.

The legal question is whether the clinician would be qualified by a court as an expert in the case in question. A professional is legally qualified as an expert witness when a court concludes that the person possesses specialized knowledge (e.g., scientific or clinical knowledge) that will assist the legal fact-finder in weighing the issues in the case. The professional must have training and experience relevant to the matters about which expert opinions will be offered. Expert witness testimony typically begins with questioning—often brief, but sometimes quite detailed—concerning the expert's training and experience relevant for the present case. How much experience and training are necessary will vary considerably depending on the circumstances of the case and judicial discretion.

Beyond judicial acknowledgment of qualifications, there is an ethical obligation to make one's own independent judgment about one's areas of competence. Courts often do not apply very rigid or demanding criteria for qualifying an expert, and sometimes a court may qualify a person to testify about matters that would be outside a clinician's area of expertise according to professional ethical standards. For example, it is not unusual to hear that a court has qualified a physician to testify about a broad range of psychological issues in a delinquency case even though the physician has had almost no training or experience in child psychiatry.

The need to weigh the matter of professional competence for oneself is created by our ethical obligation to avoid providing professional services in ways that may harm the welfare of others or do damage to the public's confidence in the profession. Thus clinicians must set their own limits in some cases, based on their own fund of knowledge and experience, the specific nature of the case, and their sense of ethical practice.

What should be taken into consideration? The clinician should have training that offered a basic understanding of the developmental, clinical, and legal issues involved in delinquency evaluations (or that are required by the specific type of evaluation that the case calls for). This training need not have been obtained in formal academic programs; it may have been acquired through continuing education activities and conscientious self-study. One should also have experience in performing the type of evaluation in question (a matter that courts weigh heavily). Early in one's work in this area, lack of experience (if backed by adequate preparation) is easily handled by having a supervisory or consultative relationship with a clinician who is recognized as experienced and qualified in the area.

Clinicians often must consider whether they are competent to take on the issues raised in *specific* cases, even if they are generally well qualified to do delinquency evaluations. Although courts will sometimes be lenient in this regard, clinicians should set a higher standard in some instances on ethical grounds. For example, some juvenile courts have allowed me to testify to the effects of certain psychiatric medications on youths although I have had no formal training in psychopharmacology and only limited direct clinical experience in working with youths for whom medication is part of their treatment. In these cases, I must set my own limits based on my sense of competent practice. For example, I have sometimes felt comfortable testifying to general information, such as the medically well-known effects of common antidepressants employed with youths. But I decline to offer opinions about the probable effects on a specific youth, the general effects of medications for which there is controversy in the literature, or situations that involve interactions of various drugs. In a rehabilitation evaluation, I am certainly capable of identifying cases that should be seen by psychiatrists to assess the probable need for medication, yet I would not offer an opinion that a *specific* medication should be part of the rehabilitation plan for a particular youth.

Recognizing one's limits of competence does not necessarily mean turning down the case. During the referral discussion, the clinician can inform the attorney about those aspects of the case that the clinician may not be willing to address, then if necessary recommend the involvement of another clinician whose specialization addresses that particular question. The specialist can then consult to the clinician who will be the primary examiner, or the specialist could perform a separate evaluation and offer testimony on that specific aspect of the case.

3.0 CLARIFYING THE SERVICES, OBLIGATIONS, AND FEES

If the clinician decides to accept the referral, there should be a discussion that makes clear to the clinician and the attorney or court what the clinician will do, what obligations the clinician is and is not accepting, and what the referral source will be expected to provide to assist the examiner.

3.1 *Anticipated Methods, Procedures, and Products*

The methods and procedures that the clinician anticipates using should be sketched out during the referral discussion so that the attorney knows what will be done. These expectancies, often general at first, can be modified later in consultation with the referral source. For example, the clinician might indicate that the case in question sounds as though it will require at least two sessions with the youth, one of them being for interview and the other for psychological testing. The nature of the tests might be described if the clinician can make that judgment based on the initial case information and past experience with similar cases. In a few instances, defense attorneys have asked that I not perform certain psychological tests—for example, the Rorschach—because they have had bad experiences in the past in defending the test's results against cross-examination. Whether to accept limitations like this on one's evaluation practices is a matter of professional judgment. When clinicians feel that they could not perform their task competently without a particular type of data, they should say so and let the attorney decide whether or not to hire them.

Possible interviews with third parties (e.g., parents) should be mentioned so that the attorney can anticipate setting up the interview appointments. Similarly, the types of records and files that the clinician hopes to review should be identified so that the attorney can anticipate obtaining those materials.

The probable need for a written report and for expert testimony should be discussed. A report is almost always written when the evaluation is requested by the court for its own use. Not all defense attorneys, however, will automatically want a written report. They may want the results to be communicated verbally to them, after which they can decide whether they want the clinician to prepare a written report in anticipation of entering the evaluation results as evidence. Similarly, not all cases will require oral testimony, and attorneys sometimes can anticipate the likelihood that this will be required.

Finally, a "schedule of events" should be discussed, developing some plan as to when the clinician will accomplish various tasks associated with the evaluation. This requires knowing when the evaluation will have to be completed for use by the referring party.

Sometimes a court date has been set for the related hearing, and clinicians should check to make sure that their professional and personal schedules will not preclude their appearance at the hearing if their expert testimony is required.

3.2 *Clarifying Expectations of Confidentiality and Privilege*

The conditions of confidentiality and privilege should be discussed so that they are clear to the clinician and the referring party. When the evaluation is for defense counsel, the conditions usually are straightforward. All communications will flow from the clinician to the defense attorney, and they will reach other parties (including the court) only through defense counsel or with the defense attorney's approval. There may be exceptions to this in certain jurisdictions, however, and the clinician should make inquiries about law and practice pertaining to this issue in local juvenile courts.

When the evaluation is ordered by the court for the court's use, the issues are sometimes more complex. Typically, no privilege is provided by law for these evaluations, except that in some cases the results of the evaluation may be used only for the specific hearing for which it is intended, not for later hearings on other issues (e.g., at the adjudication hearing in juvenile court or the trial in criminal court). In addition, legal concerns about the effects of self-incriminating statements have created special rules in some courts. For example, as noted in Section 3.2 of Chapter 6 (on waiver to criminal court), courts sometimes place special limits on the types of information that forensic examiners can obtain, especially regarding the youth's statements about anything having to do directly with the alleged offense.

In evaluations ordered by the court for the court's use, all communications about the evaluation results flow from the clinician to the court (i.e., to the judge or someone the judge authorizes such as the clerk of courts). They will reach other parties in the case (e.g., the defense attorney and prosecutor) only through the judge or with the judge's expressed authorization.

The fact that privilege is limited or does not exist in evaluations for the court does not mean that confidentiality can be ignored. Privilege refers to legal restrictions against the use of certain information in a legal proceeding against the individual. Confidentiality refers more broadly to a person's reasonable expectation that the clinician will not reveal information to others in general without proper legal authority. So nonprivileged information can still be protected by an ethical or legal obligation to refrain from (a) providing the information in contexts outside the legal proceedings and (b) revealing interview information in court that is not relevant for the legal issue.

3.3 *Caveats and Limits*

Prior to forming contractual arrangements, clinicians are obligated to fully disclose matters regarding their participation that might negatively influence the welfare or interests of the parties for whom they will provide professional services. There are several types of information that may be relevant to disclose before taking a delinquency evaluation case.

Clinicians are obligated to perform their evaluations and reach their opinions in an objective manner, making conscientious efforts to avoid influences that matters of personal gain or bias might have on their opinions. While courts typically will expect the clinician to take the case on this premise, some attorneys might not. They might presume that the clinician is agreeing to provide information that will be consistent with the argument that the defense plans to make. Therefore, clinicians are well advised to somehow communicate their intentions to do an impartial evaluation. This can be stated in a simple, straightforward way in the course of the initial discussion, or it can be conveyed in statements that imply the principle of objectivity (e.g., "You may or may not want a written report, depending on whether my findings turn out to be consistent with your defense," implying that they might or might not be supportive).

If the clinician is uncertain about an area of knowledge that is relevant to the case (see examples earlier in 7-2.2), this limitation and its implications should be discussed with the attorney. Some clinicians also maintain limits on the type of final opinion that they are willing to provide. For example, the clinician might be willing (if the data permit) to testify that the youth was "very unlikely to have understood the Miranda warnings" but might have a personal policy never to testify as though this clinical information resolved the legal question (i.e., would never testify that the youth "could not make a voluntary, knowing, and intelligent waiver of rights"). (The distinction between these forms of testimony is explained later.) Defense attorneys are entitled to know these matters before contracting with the clinician.

Finally, clinicians will sometimes get referrals from defense attorneys for cases that, on the basis of initial information about the youth, seem highly unlikely to result in data and opinions that will support the defense attorney's intended arguments. I do not believe that clinicians are obligated to "warn" attorneys when the case looks doubtful. But I have often done so just in case it is not obvious to the attorney, who is about to commit often scarce financial resources to the evaluation.

In my experience, this usually does not discontinue the inquiry. Attorneys often have reasons for obtaining evaluations that are not related to the likelihood of success (e.g., to fulfill their obligation to pursue all avenues of defense in high-stakes cases or to convince a client that the client's insistence about a defense based on a particular psychological point must be abandoned). Sometimes this leads to special arrangements in which the clinician agrees to perform part of the evaluation—for example, the review of existing records and documents—to form a first impression, then to convey that to the attorney before deciding whether to proceed further with the evaluation.

3.4 *Costs and Arrangements for Fees*

Some juvenile court systems have relatively nonnegotiable fee schedules for court-ordered evaluations. These may be either hourly rates or fixed amounts for particular types of evaluations independent of the hours expended in the specific case. Evaluations for defense attorneys typically are billed on an hourly basis at a rate set by the clinician.

When payment is by the hour, and/or when hourly rates are not determined by the court, the clinician should inform the referral source of the clinician's hourly fee, the approximate number of hours that the evaluation will require, and the additional hours that will probably be involved for a written report and testimony if they are eventually needed. Retainer fees usually are not requested by clinicians who perform evaluations in delinquency cases, presumably because fees are almost always paid by government sources, not by private parties. In many states, however, attorneys have to provide an estimate of the cost when they petition the court for authorization to use state funds for the evaluation of indigent youths. The court's authorization legally obligates the state to pay the costs (within the limit specified in the court's authorization) when the clinician submits the final bill.

The set rates for reimbursement of clinicians for juvenile court evaluations vary considerably across the states. Typically it is "adequate," but in some states it is remarkably low and does not encourage a high level of professional practice. The blanket amounts set by some jurisdictions for an evaluation in a delinquency case (for data collection, report writing, and testimony) often would not provide compensation for more than an hour or two of the clinician's total time at the clinician's usual hourly rate for clinical evaluation services. Clinicians who do a thorough job under such circumstances usually must be willing to commit more hours than they are paid for. When the rate is set on an hourly basis, the clinician may have more leeway to work the necessary hours to do an adequate job, but sometimes the hourly rate established by state policy is below the average rate for general clinical practice. (This is not the case in all jurisdictions, of course; many courts will authorize compensation at the clinician's usual fee for the reasonable number of hours anticipated.)

Professional codes of ethics encourage all clinicians to perform some services *pro bono*. Many clinicians believe that performing evaluations at the request of defense counsel in delinquency cases is a good way to fulfill that obligation, assuring that youths have adequate services despite the very limited budget that most states provide for meeting the need.

3.5 *Obligations of the Referral Party*

All of the evaluations discussed in this book require reviews of various records and documents: for example, police reports and court records, school records, past mental health records, and current records of the detention center where the youth is being held. Often these are not easy or legally possible for the clinician to obtain independently, and the clinician is dependent upon the referring party to supply them. Social service workers at the juvenile court that request the examiner's services may be able to provide such records, and the clinician should request that they do so. Defense attorneys typically expect to play this role for clinicians especially since attorneys are in the legal position to obtain their client's consent to release of documents by the agencies that have them on record. The nature of the documents that the clinician needs should be reviewed with the referring party and some arrangement made for their transport to the clinician's office.

The court or the attorney also must provide access to the youth and to others who must be interviewed in the evaluation process. For example, typically the referring party should make advance arrangements for the clinician to gain entry to the detention center where the youth can be interviewed and should make the initial contact with the parents either to arrange a time and place for the interview or to indicate that the clinician will be calling them. Clinicians who take on these tasks without assistance and explicit authorization by the court or attorney may contribute to confusion about the clinician's relationships with youths, parents, and the referral parties themselves and may interfere with the youth's right to a fair trial.

4.0 PROFESSIONAL RELATIONSHIPS

Some of the most potent threats to the clinician's ability to strive for objectivity in the evaluation process are the clinician's relationships with other professionals in the juvenile justice system, and to some extent their relationships with youths themselves. The power of these relationships is sometimes so strong or so subtle that it is hard to avoid even when one is aware of it. Awareness, though, is the first line of defense.

4.1 *Co-Optation*

Clinicians who routinely provide evaluations in delinquency cases work in a world far different from their colleagues in purely clinical settings. They are outsiders in a system of legal definitions and procedures devised and managed by legal professionals. Legal professionals in these settings regard clinicians sometimes with awe and deference and at other times as ancillary professionals on the fringe of the legal system. In either case, most clinicians who perform services for juvenile courts and attorneys recognize that they work in a context that does not fit a clinical paradigm. Although juvenile courts may be more compatible to clinical ways of thinking than criminal courts, most juvenile courts are nevertheless more like courts than mental health centers.

Clinicians must learn to tolerate these differences and to adapt to the needs of the judges and attorneys with whom clinicians work. There are effective and exciting ways to adapt to this world of laws, legal procedures, and legal professionals. One can accommodate by working closely with it, finding the common ground between its legal concepts and objectives and those of one's own profession, and adapting one's clinical expertise in ways that will best serve the needs of youths and the justice system. Not to draw too extreme an analogy, but being a clinician in a juvenile court can be like finding a very important role and function within a foreign culture where one will never be a "native" but may find satisfaction in the work and be appreciated for one's efforts.

There is a twilight area, however, in which accommodation fades into assimilation. Unless clinicians exercise caution, they may become so intimately a part of the culture itself that they are co-opted. Their clinical identities blur and the adversarial dynamics of the legal process gradually dominate their work. When this happens, it threatens clinical objectivity.

Court clinicians, for example, are in daily contact with police officers, prosecutors, and others for whom a primary objective is law enforcement. Co-optation to their perspective can result in clinical work that one-sidedly focuses on youths' guilt, their harm to victims, and their detainment and punishment. Clinicians who perform evaluations primarily for defense attorneys have similar problems. Co-optation to the defense attorneys' perspective and their role can bias one's practice so that one sees only the excusing circumstance, while missing the ways in which youths' character might really matter when accounting for their violent behavior.

Having said this, it is important to recognize that co-optation is not inevitable and, in my opinion, is not the norm among clinicians who perform delinquency evaluations. I have encountered few juvenile court clinics in which the clinicians did their job as though they were law enforcement officers. Moreover, by far the most common situation in most communities is to find that when the juvenile court clinician and the clinician called by the defense have independently evaluated the same youth, they have come up with the same data and provided only slightly different interpretations. When they disagree, the case tends to be one in which there is room for honest differences of opinion, and the court is thereby given alternative views that can be weighed for their respective value.

When co-optation occurs, it usually arises through a socialization process involving clinicians' responses to day-to-day immersion in the world of legal professionals and juvenile court proceedings. One of the best hedges against co-optation is to maintain frequent contact with other clinicians, especially clinicians who do not do forensic work. This keeps the clinician in touch with the knowledge base, ethics, objective methods of analysis, and other features of clinical psychology and psychiatry that constitute important parts of our professional identity.

4.2 *Reputation*

Like everyone else, clinicians must pay their children's college tuition, chip away at the mortgage on their house, and prepare for their retirement. They know that their prospects for meeting these personal obligations depend in part on their ability to get work. This, in turn, depends in large part on their reputation. How they are perceived by their clients in the juvenile court or the community of prosecutors and defense attorneys is important for their livelihood.

Like other areas of legal practice, the world of juvenile law practice is result oriented. When attorneys contact a clinician for an evaluation in a delinquency case, they hope to obtain strong evidence in favor of their position and their arguments. One of the substantial threats to clinicians' objectivity when performing forensic evaluations is the subtle pressure to meet clients' objectives lest the flow of referrals begins to wane.

It does no good for clinicians to imagine that they are above this sort of economic pressure. It is better to recognize it and to use it to produce better evaluations that have no trouble meeting ethical standards of practice. For example, because lawyers are result oriented, most of them realize that a clinician's bottom-line opinion is not all that matters. An opinion will have little value if it is not accompanied by the clinician's credibility. This is especially true in juvenile court, where a judge often hears the same clinicians testifying in cases from day to day and is able to compare the quality and nature of their work. Judges soon learn who they can and cannot trust. When that is reflected in judges' decisions about cases, lawyers soon learn which clinicians have the necessary credibility.

Credibility is not gained by making sure that one produces the opinion that the client wants to hear. It is gained, for example, by actively searching for data and interpretations that will challenge *all* of the arguments in the case, not merely amassing data that support a particular argument. A reputation for credibility is enhanced by doing careful, thoughtful evaluations that reach conclusions based on balanced, straightforward interpretation of the data, then having the skills to communicate the strength of one's evaluation process and interpretations. Credibility is enhanced by being open and forthright on matters about which one is unsure, pointing out alternative hypotheses to one's own and showing the limitations of one's own conclusion. These can all be done without detracting from the value of one's clinical opinion.

In the long run, most successful attorneys learn to value the power of a clinician's credibility more than the assurance that the clinician will find exactly what the attorney wanted to hear. And clinicians who recognize this can build a reputation and a career that will ensure that the college tuition gets paid.

4.3 *Conflicts of Interest*

Some clinicians who take referrals for delinquency evaluations also have a clinical practice in which they treat delinquent youths and their families. This can produce conflicts of interest that threaten objectivity in evaluations for the court or attorneys.

Performing a court-ordered evaluation of a youth whom one is treating or has treated in the past runs the risk of being influenced by biases related to concerns for the youth that are rooted in the advocacy of the therapeutic relationship. For example, the clinician may be reluctant to recognize negative aspects of the youth's character, because its acknowledgment might harm the thera-peutic relationship if reported by the clinician in the evaluation.

A delinquency evaluation should proceed with no prospects or expectations that the youth might be referred to the clinician for treatment as a result of the court's decision on rehabilitation. Such prospects might incline the clinician toward treatment recom-mendations that are motivated by economic benefit, or at least can create a perception of personal gain that threatens the credi-bility of the clinician's evaluation.

5.0   <u>METHODS AND PROCEDURES</u>

Clinicians must be careful to conduct delinquency evaluations in ways that protect the rights of youths, ensure the integrity of their data, and promote opinions that are informed by adequate data. Circumstances associated with evaluations in delinquency cases raise some special concerns in these areas.

5.1   *Disclosures about*   <u>*Confidentiality and Privilege*</u>

As noted earlier, prior to the evaluation the clinician should be clear on the limits of privilege and confidentiality. Those limits will vary across juvenile court jurisdictions. They also vary for different types of evaluations discussed in this book and according to whether the evaluation is being performed for the court or for the youth's defense attorney. Be aware, therefore, that the discussion that follows may not necessarily be accurate for one's own jurisdiction. Check local sources for guidance.

In general, all information provided by a youth for an evalua-tion that is being done for the juvenile court will be made avail-able to the juvenile court judge. It is confidential for other purposes (e.g., the clinician is not free to disclose the results to most people outside the court) but not for the proceeding for which it is being performed. In contrast, evaluations done for defense counsel typically are protected under the rules of attorney-client privilege. Results will be seen only by the defense attorney unless the client and attorney decide to release the information. In most states, evaluations performed pretrial (e.g., for waiver of

Miranda rights, competence to stand trial, and waiver to criminal court) may not be used in evidence at the delinquency adjudication hearing or in any later trial in criminal court unless defense counsel enters the information. Again, there may be exceptions in one's own state, as well as unusual cases in which prosecutors may attempt to rebut a defendant's statements at trial using information from an earlier and otherwise privileged evaluation.

In some states, court-ordered evaluations cannot proceed before a youth's attorney has been notified of the time, place, and purpose of the evaluation. This provides an opportunity for defense counsel to explain the nature of the evaluation to the youth and to discuss any matters that might be troubling to the defense, such as the potential for self-incriminating statements. In states that do not require this, it is nevertheless consistent with ethical guidelines (e.g., Committee on Ethical Guidelines for Forensic Psychologists, 1991) for the clinician to notify defense counsel prior to the evaluation.

In many states, the clinician is also required by law to inform youths of the limits of confidentiality before proceeding with interviews and testing related to a court-ordered evaluation. The description should include

- who the clinician is
- who has requested the evaluation
- what the evaluation is for
- generally what the evaluation will entail
- who will see the results
- the extent and limits of confidentiality

Some clinicians also tell youths that they can refuse to talk about anything that they do not want to reveal. Youths for whom an evaluation is ordered typically must present themselves for the evaluation, but they are not required to provide any information that they do not wish to provide.

Exactly what the clinician will tell the youth about each of these things will vary, of course, depending on the type of evaluation, who has requested it, and what the limits of confidentiality actually are. The description should be fairly simple and worded in a way that the youth is most likely to understand. Some states do not require this disclosure process, but it is consistent with ethical guidelines to do so even when it is not required.

The purpose of this disclosure to the youth is not to obtain a "waiver of confidentiality." In the typical evaluation for the court, there is no confidentiality to waive; in evaluations for defense attorneys, confidentiality is protected and should not be waived. The disclosure also should not be construed as part of "informed consent." Informed consent is a process in which a person, on the basis of adequately disclosed information, makes a competent and voluntary decision to allow a professional to do something that would otherwise be a violation of one's right to privacy. This does not fit the present situation. It is questionable in some cases whether youths are "competent" to make decisions related to informed consent. Moreover, for court-ordered evaluations, the clinician is legally authorized to perform the evaluation, regardless of the youth's desires. If the youth decides not to participate in the evaluation, the clinician may still use other data sources to form opinions (often at some reduced level of confidence) that might be helpful to the court.

The disclosure regarding confidentiality and its limits, therefore, allows youths to understand what is happening and to decide whether, how much, and what they want to reveal to the examiner. Likewise, if the youth decides to participate but not to provide certain types of information, the clinician simply forms opinions that, if necessary, are limited due to lack of access to that information.

5.2 *Interview and Testing Conditions*

The clinician should conduct interviews and tests with youths in conditions that do not unduly compromise the validity of the results. Delinquency evaluations often present challenges in this regard.

Quite often the evaluations described in this book take place while youths are in custody in detention facilities prior to their juvenile court trials. Typically these facilities have interview rooms that are used by attorneys and clinicians. When such rooms are not available, clinicians run the risk of harming the integrity of the evaluation data when they simply "make do" with inadequate conditions. For example, in lieu of an interview room, the clinician should not opt for a corner of the day room or the cot in the youth's cell. The court or defense attorney should be asked to arrange for the youth's transportation to an appropriate place for the interview and testing. The same request should be made if the facility's interview room does not provide adequate privacy or if internal windows looking onto the day room (where there are inevitable distractions, some inadvertent and some purposeful) cannot be dealt with by covering the window or seating the youth with the windows to his or her back. If testing requires a table, do not offer to make do with a clipboard.

In some communities, it is fairly common in delinquency evaluations for defense attorneys to indicate that they want to be present while youths are being interviewed for an evaluation that is being done for the court. In a few states they have the right to do so, while in most states it is allowed at the discretion of the clinician (or if the attorney objects to the clinician's refusal, at the discretion of the judge).

Attorneys offer several reasons for wanting to be present. They can hear exactly what questions the clinician asks and what responses the youth gives, which attorneys believe may be important in challenging the examiner's opinions if they are based on aspects of the interview that admit to differing interpretations. Sometimes they do not trust the youth's ability to avoid talking about the alleged offense, and they wish to be there to warn the youth if that should happen. At times they simply believe that they will learn something about their client by listening to a skillful clinician performing a diagnostic and clinical history interview.

From the clinician's perspective, the main issue is the integrity of the evaluation process. The potential for distractions or inhibitions to compromise the evaluation are probably greater in juvenile evaluations than in evaluations of adult defendants, especially when the youth is fearful, is dependent on adults, or has a developmental disability that increases distractibility. Frequent interruptions by attorneys might create an argumentative tone that disrupts the flow of the interview process.

Some clinicians never agree to an attorney's presence when they evaluate a youth. Others have a personal policy of allowing it under certain conditions. Among those conditions are the placement of the attorney (behind and some distance away from the youth) and the attorney's agreement to say nothing after introductions are made (except, perhaps, to stop the youth from talking directly about the alleged offense). If the clinician adopts this policy, the conditions should be rigidly enforced. Even the slightest deviation should result in an immediate postponement of the session with an explanation to the attorney after the youth has left the room.

5.3 *Time and Resources*

Certain conditions in juvenile justice systems sometimes threaten the clinician's ability to fulfill an ethical obligation to perform a careful and professional evaluation. Specifically, the amount of time that the court (or statutes) provides for the evaluation may not be enough to do an adequate job. Moreover, earlier we discussed the limited financial compensation for delinquency evaluations in some juvenile justice jurisdictions.

Clinicians have three responsibilities when they encounter these frustrations. First, when the issues arise in the context of an evaluation, clinicians must do as well as they can and, in some cases, do somewhat more than they will be paid to do, in order to perform the task in a way that least compromises the evaluation process. But if the evaluation conditions severely limit clinicians' confidence in their conclusions, they should say so. If they have the appropriate opportunity, they might sometimes politely inform the court of the way in which the system's conditions limited their ability to provide the best information for the court.

Second, if the problem is chronic, clinicians may discuss the issue with the juvenile court judge as a general problem (not in relation to any specific ongoing case) and explore ways that the conditions could be modified for the benefit of youths and the court.

Third, for both of the previous responses to occur "in good faith," clinicians must take a hard look at their evaluation practices to determine what is truly needed to perform an "adequate" evaluation. A complete battery of the "usual" psychological tests (intelligence, objective personality, projective methods) is not necessary in every type of evaluation or in every case. As described in Chapter 5, there are several types of risk and rehabilitation evaluations for different questions that come before the court. Some may be fairly brief, and others (such as evaluations in criminal court waiver cases involving serious charges) may need to be comprehensive, involving a greater amount of time.

Clinicians, therefore, should develop a very clear view of the most *efficient* way to perform evaluations (while still satisfying professional standards), and they should conduct their evaluations accordingly. This is good business and good ethics. It also gives the clinician the high ground when making arguments for increased time and resources to provide the quality of service that youths and juvenile courts should obtain.

6.0   COMMUNICATIONS

There are only a few points to discuss regarding report writing and testimony that are specific to delinquency evaluations and juvenile courts. Most of the guidelines for this final and important part of the evaluation are the same as for other forensic cases, for which one should consult the organizational guidelines cited earlier for forensic psychology and forensic psychiatry, as well as texts (e.g., for report writing, see Melton et al., 1997; for expert testimony, see Brodsky, 1991). In addition, Chapters 2 through 6 of this book offer comments on report writing for various types of delinquency evaluations.

6.1   *Report Writing*

The following are some of the most important tips for writing reports for courts, as described in the forensic mental health literature:

- Use a *consistent outline* that takes into account the needs of the court and the legal context for the evaluation. (This often makes forensic reports look considerably different than reports written for clinical treatment settings.)
- Write *concisely and clearly*, using *no clinical jargon* (or defining it when it is used).
- *Describe the purpose* of the evaluation.
- *List all sources of data* for the evaluation (every document, telephone call, interview, and test).

- Include *all data that are necessary* in order to support or question your opinion.
- Include *no more data or inferences than are necessary* to reach the relevant opinion.
- Offer *interpretations and conclusions* only *after* all of your data have been described.
- *Provide clear explanations for each of your opinions* (i.e., spell out the reasoning that links your data to your conclusions).
- *Offer opinions on matters directly pertaining to the legal question* (e.g., "In my opinion, it is unlikely that the youth can be rehabilitated in the juvenile justice system by his 18th birthday"), although careful consideration should be given to *avoiding opinions that claim to answer the ultimate legal question* (e.g., "In my clinical opinion, the youth should be waived to criminal court"). (This point will be discussed in 7-6.3.)

6.2 *Prehearing Communications*

Virtually all texts on expert testimony urge clinicians to meet with attorneys prior to the hearing if they are being asked to testify. Typically they should discuss how questions on direct examination will flow, what conclusions the clinician will reach, and some of the things that the clinician should expect on cross-examination.

Many attorneys in delinquency cases are somewhat less conscientious about this process than are attorneys in adult criminal cases. This may be due to the more informal nature of juvenile court proceedings in some jurisdictions. In addition, the American Bar Association has been concerned for some time about deficiencies in the quality of legal representation for youths in some juvenile courts (American Bar Association Juvenile Justice Center, Juvenile Law Center, and Youth Law Center, 1995). Therefore, clinicians may have to take the initiative in arranging for a discussion with the attorney about the testimony if the attorney does not raise it. Face-to-face meetings are best for very difficult cases, but a telephone conversation will suffice for many less-demanding cases.

Clinicians sometimes prefer to have a brief session with the youth and another with members of the family prior to the hearing at which testimony will be given. The purpose is to prepare them for what they will hear in court by way of the clinician's descriptions of the youth. This is not too difficult to arrange especially when one is testifying at the request of defense.

The primary reason for considering this is to prevent the youth's or parents' misunderstanding of difficult evaluative or descriptive comments by the clinician during the testimony, which could lead to serious psychological discomfort for the youth, the parents, or their relationship. Some cases require disclosure of the youth's psychological dynamics or social relationships that clinicians would never ordinarily spell out to youths in the absence of a therapeutic relationship in which the timing of the interpretation and its effects can be managed. For example, in one case it was very necessary for the court to understand a youth's underlying anger and mistrust of his mother, which neither the youth nor her mother seemed to acknowledge. What would be the effects upon them if they heard this interpretation for the first time from a clinician on the witness stand testifying to a roomful of strangers? Does a prehearing discussion have a protective function?

The answers are not simple. Some youths and parents might greatly benefit from a discussion of the matter prior to the trial, especially of the reasons why the information is important to the welfare of the youth and the potential outcome of the hearing. But it is possible that some youths and parents can best cope with this information by hearing it for the first time in court, where they can protect themselves from the interpretation by reacting with defensive outrage or denial.

Forensic ethical guidelines do not specifically require feedback sessions with examinees, but clinicians are obligated to avoid psychological harm when it is feasible to do so. When and how this should be done, however, is a matter for individual clinical judgment. Pretrial feedback need not occur routinely, but occasionally one encounters cases in which it seems necessary.

6.3   *Court Testimony*

One difference between testimony in juvenile court cases and in other forensic cases is that one will almost never testify before a jury in juvenile court. (There are exceptions, however.

Juveniles have the right to a jury trial in Massachusetts although the right is rarely invoked.) Attorneys' strategies for presenting and challenging evidence are usually different for jury trials than for trials decided by judges alone. For example, presentation intended to appeal to emotion is usually far less effective with judges than with juries. Attempts to discredit expert witnesses or to make them look "foolish" are more common in jury trials than in bench trials.

In addition, until the reforms brought about by *In re Gault* (1967), juvenile court hearings were relatively informal matters devoid of adversarial argument, with all participants claiming simply to be trying to determine what was best for the youth. Although juvenile court hearings now are conducted with some of the due process and formality of criminal courts, some juvenile courts continue to maintain a less formal atmosphere.

As a consequence, experts testifying in juvenile courts experience the rigors of brutal cross-examination less often than their colleagues in criminal courts and civil litigation cases. These differences diminish, however, when the stakes for the youth or society are very high: for example, in many waiver to criminal court cases involving murder charges when both the state and the youth are represented by effective attorneys.

One of the questions frequently raised in continuing education seminars regarding expert testimony pertains to the nature of experts' opinions. Should experts testify to the "ultimate legal question"?

A colleague of mine, Robert Kinscherff, likes to illustrate the issue with a hypothetical. Imagine that a highly respected nuclear engineer provides expert testimony at a legal hearing to determine whether a nuclear power plant should be built in a particular town. The engineer testifies to the benefits of the proposed plant: the number of kilowatts daily that will be produced, the specific reductions in cost, and the increased efficiency compared to existing hydroelectric plants. She testifies also to the risks: the specific probability of a nuclear accident and the effects on neighborhood families if it were to happen. As the engineer concludes her testimony, the judge turns to her and says, "Thank you very much for educating us to the benefits and risks of this project. That was excellent. Now, tell me: Should we build it or not?"

The last question is far different from the others for which the engineer formed opinions. It requires deciding whether it is reasonable or desirable for citizens to bear the risk of suffering in order to enjoy the benefits of the proposed plant. What qualifies the witness, as a professional in nuclear engineering, to form an *expert* opinion about what the citizens of the town should or should not want or the stress that they should or should not be required to endure?

Replace the final question in this hypothetical with "Should the youth be found competent to stand trial," or "Should we waive this youth to criminal court." The clinician who offers opinions on these questions in testimony answers the same type of question the judge asked the engineer. Every waiver case, for example, is a test of the degree of risk that the court (or society) wishes to tolerate, in light of (a) the probability of danger (risk of harm to others) weighed together with (b) the likelihood of benefit (degree of prospect for rehabilitation). Our professional ethics require that we consider whether we should form opinions in court about what society should or should not tolerate.

Considering these matters, some clinicians (perhaps most) decide nevertheless to testify to what is called the "ultimate legal question." They claim that judges often require it and that clinicians would not (or should not) be allowed to testify at all if they have no opinion about the ultimate legal question. They note also that stating an opinion on the ultimate legal question does no harm because judges are not required to agree with the clinician. Finally, they point out that once one has answered the penultimate legal question (e.g., "Is the youth amenable to reha- bilitation in the juvenile justice system") their answer to the ulti- mate legal question ("Should the youth be waived to criminal court") is obvious and might as well be stated.

Other clinicians (probably a minority) will not answer either the ultimate or the penultimate legal question. For my own part, I will testify to the latter, but never with a "yes" or "no." I answer with a short sentence that captures the essence of the clinical inferences that I have formed in the case. For example, when asked whether the youth is amenable to rehabilitation, I may reply, "Given that the youth receives the rehabilitation program I will be describing (or have described) in my testimony, the prospects are good for substantially reducing the risk of future danger to others within 2 or 3 years." No judge or attorney has ever complained to me that this type of testimony did not satisfy their legal needs for a "bottom-line" expert opinion.

6.4   *Public Scrutiny and Public Statements*

Hearings and expert witnesses in juvenile court typically receive less scrutiny than in criminal court. By long tradition, juvenile court proceedings have been closed to the general public and to representatives of the media, consistent with the juvenile court's interest in fulfilling rehabilitative objectives and shielding the youth from stigma that might work against rehabilitation. This is rapidly changing, however. Within the past few years, many states opened some delinquency hearings to the public and the media, especially those involving murder or other very serious charges.

This can make a dramatic difference in the nature of the hearing and the experience for the expert witness. A few years ago I testified in one of the first juvenile hearings open to the public under a new Massachusetts law. The case involved a brutal murder of a high school cheerleader by her boyfriend. Accustomed to the relatively quiet and orderly nature of juvenile proceedings in Massachusetts, I suddenly found myself speaking to a packed and noisy gallery (friends of the victim on one side, those having empathy for the accused on the other), three television cameras, several still cameras with flashes, and a cluster of microphones. (Years later I continue to get messages from friends and acquaintances around the world that "I saw you on TV last night," referring to a 10-second TV-file sound bite that made its way into countless news specials on juvenile violence.)

Like clinicians in criminal cases, expert witnesses in juvenile cases now find that they are approached by the media outside the courtroom to provide material for news articles on cases that have gained local notoriety. One should *never* respond to media requests for information prior to providing testimony. But there are two schools of thought on the ethical propriety of discussing with the media cases in which one has already testified (Grisso, 1990).

One view emphasizes the public benefit of interviews about one's completed testimony. This argument is strongest when the testimony was public (i.e., the press was allowed to attend) and when the public is likely to misconstrue the meaning of the clinician's testimony because of ways in which it emerged under cross-examination, which may have distorted the meaning of the clinician's data. Supporters of this view point out that clinicians have an ethical duty to educate the public about psychology's and psychiatry's insights in legal cases and to foster their accurate interpretation.

The other point of view cautions that this practice may inadvertently teach the public to doubt the confidentiality they expect from mental health professionals. Questioning by the press also might cause the clinician inadvertantly to reveal information about the youth that was not actually a part of the clinician's testimony and therefore was not a matter of public record, thus risking a breach of confidentiality and potential damage in further legal proceedings involving the youth. Moreover, although the hearing may have been recorded in an open legal forum, clinicians must consider the possibility that their interviews with the press will magnify the potentially negative impact of public exposure on the youth.

7.0   EXAMINING ONE'S PERSONAL VALUES

The law frequently allows what professional ethics do not. Similarly, professional ethical guidelines sometimes allow what one's own values and conscience cannot accept. At this time in the history of the juvenile justice system, clinicians need to examine their assessment activities in light of their own moral principles, which may differ from both the law's and their profession's notions of what is right and fair.

Juvenile law in most states has recently evolved to ensure harsh punishment of even very young adolescents at the expense of rehabilitation, when they commit very serious offenses. Some juvenile courts, policy makers, and segments of the public have largely abandoned the notion that society's response to adolescent offenders should be different than for adults.

If there is any value in death sentences and lengthy adult prison terms for some serious adolescent offenders, it is gained at the cost of throwing away some unknown percentage of youths who otherwise would have been rehabilitated or whose acts were a consequence of immaturity rather than an enduring criminal character. Current laws have lowered the standard required to show nonamenability, thus increasing the likelihood of waiver to criminal court for some "difficult" rehabilitation cases—often involving youths with mental disorders—that might have been retained in juvenile court a few years ago.

Clinicians who perform evaluations for waiver cases contribute to those outcomes. Indeed, when their data indicate that a youth is dangerous and will be difficult to treat, they must be willing to accept those data and their implications. Clinicians who choose to perform certain evaluations for juvenile courts must participate in a process that inevitably harms some youths for the sake of public protection and society's desire for retribution.

Is it ethical for psychologists to participate in such proceedings? A similar question has been asked for years about mental health professionals' evaluations in legal proceedings that may result in the death penalty for convicted adult criminals. Many psychiatrists especially have argued that the ethical requirement "First do no harm" places these types of forensic involvements by clinicians outside the boundaries of ethical clinical practice.

Others, however, contend that when psychiatrists and psychologists take the role of forensic examiner, they function under a different, but equally viable, set of ethical imperatives compared to those that apply to general clinical practice. Paul Appelbaum (1997), for example, points out that when psychiatrists are forensic examiners, society assigns them a different role than the one that is expected of other physicians. They are not expected to take responsibility for the health of the individuals whom they are evaluating. Their primary ethical imperative is not to avoid doing harm but to strive to be fair to defendants within the framework of the legal process of which they are a part and to tell the truth consistent with their obligation to assist society in resolving legal questions. Within this special role that society recognizes for the forensic psychiatrist, practice that holds true to the truth-telling principle is ethically defensible, Appelbaum argues, despite the fact that some individuals may be harmed in the interest of the cause of legal justice to which the forensic psychiatrist contributes.

Therefore, one can construct a professional ethic that will permit clinicians to participate in societally approved, legally sanctioned proceedings that may result in harm to some youthful defendants. The question beyond this is whether one's own personal sense of justice comports with the current trend toward punishment of youths for their crimes of adolescence. Some may feel quite comfortable with it, while others may find it appalling. The important point is that clinicians need to know where they stand on these questions because their values might be inconsistent with their obligation to approach their cases with the objectivity required by the forensic clinician's role.

Even if there are some types of cases that some clinicians might decide they should avoid, they can still perform other types of evaluations that arise in delinquency cases. Rehabilitation evaluations in disposition cases, for example, typically involve beneficent objectives with which we are familiar in general clinical practice. Like most evaluations for juvenile courts, they provide clinicians the exciting opportunity to apply their clinical skills in a legal context for the benefit of youths and the protection of society.

References

Achenbach, T. (1991a). *Manual for the Child Behavior Checklist/4-18 and 1991 Profile.* Burlington, VT: University of Vermont, Department of Psychiatry.

Achenbach, T. (1991b). *Manual for the Teacher's Report Form and 1991 Profile.* Burlington, VT: University of Vermont, Department of Psychiatry.

Achenbach, T. (1991c). *Manual for the Youth Self-Report and 1991 Profile.* Burlington, VT: University of Vermont, Department of Psychiatry.

Ambrosini, P. (1992). *Schedule for Affective Disorders and Schizophrenia for School-Age Children (6-18 Years): Kiddie-SADS (K-SADS).* Philadelphia: Medical College of Pennsylvania.

American Academy of Psychiatry and the Law. (1995). *Ethical Guidelines for the Practice of Forensic Psychiatry.* Bloomfield, CT: Author.

American Bar Association Juvenile Justice Center, Juvenile Law Center, and Youth Law Center. (1995). *A Call for Justice: An Assessment of Access to Counsel and Quality of Representation in Delinquency Proceedings.* Washington, DC: Office of Juvenile Justice and Delinquency Prevention.

American Psychiatric Association. (1987). *Diagnostic and Statistical Manual of Mental Disorders* (3rd ed. rev.). Washington, DC: Author.

American Psychiatric Association. (1994). *Diagnostic and Statistical Manual of Mental Disorders (4th ed.).* Washington, DC: Author.

American Psychiatric Association. (1995). *Principles of Medical Ethics with Annotations Especially Applicable to Psychiatry.* Washington, DC: Author.

American Psychological Association. (1992). Ethical principles of psychologists and code of conduct. *American Psychologist, 47,* 1597-1611.

Appelbaum, P. (1997). A theory of ethics for forensic psychiatry. *Journal of the American Academy of Psychiatry and the Law, 25,* 233-247.

Archer, R. (1992). *MMPI-A: Assessing Adolescent Psychopathology.* Hillsdale, NJ: Erlbaum.

Arnett, J. (1992). Reckless behavior in adolescence: A developmental perspective. *Developmental Review, 12,* 339-373.

Barbaree, H., Hudson, S., & Seto, M. (1993). *The Juvenile Sex Offender.* New York: Guilford.

Barkley, R. (1990). *Attention-Deficit Hyperactivity Disorder: A Handbook for Diagnosis and Treatment.* New York: Guilford.

Barnum, R. (1990). Self-incrimination and denial in the juvenile transfer evaluation. *Bulletin of the American Academy of Psychiatry and the Law, 18,* 413-428.

Barrera, M., & Garrison-Jones, C. (1988). Properties of the Beck Depression Inventory as a screening instrument for adolescent depression. *Journal of Abnormal Child Psychology, 16,* 263-273.

Barthel, J. (1977). *A Death in Canaan.* New York: Dell.

Bernard, T. (1992). *The Cycle of Juvenile Justice.* New York: Oxford University Press.

Blake, D., Weathers, F., Nagy, L., Kaloupek, D., Lauminzer, G., Charney, D., & Keane, T. (1990). A clinician rating scale for assessing current and lifetime PTSD: The CAPS-1. *Behavior Therapist, 18,* 187-188.

Bonnie, R. (1992). The competence of criminal defendants: A theoretical reformulation. *Behavioral Sciences and the Law, 10,* 291-316.

Borum, R., Swartz, M., & Swanson, J. (1996). Assessing and managing violence risk in clinical practice. *Journal of Practice in Psychiatry and Behavioral Health, 4,* 205-215.

Brandt, J., Kennedy, W., Patrick, C., & Curtin, J. (1997). Assessment of psychopathy in a population of incarcerated adolescent offenders. *Psychological Assessment, 4,* 429-435.

Breckinridge, S., & Abbott, E. (1970). *The Delinquent Child and the Home.* New York: Arno. (Original work published 1912)

Brodsky, S. (1991). *Testifying in Court: Guidelines and Maxims for the Expert Witness.* Washington, DC: American Psychological Association.

Butcher, J., Williams, C., Graham, J., Archer, R., Tellegen, R., Ben-Porath, Y., & Kaemmer, B. (1992). *MMPI-A: Manual for Administration Scoring and Interpretation.* Minneapolis, MN: University of Minnesota Press.

Cauffman, E. (1996). *Maturity of Judgment in Adolescence: Psychosocial Factors in Adolescent Decision-Making.* Unpublished doctoral dissertation, Temple University, Philadelphia, PA.

Cicourel, A. (1968). *The Social Organization of Juvenile Justice.* New York: John Wiley.

Cocozza, J. (Ed.). (1992). *Responding to the Mental Health Needs of Youth in the Juvenile Justice System.* Seattle, WA: National Coalition for the Mentally Ill in the Criminal Justice System.

Committee on Ethical Guidelines for Forensic Psychologists. (1991). Specialty guidelines for forensic psychologists. *Law and Human Behavior, 15,* 655-665.

Cooper, D. (1997). Juveniles' understanding of trial-related information: Are they competent defendants? *Behavioral Sciences and the Law, 15,* 167-180.

Cooper, D., & Grisso, T. (1997). Five-year research update (1990-1995): Evaluations for competence to stand trial. *Behavioral Sciences and the Law, 15,* 347-364.

Cormier, B., & Markus, B. (1980). A longitudinal study of adolescent murderers. *Bulletin of the American Academy of Psychiatry and the Law, 8,* 240-260.

Cornell, D., Benedek, E., & Benedek, D. (1989). A typology of juvenile homicide offenders. In E. Benedek & D. Cornell (Eds.), *Juvenile Homicide* (pp. 61-84). Washington, DC: American Psychiatric Press.

Cowden, V., & McKee, G. (1995). Comptency to stand trial in juvenile delinquency proceedings: Cognitive maturity and the attorney-client relationship. *Journal of Family Law, 33,* 629-660.

Daubert v. Merrell Dow Pharmaceuticals, Inc., 112 S.Ct. 2786 (1993).

Derogatis, L. (1993). *Brief Symptom Inventory: Administration, Scoring, and Procedures Manual.* Minneapolis, MN: National Computer Systems.

Drukteinis, A. (1986). Criminal responsibility of juvenile offenders. *American Journal of Forensic Psychology, 4,* 33-48.

Dunn, L., & Dunn, L. M. (1981). *Peabody Picture Vocabulary Test-Revised.* Circle Pines, MN: American Guidance Service.

DuPaul, G., Power, T., Anastopoulus, A., Reid, R., McGoey, K., & Ikeda, M. (1997). Teacher ratings of Attention Deficit Hyperactivity Disorder symptoms: Factor structure and normative data. *Psychological Assessments, 4,* 436-444.

Dusky v. U.S., 362 U.S. 402 (1960).

Elliott, D. (1994). Serious violent offenders: Onset, developmental course, and termination—American Society of Criminology presidential address. *Criminology, 32,* 1-21.

Elliott, D., Ageton, S., Huizinga, D., Knowles, D., & Canter, R. (1983). *The Prevalence and Incidence of Delinquent Behavior: 1976-1980* (The National Youth Survey Report No. 26). Boulder, CO: Behavioral Research Institute.

Elliott, D., Huizinga, D., & Morse, B. (1986). Self-reported violent offending: A descriptive analysis of juvenile violent offenders and their offending careers. *Journal of Interpersonal Violence, 1,* 472-514.

Ennis, B., & Litwack, T. (1974). Psychiatry and the presumption of expertise: Flipping coins in the courtroom. *California Law Review, 62,* 693-752.

Everington, C. (1990). The Competence Assessment for Standing Trial for Defendants with Mental Retardation (CAST-MR). *Criminal Justice and Behavior, 17,* 147-168.

Ewing, C. (1990). *When Children Kill: Dynamics of Juvenile Homicide.* Lexington, MA: Lexington Books.

Fare v. Michael C., 442 U.S. 707 (1979).

Feld, B. (1980). Juvenile court legislative reform and the serious young offender: Dismantling the "rehabilitative ideal." *Minnesota Law Review, 65,* 16-242.

Feld, B. (1988). The juvenile court meets the principle of offense: Punishment, treatment, and the difference it makes. *Boston University Law Review, 68,* 821-898.

Fletcher, K. (1996). Psychometric review of Childhood PTSD Interview. In B. H. Stamm (Ed.), *Measurement of Stress, Trauma, and Adaptation* (pp. 87-89). Lutherville, MD: Sidran Press.

Forth, A., Hart, S., & Hare, R. (1990). Assessment of psychopathy in male young offenders. *Psychological Assessment, 2,* 342-344.

Frick, P., O'Brien, H., Wootton, J., & McBurnett, K. (1994). Psychopathy and conduct problems in children. *Journal of Abnormal Psychology, 103,* 700-707.

Frye v. U.S., 293 F. 1013 (D.C. Cir. 1923).

Furby, M., & Beyth-Marom, R. (1992). Risk-taking in adolescence: A decision-making perspective. *Developmental Review, 12,* 1-44.

Gerard, A. (1994). *Parent-Child Relationship Inventory (PCRI): Manual.* Los Angeles: Western Psychological Services.

G.J.I. v. State, 778 P.2d 485 (Okla. Crim. 1989).

Godinez v. Moran, 113 S.Ct. 2680 (1993).

Gottfredson, M., & Hirschi, T., (1990). *A General Theory of Crime.* Stanford, CA: Stanford University Press.

Grisso, T. (1980). Juveniles' capacities to waive Miranda rights: An empirical analysis. *California Law Review, 68,* 1134-1166.

Grisso, T. (1981). *Juveniles' Waiver of Rights: Legal and Psychological Competence.* New York: Plenum.

Grisso, T. (1986). *Evaluating Competencies: Forensic Assessments and Instruments.* New York: Plenum.

Grisso, T. (1988). *Competency to Stand Trial Evaluations: A Manual for Practice.* Sarasota, FL: Professional Resource Exchange.

Grisso, T. (1990). Forensic evaluations and the fourth estate. *Forensic Reports, 3,* 427-437.

Grisso, T. (1992). Five-year research update (1986-1990): Evaluations for competence to stand trial. *Behavioral Sciences and the Law, 10,* 353-369.

Grisso, T. (1996). Society's retributive response to juvenile violence: A developmental perspective. *Law and Human Behavior, 20,* 229-247.

Grisso, T. (1997). The competence of adolescents as trial defendants. *Psychology, Public Policy, and Law, 3,* 3-32.

Grisso, T., Cocozza, J., Steadman, H., Fisher, W., & Greer, A. (1994). The organization of pretrial forensic evaluation services: A national profile. *Law and Human Behavior, 18,* 377-393.

Grisso, T., Miller, M., & Sales, B. (1987). Competency to stand trial in juvenile court. *International Journal of Law and Psychiatry, 10,* 1-20.

Grisso, T., & Pomicter, C. (1977). Interrogation of juveniles: An empirical study of procedures, safeguards, and rights waiver. *Law and Human Behavior, 1,* 321-342.

Grisso, T., & Ring, M. (1979). Parents' attitudes toward juveniles' rights in interrogation. *Criminal Justice and Behavior, 6,* 221-226.

Groth, A., & Loredo, C. (1981). Juvenile sex offenders: Guidelines for assessment. *International Journal of Offender Therapy and Comparative Criminology, 25,* 31-39.

Gudjonsson, G. (1984). A new scale of interrogative suggestibility. *Personality and Individual Differences, 5,* 303-314.

Gudjonsson, G. (1992). *The Psychology of Interrogations, Confessions and Testimony.* New York: John Wiley.

Hare, R. (1991). *The Hare Psychopathy Checklist-Revised Manual.* Tonawanda, NY: Multi-Health Systems, Inc.

Harrington, M., & Keary, A. (1980). The insanity defense in juvenile delinquency proceedings. *Bulletin of the American Academy of Psychiatry and the Law, 8,* 272-279.

Heide, K. (1992). *Why Kids Kill Parents.* Columbus: Ohio State University Press.

Heilbrun, K. (1992). The role of psychological testing in forensic assessment. *Law and Human Behavior, 16,* 257-272.

Heilbrun, K., Leheny, C., Thomas, L., & Huneycutt, D. (1997). A national survey of U.S. statutes on juvenile transfer: Implications for policy and practice. *Behavioral Sciences and the Law, 15,* 125-149.

Hertzig, M. (1992). Personality disorders in children and adolescents. In R. Michels (Ed.), *Psychiatry* (Vol. I, pp. 1-11). Philadelphia: Lippincott.

Hoge, R., & Andrews, D. (1996). *Assessing the Youthful Offender.* New York: Plenum.

Hoge, S., Poythress, N., Bonnie, R., Monahan, J., Eisenberg, M., & Feicht-Haviar, T. (1997). The MacArthur Adjudication Competence Study: Diagnosis, psychopathology, and adjudicative competence-related abilities. *Behavioral Sciences and the Law, 15,* 329-345.

Holinger, P., Offer, D., Barter, J., & Bell, C. (1994). *Suicide and Homicide Among Adolescents.* New York: Guilford.

Howell, J., Krisberg, B., Hawkins, J., & Wilson, J. (Eds.). (1995). *A Sourcebook: Serious, Violent, and Chronic Juvenile Offenders.* Thousand Oaks, CA: Sage.

In re Causey, 363 So.2d 472 (La. 1978).

In re Gault, 387 U.S. 1 (1967).

In the Interest of S.H., 469 S.E.2d 810 (Ga. Ct. App., 1996).

Inbau, F., Reid, J., & Buckley, J. (1986). *Criminal Interrogation and Confessions* (3rd ed). Baltimore, MD: Williams and Wilkins.

Jackson, D. (1995). *The Basic Personality Inventory Manual.* Port Huron, MI: Sigma Assessment Systems.

Jackson v. Indiana, 406 U.S. 715 (1972).

Janis, I. (1982). Decision making under stress. In L. Goldberger & S. Brezmitz (Eds.), *Handbook of Stress: Theoretical and Clinical Aspects* (pp. 69-80). New York: Van Nostrand Reinhold.

Jastak, S., Wilkinson, G., & Jastak, J. (1984). *Wide Range Achievement Test-Revised.* Wilmington, DE: Jastak Associates.

Jesness, C., & Wedge, R. (1984). Validity of a revised Jesness Inventory I-Level classification with delinquents. *Journal of Consulting and Clinical Psychology, 52,* 997-1010.

Jesness, C., & Wedge, R. (1985). *Jesness Inventory Classification System: Supplementary Manual*. Palo Alto, CA: Consulting Psychologists Press.

Kaufman, A., & Kaufman, N. (1985). *Kaufman Test of Educational Achievement*. Circle Pines, MN: American Guidance Service.

Kent v. U.S., 383 U.S. 541 (1966).

Kohlberg, L. (1976). Moral stages and moralization: The cognitive-developmental approach. In T. Lickona (Ed.), *Moral Development and Behavior*. New York: Holt, Rinehart & Winston.

Lachar, D., & Kline, R. (1994). Personality Inventory for Children and Personality Inventory for Youth. In M. Maruish (Ed.), *The Use of Psychological Testing for Treatment Planning and Outcome Assessment* (pp. 479-516). Hillsdale, NJ: Erlbaum.

Lewis, D., Pincus, J., Bard, B., & Richardson, B. (1988). Neuropsychiatric, psychoeducational, and family characteristics of 14 juveniles condemned to death in the United States. *American Journal of Psychiatry, 145*, 585-589.

Lipsey, M. (1992). *Juvenile Delinquency Treatment: A Meta-Analytic Inquiry into the Variability of Effects*. In T. Cook, H. Cooper, D. Cordray, H. Hartmann, L. Hedges, R. Knight, T. Lewis, & F. Mosteller (Eds.), Meta-analysis for explanation (pp. 83-127). New York: Russell Sage.

Lipsitt, P., Lelos, D., & McGarry, A. L. (1971). Competency for trial: A screening instrument. *American Journal of Psychiatry, 128*, 105-109.

Loeber, R., & Stouthamer-Loeber, M. (1998). Development of juvenile aggression and violence: Some common misconceptions and controversies. *American Psychologist, 53*, 242-259.

Lynam, D. (1996). Early identification of chronic offenders: Who is the fledgling psychopath? *Psychological Bulletin, 120*, 209-234.

Mack, J. (1909). The juvenile court. *Harvard Law Review, 23*, 104-122.

Markwardt, F. (1989). *Peabody Individual Achievement Test-Revised*. Circle Pines, MN: American Guidance Service.

Martinson, R. (1974). What works? *The Public Interest, 35*, 22-54.

Mattanah, J., Becker, D., Levy, K., Edell, W., & McGlashan, T. (1995). Diagnostic stability in adolescents followed up 2 years after hospitalization. *American Journal of Psychiatry, 152*, 889-894.

McCann, J. (1997). The MACI: Composition and clinical application. In T. Millon (Ed.), *The Millon Inventories: Clinical and Personality Assessment* (pp. 363-388). New York: Guilford.

McCann, J. (1998). *Malingering and Deception in Adolescents: Assessing Credibility in Clinical and Forensic Settings.* Washington, DC: American Psychological Association.

McCann, J., & Dyer, F. (1996). *Forensic Assessment with the Millon Inventories.* New York: Guilford.

McGarry, L. (1973). *Competency to Stand Trial and Mental Illness* (Publication No. ADM 77-103). Rockville, MD: Department of Health, Education and Welfare.

Megargee, E. (1971). The role of inhibition in the assessment and understanding of violence. In J. Singer (Ed.), *The Control of Aggression and Violence.* New York: Academic Press.

Megargee, E. (1984). A new classification system for criminal offenders: VI: Differences among the types on the adjective checklist. *Criminal Justice and Behavior, 11,* 349-376.

Megargee, E., & Bohn, M. (1979). *Classifying Criminal Offenders: A New System Based on the MMPI.* Beverly Hills, CA: Sage.

Melton, G. (1980). Children's concepts of their rights. *Journal of Clinical Child Psychology, 9,* 186-190.

Melton, G., Petrila, J., Poythress, N., & Slobogin, C. (1997). *Psychological Evaluations for the Courts* (2nd ed.). New York: Guilford.

Millon, T. (1993). *Millon Adolescent Clinical Inventory.* Minneapolis, MN: National Computer Systems.

Millon, T., Green, C., & Meagher, R. (1982). *Millon Adolescent Personality Inventory.* Minneapolis, MN: National Computer Systems.

Miranda v. Arizona, 384 U.S. 436 (1966).

Moffitt, T. (1993). Adolescence-limited and life-course-persistent antisocial behavior: A developmental taxonomy. *Psychological Review, 100,* 674-701.

Monahan, J. (1981). *The Clinical Prediction of Violent Behavior.* Rockville, MD: National Institute of Mental Health.

Moos, R., & Moos, B. (1986). *The Family Environment Scale Manual* (2nd ed.). Palo Alto, CA: Consulting Psychologists Press.

Nader, K. (1997). Assessing traumatic experiences in children. In J. Wilson & T. Keane (Eds.), *Assessing Psychological Trauma and PTSD* (pp. 291-348). New York: Guilford.

National Institute of Mental Health. (1991). *NIMH Diagnostic Interview for Children, Version 2.3.* Rockville, MD: Author.

Nicholson, R., & Kugler, K. (1991). Competent and incompetent defendants: A quantitative review of comparative research. *Psychological Bulletin, 109,* 355-370.

Nicholson, R., Robertson, H., Johnson, W., & Jensen, G. (1988). A comparison of instruments for assessing competency to stand trial. *Law and Human Behavior, 12*, 313-321.

Otto, R. (1992). Prediction of dangerous behavior: A review and analysis of "second-generation" research. *Forensic Reports, 5*, 103-113.

Otto, R., Greenstein, J., Johnson, M., & Friedman, R. (1992). Prevalence of mental disorders among youth in the juvenile justice system. In J. Cocozza (Ed.), *Responding to the Mental Health Needs of Youth in the Juvenile Justice System* (pp. 7-48). Seattle, WA: National Coalition for the Mentally Ill in the Criminal Justice System.

People v. Lara, 432 P.2d 202 (1967).

Piaget, J. (1972). *The Child's Conception of the World*. Totowa, NJ: Littlefield, Adams.

Platt, A. (1969). *The Child Savers*. Chicago: University of Chicago Press.

Poythress, N., Hoge, S., Bonnie, R., Otto, R., Edens, J., Monahan, J., Nicholson, R., Eisenberg, M., & Feucht-Haviar, T. (1997). *The MacArthur Competence Assessment Tool-Criminal Adjudication (MacCAT-CA): Introduction and Preliminary Research Findings*. Unpublished manuscript, Florida Mental Health Institute, University of South Florida, Tampa, FL.

Quay, H. (1964). Personality dimensions in delinquent males as inferred from the factor analysis of behavior ratings. *Journal of Research in Crime and Delinquency, 1*, 33-37.

Quay, H. (1966). Personality patterns in preadolescent delinquent boys. *Educational and Psychological Measurement, 16*, 99-110.

Quay, H. (1987). Patterns of delinquent behavior. In H. Quay (Ed.), *Handbook of Juvenile Delinquency* (pp. 118-138). New York: John Wiley.

Quay, H., & Peterson, D. (1987). *Manual for the Revised Behavior Problem Checklist*. Miami, FL: University of Miami.

Reich, W., Shayka, J., & Taibleson, C. (1991). *Diagnostic Interview for Children and Adolescents (DICA-R-A): Adolescent Version*. St. Louis, MO: Washington University.

Reitan, R., & Wolfson, D. (1985). *The Halstead-Reitan Neuropsychological Test Battery*. Tucson, AZ: Neuropsychology Press.

Resnick, P. (1984). The detection of malingered mental illness. *Behavioral Sciences and the Law, 2*, 21-37.

Reynolds, W. (1991). A school-based procedure for the identification of adolescents at risk for suicidal behaviors. *Family and Community Health, 14*, 64-75.

Richardson, G., Gudjonsson, G., & Kelly, T. (1995). Interrogative suggestibility in an adolescent forensic population. *Journal of Adolescence, 18,* 211-216.

Roesch, R., & Golding, S. (1980). *Competency to Stand Trial.* Champaign, IL: University of Illinois Press.

Roesch, R., Webster, C., & Eaves, D. (1994). *The Fitness Interview Test-Revised: A Method for Examining Fitness to Stand Trial.* Burnaby, British Columbia: Department of Psychology, Simon Fraser University.

Rogers, R. (1995). *Diagnostic and Structured Interviewing.* Odessa, FL: Psychological Assessment Resources.

Rogers, R., Bagby, R., & Dickens, S. (1992). *Structured Interview of Reported Symptoms: Professional Manual.* Odessa, FL: Psychological Assessment Resources.

Rogers, R., Harrell, E., & Liff, C. (1993). Feigning neuropsychological impairment: A critical review of methodological and clinical considerations. *Clinical Psychology Review, 13,* 255-274.

Rogers, R., Hinds, J., & Sewell, K. (1996). Feigning psychopathology among adolescent offenders: Validation of the SIRS, MMPI-A, and SIMS. *Journal of Personality Assessment, 67,* 244-257.

Rogers, R., & Resnick, P. (1988). *Malingering and Deception: The Clinical Interview: Practitioner's Manual.* New York: Guilford.

Rosner, R., & Schwartz, H. (Eds.). (1989). *Juvenile Psychiatry and the Law.* New York: Plenum.

Ross, J., & Loss, P. (1991). Assessment of the juvenile sex offender. In G. Ryan & S. Lane (Eds.), *Juvenile Sexual Offending: Causes, Consequences, and Correction* (pp. 199-251). Lexington, MA: Lexington Books.

Schetky, D., & Benedek, E. (Eds.). (1980). *Child Psychiatry and the Law.* New York: Brunner/Mazel.

Schetky, D., & Benedek, E. (Eds.). (1985). *Emerging Issues in Child Psychiatry and the Law.* New York: Brunner/Mazel.

Schetky, D., & Benedek, E. (Eds.). (1992). *Clinical Handbook of Child Psychiatry and the Law.* Baltimore, MD: Williams and Wilkins.

Scott, E. (1992). Judgment and reasoning in adolescent decision making. *Villanova Law Review, 37,* 1607-1669.

Scott, E., Reppucci, N., & Woolard, J. (1995). Evaluating adolescent decision making in legal contexts. *Law and Human Behavior, 19,* 221-244.

Seeburger, R., & Wettick, R. (1967). Miranda in Pittsburgh: A statistical study. *University of Pittsburgh Law Review, 29,* 1-26.

Shaffer, D., Schwab-Stone, M., Fisher, P., Cohen, P., Piacentini, J., Davies, M., Conners, C., & Regier, D. (1993). The Diagnostic Interview Schedule for Children Revised Version (DISC-R): Preparation, field testing, inter-rater reliability and acceptability. *Journal of the American Academy of Child and Adolescent Psychiatry, 32,* 643-650.

Smith, C., Lizotte, A., Thornberry, T., & Krohn, M. (1995). Resilient youth: Identifying factors that prevent high-risk youth from engaging in delinquency and drug use. In J. Hagan (Ed.), *Delinquency in the Life Course* (pp. 217-247). Greenwich, CT: JAI.

Stapleton, W., & Teitelbaum, L. (1972). *In Defense of Youth.* New York: Russell Sage.

Steinberg, L., & Cauffman, E. (1996). Maturity of judgment in adolescence: Psychosocial factors in adolescent decision making. *Law and Human Behavior, 20,* 249-272.

Tarter, R. (1990). Evaluation and treatment of adolescent substance abuse: A decision tree method. *American Journal of Drug and Alcohol Abuse, 16,* 1-46.

Tate, D., Reppucci, N., & Mulvey, E. (1995). Violent juvenile delinquents: Treatment effectiveness and implications for future action. *American Psychologist, 50,* 777-781.

Torbet, P., Gable, R., Hurst, H., Montgomery, I., Szymanski, L., & Thomas. D. (1996). *State Responses to Serious and Violent Juvenile Crime.* Washington, DC: Office of Juvenile Justice and Delinquency Prevention.

Warren, M. (1966). *Interpersonal Maturity Level Classification: Juvenile Diagnosis and Treatment of Low, Middle, and High Maturity Delinquents.* Sacramento, CA: California Youth Authority.

Warren, M. (1976). Intervention with juvenile delinquents. In M. Rosenheim (Ed.), *Pursuing Justice for the Child* (pp. 176-204). Chicago: University of Chicago Press.

Wechsler, D. (1981). *Wechsler Adult Intelligence Scale-Revised.* San Antonio, TX: Psychological Corporation.

Wechsler, D. (1991). *Wechsler Intelligence Scale for Children-III.* San Antonio, TX: Psychological Corporation.

Weinberg, W., & Emslie, G. (1988). Weinberg Screening Affective Scales (WSAS and WSAS-SF). *Journal of Child Neurology, 3,* 294-296.

Weinrott, M. (1996). *Juvenile Sexual Aggression: A Critical Review.* Boulder, CO: Center for the Study and Prevention of Violence, University of Colorado.

West v. U.S., 399 F.2d 467 (1968).

Widom, C. (1989). Does violence beget violence? A critical examination of the literature. *Psychological Bulletin, 106*, 3-28.

Widom, C., & Maxfield, M. (1996). A prospective examination of risk for violence among abused and neglected children. In C. Ferris & T. Grisso (Eds.), *Understanding Aggressive Behavior in Children* (pp. 224-237). New York: Annals of the New York Academy of Sciences.

Wiebush, R., Baird, C., Krisberg, B., & Onek, D. (1995). Risk assessment and classification for serious, violent, and chronic juvenile offenders. In J. Howell, B. Krisberg, J. D. Hawkins, & J. Wilson (Eds.), *A Sourcebook: Serious, Violent, and Chronic Juvenile Offenders* (pp. 171-212). Thousand Oaks, CA: Sage.

Woodcock, R., Johnson, M., McGrew, K., & Werder, J. (1989). *Woodcock-Johnson Psycho-Educational Battery-Revised*. Chicago: Riverside Publishing Company.

Zager, L. (1988). The MMPI-based criminal classification system: A review, current status, and future directions. *Criminal Justice and Behavior, 15*, 39-57.

Zapf, P., & Roesch, R. (1997). Assessing fitness to stand trial: A comparison of institution-based evaluations and a brief screening interview. *Canadian Journal of Community Mental Health, 16*, 53-66.

Zimring, F. (1982). *The Changing Legal World of Adolescence*. New York: Free Press.

Zuckerman, M., Eysenck, S., & Eysenck, H. (1978). Sensation seeking in England and America: Cross-cultural, age, and sex comparisons. *Journal of Consulting and Clinical Psychology, 46*, 139-149.

Glossary of Terms

Adjudication To hear and settle a case by judicial procedure. As used in this book, the judicial process for determining guilt in criminal or juvenile court.

Adolescence-Limited Delinquency A pattern of delinquent behavior in which harmful or illegal behaviors have their onset during adolescence and tend to subside with development from adolescence to adulthood.

Amenability to Rehabilitation Likelihood of responsiveness to rehabilitation within the resources of the juvenile justice system.

Bench Trial A trial in which the judge is the trier of fact (has the legal authority to reach a verdict).

Bindover Another term for *Waiver of Jurisdiction* (referring to a juvenile case that is "bound over" to criminal court for trial).

Causal Component A characteristic of all legal competencies, referring to the fact that explanations must be provided for deficits in functional abilities related to the legal question, and that only certain explanations are consistent with legal incompetence. For example, in most states, incompetence to stand trial in criminal court requires functional deficits (see *Functional Component*) that are due to mental illness or mental retardation.

Certification	Another term for *Waiver of Jurisdiction* (referring to a juvenile case that is "certified" to criminal court for trial).
Competence to Stand Trial	In a criminal proceeding, a finding that the defendant has sufficient present ability to consult with his or her attorney with a reasonable degree of rational understanding and a rational as well as factual understanding of the proceedings against him or her.
Continuance	A court's decision to delay a legal decision. In juvenile court disposition cases, to delay the disposition decision as a way to provide incentive for the youth to avoid further juvenile court intervention by avoiding further illegal acts that might again bring the youth to the attention of the court (thereby triggering a dispositional penalty).
Court Clinic	One or more mental health professionals who are employed, or have a contract, to meet the daily needs of a court for mental health services, especially forensic mental health evaluations.
Desistance Phenomenon	A tendency toward reduced offending during the transition from adolescence to adulthood.
Detention	Holding in secure custody prior to trial or after trial in anticipation of sentencing and placement.
Determinate Sentencing	Uniform sentencing based on the nature of the offense rather than considerations based on characteristics of the individual offender.
Disposition	A juvenile court decision about the consequences of a finding of delinquency. (Similar to the sentencing phase of a criminal court trial.) Also, the consequence itself (e.g., "The disposition of the case was placement in the custody of the state's youth authority").

Extension of Jurisdiction	A legal mechanism whereby the juvenile court may, under certain circumstances, retain its custody over a youth beyond the maximum age of juvenile court jurisdiction.
Fitness	Another term for *Amenability to Rehabilitation* (referring to whether the juvenile is a "fit and proper subject" for rehabilitation within the juvenile justice system). ***Note***: The term "fitness" also is used in some states and Canada to refer to *Competence to Stand Trial*. The two uses of this term, however, are completely unrelated with regard to legal meaning.
Floor Effects	On a test, the lowest score made by most people with a particular type of disability. May be used as a strategy in detecting the possibility of malingering, in that persons who attempt to malinger a particular disability may intentionally try to answer incorrectly as much as possible and thereby score below the lowest scores of persons who truly have the disability.
Formal Operations	A developmental transition during which youths attain, among other things, the ability to use abstractions and hypotheticals in thinking about the world. Typically said to develop around age 12 to 14, although age of attainment may vary widely among youths and may develop unevenly across social contexts in a youth's life (Piagetian theory).
Functional Component	A characteristic of all legal competencies, referring to the fact that they are concerned with people's functioning in a specific performance domain. For example, in competence to stand trial, what people actually understand, believe, or can do related to performance in the role of defendant.

271

Informal Adjustment	Typically, a juvenile court intake worker's agreement with a youth and the youth's family that the case will not be filed for adjudication if the youth and family agree to certain conditions (e.g., counseling, community services) designed to reduce the likelihood that the youth will engage in illegal behaviors in the future.
Informed Consent	A legal doctrine that requires that a person's consent to intrusive procedures by medical and mental health professionals (e.g., medication, surgery, psychological testing), in order to be valid, must be made by the person under three conditions: (a) adequate disclosure of information, (b) voluntariness, and (c) the competence of the person providing consent.
Interactive Component	A characteristic of all legal competencies, referring to competence as, in part, a question of the match or mismatch between a person's degree of functional abilities and the demands of the person's specific situation. For example, a person's functional deficits may or may not contribute to a finding of incompetence to stand trial, depending on the nature and complexity of the person's own trial process.
Judgment Component	A characteristic of all legal competencies, referring to the fact that ultimately a judgment must be made concerning whether the defendant's capacities, in light of the demands of the situation the defendant faces, are enough to satisfy legal standards of fairness associated with the purpose of the legal construct of competence. For example, the judgment that a defendant's incapacities are sufficiently great that it would be unfair to put him or her to trial, therefore calling for a decision that the defendant is incompetent to stand trial.

Jursidiction	A court's scope of authority for interpreting and applying the law.
Jurisdictional Age	The lower or upper age that defines the age groups for whom courts are authorized to interpret and apply the law. For juvenile courts, the age range for which the juvenile justice system is authorized to make legal decisions and retain custody.
Least Restrictive Alternative	The rehabilitation option that allows for the greatest degree of individual liberty while satisfying society's interests in safety and rehabilitation of the individual.
Legal Standard	The criterion that a court must apply when deciding whether the facts of a case meet a legal definition. For example, the legal standard for deciding that a defendant's waiver of Miranda rights is admissible as evidence at trial is whether the waiver was made "voluntarily, knowingly, and intelligently."
Life-Course-Persistent Delinquency	A pattern of delinquent behavior in which harmful or illegal behaviors have their onset in early childhood and tend to persist through adolescence into adulthood.
Offense-Based Sentencing	See *Determinate Sentencing*.
Over-Controlled Hostility	A personality type, referring to persons who deal with excessive anger by rigidly restricting its expression (e.g., by psychological defenses or learned patterns of behavior), and who are therefore at higher risk of infrequent but suddenly explosive aggression.
Parens Patriae	The authority of the state to act as a parent who provides for the needs and welfare of a youth.

273

Performing Curve Strategy	Refers to a strategy for detecting possible malingering of cognitive deficits. When a test-taker's performance on a set of items graded from easy to difficult does not show the usual pattern of progression from predominately correct to predominately incorrect answers (e.g., many easy items are missed while some harder ones are answered correctly).
Prediction of Violence	A clinical judgment that a person will or will not engage in an aggressive or delinquent act in the future. A binary or dichotomous conclusion about future violent acts.
Probable Cause	A determination by a court that there is sufficient evidence concerning the acts of which the accused is charged to justify arrest, referral, detention, or other processing of the case toward adjudication.
Prosecutor Direct File	In some states, statutes that allow prosecutors to decide whether they wish to file a case in juvenile court or in criminal court. Typically restricted to certain serious offenses and specifying a lower age limit (e.g., 14 or older).
Recidivism	To relapse to a former pattern of behavior; to offend again after efforts have been made to reduce the likelihood of further offending.
Referral	Any process by a person with legal authority that passes a case to another legal authority. For example, a police officer's referral of a case to the juvenile court for processing, a juvenile court's referral of a case to criminal court for trial.
Resiliency Factors	Personal or environmental variables that are associated with a lower risk of aggression or delinquency among youths who otherwise are identified with populations of youths who are at increased risk of aggression or delinquency.

Restitution	A juvenile court disposition requiring that the youth perform service for or otherwise repay a victim of the youth's illegal behavior.
Restoration of Competence	After a finding of incompetence to stand trial, the condition of a sufficient increase in relevant functional abilities, usually as a result of treatment, so that the person can be found competent to stand trial and the trial can proceed.
Reverse Transfer (or Reverse Waiver)	In some states, a legal mechanism whereby a criminal court, in a case involving a defendant of juvenile age, may waive jurisdiction and transfer the case to juvenile court.
Risk Estimate	A clinical judgment about the probability or relative likelihood of a person's future aggression or delinquency so as to convey the degree of risk to society. Contrasted with binary *Prediction of Violence*.
Risk Factor	A personal or environmental variable that is associated with an increased risk of aggression or delinquency.
Staff-Secure Placement	A residential facility for delinquent youths that does not have perimeter security, but in which youths' movement into and from the facility is controlled by staff members.
Status Offender	A youth who has violated a law that would not be a crime if the youth were an adult (e.g., truancy, runaway, incorrigible).
Statutory Exclusion	Statutes in some states requiring that cases involving charges for certain serious offenses must be filed in criminal court, even when the accused is a youth. (That is, cases involving certain offenses that are "excluded" from juvenile court jurisdiction and adjudication.) Statutes typically state a lower age limit (e.g., 14 and older).

Totality of Circumstances	A legal standard emphasizing that no particular fact(s) (e.g., no specific age) is (are) dispositive of a legal question across cases, and that a decision must be made by weighing all relevant factors on a case-by-case basis.
Transfer	Any form of referral of a juvenile to criminal court for trial on allegations of offending. Includes judicial waiver of jurisdiction and various laws that exclude certain juvenile cases from juvenile court automatically based on variables such as type of offense, age, and offense history.
Ultimate Legal Question	A question of law for which the answer disposes of the matter of law before the court. For example, "Is the defendant guilty or not guilty?" and "Is the defendant competent or incompetent to stand trial?" are ultimate legal questions.
Waiver Hearing	A juvenile court hearing to determine whether the court should waive jurisdiction and thereby transfer the youth to criminal court for trial. See *Waiver of Jurisdiction*.
Waiver of Jurisdiction	A juvenile court judge's decision that a juvenile should be referred to criminal court for trial. Requires a judicial hearing and decision that a youth who is under the juvenile court's custody meets the legal standard for waiver of the court's jurisdiction (see *Amenability to Rehabilitation*).
Youthful Offender	In general, any child found delinquent in juvenile court. In recent years, however, new laws have given the term a more specific meaning. In states that have created "youthful offender" laws, youths with certain serious offenses may be provided sentences greater than for findings of ordinary delinquency, often extending well beyond the maximum age of juvenile court jurisdiction.

Subject Index